BOOMER GURU

How M. Scott Peck Guided Millions
but Lost Himself on the Road Less Traveled

ARTHUR JONES

Capparoe Books

Published by Capparoe Books, Maryland, USA
    ISBN 10: 9768751-1-X
    ISBN 13: 978-0-9768751-1-6

The publication of this North American edition marks the tenth anniversary of M. Scott Peck's death. This book is a revised edition of *The Road He Travelled: The Revealing Biography of M. Scott Peck* by Arthur Jones, published in the United Kingdom by Random House/Ebury (2007).

Visit the author's website: arthurjonesbooks.net

My lot was not much different from all men and women. We have the same longings, the same fears and frustrations, the same fleeting successes and inconsolable losses, the same secret shames and muted self-doubts.

I believe that, if and when we face our flawed likeness, and finally come to change what we can, we may be able to accept being merely human.

—Gail Sheehy, *Daring: My Passages, a Memoir*

Life is difficult.

—M. Scott Peck, MD, *The Road Less Traveled*

CONTENTS

INTRODUCTION

I actually believe The Road Less Traveled *began a movement of writing that looks to spiritual journeys—something we Baby Boomers seem to dwell upon. I'm just glad I read it when I did.*

—Paula Matuskey
Former Dean
Montgomery College, Maryland

It was the 1970s. Americans were troubled; they were in therapy. They were drinking too much; they were in AA. They were doing drugs too much; they fried their brains. They engaged too widely and wildly in Free Love; they could find neither true love nor the path to settling down. They were navel-gazing too much and thinking too little. It was among those struggling out of this maelstrom, and those who had been standing around its perimeter looking on with a mix of awe and fear, who in the 1970s and 1980s found a new, definable, understandable, graspable handhold. It was *The Road Less Traveled: a New Psychology of Love, Traditional Values and Spiritual Growth*, by M. Scott Peck, MD.

Peck was Park Avenue "silver spoon," a New York-born and raised psychiatrist. He was the Boomers' guide out of their personal and social wilderness. He provided a psychotherapeutic commonsense that unlocked their psychological blocks—it was commonsense with a spiritual lodestone. He searched for God; he was seeking God for himself and for others. He wrote, prayed, meditated, and preached a God in whom he desperately wanted to believe. More than ten million Americans read Dr. Peck's dozen books. Over a quarter-century span, thousands attended his talks and workshops, work that continued into the 1990s. Yet a decade later, scarcely a hundred people were present at his 2005 memorial service, and six weeks earlier, only two of his three children had shown up for his private family-and-friends funeral.

The man once known as "the Nation's Shrink," had shrunk into oblivion. Peck, the Boomers' Guru, the practicing psychotherapist who inspired an entire generation to surmount the hurdles that prevented them from living a full life, could not assist himself. The man who'd blended psychiatry and religion, who'd spoken comfortingly of God's love and one's own death, at his own end, when gripped by Parkinson's Disease and dying of pancreatic cancer, never mentioned God at all.

Was it all a hoax? No. It was a tragedy. Scott Peck lived a life of narcissism writ large while achingly wanting to be different—except the cost was too high. He couldn't express the remorse that his behavior—toward his wife and family—sorely and surely warranted. Had they forgiven him, he probably couldn't have handled that, either.

Scott Peck was the poor little rich boy who never felt loved by a father who openly favored his older brother, David. Scott Peck consequently could never separate his ego from the hurts, real and imagined.

He never forgave or forgot a slight. At age eight, when his father played a thoughtless joke on him, Peck vowed to never cry again. As he told it, he was a thirty-six-year-old psychiatrist and a U.S. Army Lieutenant-Colonel the next time he gave way to uncontrollable sobbing.

Scott Peck, who could candidly describe his early sexual life with partners of both sexes, and reflect with extreme frankness on his extra-marital affairs, was nonetheless into denial. What could not be denied was that as a writer, at a sparkling moment in time for him and them, he found the words and phrasings, concepts and maxims of encouragement that brought the Boomer Generation through the hedonism of the late 1960s and early 1970s into a mature stability he failed to achieve himself. In the 1980s, *The Road Less Traveled* moved onto *The New York Times* bestseller list and stayed there for twelve years, a new record for a living author in that category.

"Guru" was a term M. Scott Peck, MD, loathed, but the role was one he thrived on emotionally, and profited from financially. "Gu," in Hindi, means "darkness." "Ru," means "light." Combined, the word, with its paradoxical and mystical overtones, means teacher or advisor. Peck paraded his "ru" but hid his "gu."

The Peck who emerges in this biography meets all P.G. Wodehouse's requirements for biographical writing—an eccentric father, a miserable, misunderstood childhood, and a prep school that was living hell. Off-screen, Peck was a control freak with an addictive personality, a narcissist with a gift. The hell was inflicted to a great or lesser degree on his family.

His beneficiaries numbered in the hundreds and thousands, possibly millions. His mailbox—the letters in his archives—attests to it. Through his books, his workshops, and the Foundation for Community Encouragement (FCE), which he and his Chinese first wife, Lily, created, Peck's light illuminated for millions of Americans their own strategies for overcoming the limitations, the pain and the obstacles with which life had burdened them up to that point. At his best, the Peck of the printed word and public platform was an exemplary Western guru who, in the place of the East's ancient spiritual-and-asceticism-based wisdom, offered Western psychiatric wisdom. He made respectable what are now commonplace psychotherapy-based self-help encapsulations. He coupled them to a spiritual search. As a psychiatrist and physician he legitimized "self-help," another phrase he detested, yet he wrapped it in the respectable cloak of psychotherapy.

Peck accomplished much of what he did because, in that first book, he had the facility to find the language that could duplicate on the printed page the kind of personal therapeutic reassurances he was capable of providing in his clinic, the former dining room of his home on Bliss Road, New Preston, Connecticut. As Peck placed first, the Boomer Generation, and next, the nation, on the couch he normally reserved for individuals, Dr. James Guy, then dean of Fuller Theological Seminary's Graduate School of Psychology, called Peck "a prophet to the Seventies' Generation."

The Road, except for its riffs on the death of romantic love in marriage, and the right to go extra-marital—which Peck's readers spiritedly tackled him on—is a quite conservative book. Its main theme is discipline, self-discipline. It was a runaway success. At the 2005 Peck memorial service in Park Avenue's Christ Church, one attendee remarked, "God wrote Scotty's first book. Scotty wrote the rest."

By the 1980s and 90s, Peck's *Roadies,* turning up in their hundreds for Peck's lectures and workshops were, and remained, seekers and questioners. His book is still in print.

Yet, as there is no denying Peck's finest achievements there is no hiding his major personal flaws and failings. He denied himself nothing.

Good-looking with a lithe, perpetually boyish attractiveness behind his circular frame glasses, he was an entertaining yet seemingly vulnerable intellectual—a practicing psychiatrist turned public performer who was well aware he was adulation susceptible. His readers and listeners, some 90 per cent of them women, responded to his warmth and encouragement. If, in that first flush of awakened possibilities, they found themselves too close to Peck, he was not one to deny himself the advantage. One woman, who claimed he'd seduced her following one of his workshops, went public. Others complained privately. Some didn't complain at all.

Peck told his readers "life is difficult." If he held them by the hand and led them through the chapters until they were able to tackle their lives on their own, they accepted his handholding because he was a psychiatrist. Peck spent his life trying to find someone to hold his hand. Someone he trusted. The tragedy is he barely trusted even himself, and if he had, his trust may have been misplaced. His second wife, Kathy, said she wondered if, finally, he even trusted God.

Despite a media blaze that for years followed his progress, and finally threatened his reputation, his interviewers and article writers never quite pinned him down.

Everyone who knew him, said Gail Puterbaugh, his long-time executive secretary, "saw a different Scotty."

This book—much of the time in Peck's own words—reveals who and what they saw.

This is that rare phenomenon in the annals of psychotherapy: the world-famous psychiatrist on the couch.

CHAPTER ONE

Park Avenue Baby

M. Scott Peck was a performer. Watch any of the television self-helpers—from soothing psychiatrists to money-manager mavens—and the type is revealed, with this difference. Peck was a WASP. He possessed the easily recognized inbred White Anglo-Saxon Protestant self-assuredness and insouciance—the slight aloofness and requisite charm common to those who modeled themselves on the English upper classes. Peck, even during his slightly giddier moments on Oprah, was comparable in manner, method and accent to a John F. Kennedy in his ability to charm, to woo, an audience. Like Kennedy, though warmer in platform personality, Peck exuded class.

The fact Peck was indeed a psychiatrist in the "Golden Age of Psychotherapy," that Golden Age captured in Faye Dunaway's role in *The Thomas Crown Affair* remake—the psycho-therapist as respected by the power elite.

On the road, as in *The Road*, Peck offered strength and solace. On stage, he'd developed himself into a fine art. Offstage, at this moment, he was stretched out on a bed in an Edison, New Jersey, motel, nursing his now perennially bad back. He was smoking the inevitable Camel, and sipping the first of the evening's Lake Waramaug gin cocktails. Lake Waramaug, the second largest natural lake in Connecticut, was just across the road from his home. Right now Peck was the star off-stage, between acts.

Magazine writer Ben Yagoda was with him. Yagoda was one of the rarer breed of writers to interview Peck, a person of wit, not awe. "The scene isn't without irony," wrote Yagoda, who was seated at the side of Peck's bed, "considering I'm not a psychiatrist and the prone fellow on the bed is." He described Peck as having "a pleasant face, graying, thinning, blond hair and horn-rimmed glasses."

When Peck returned to the auditorium, Yagoda went into the hall to catch part of the show. Yagoda describes it this way:

Peck was saying, "People ask me if I was born again." He pauses, then, with expert timing, continues, "It was a very protracted labor and difficult delivery." Laughter. Peck is sitting in a large wing chair—his back again—a microphone in his hand, a carafe of coffee at his side. He waits out the laugh by slowly panning his head from left to right—another stand-up comic's move. He sounds like a cross between Garrison Keillor and Billy Graham, with a dash of William F. Buckley, especially in the patrician pronunciation of words like littrachure.

Yagoda's summary was that, "It all sounds good. Actually a little *too* good, a little too smooth and easy. I talk to Peck a few weeks later on the phone, and he tells me he's had some trouble with his personal staff in New Preston and they've had a retreat to try to iron out the problems. Another crisis. He almost sounds relieved." Two-plus decades later, Yagoda described *The Road Less Traveled* as "an attempt to combine more or less conventional ideas about psychotherapy with one of its traditional enemies, religion." He said he never quite figured Peck out.

For Peck, psychotherapy and religion were twin lodestars he tried to meld. He was attempting to heal himself. That's a difficult task in a person whose lack of detachment does not allow him to examine self-inflicted wounds.

For young, Park Avenue-raised Morgan Scott Peck, life wasn't difficult; it was as comfortable as a series of warm scenes from a 1940s black-and-white feel-good movie. In the early 1940s, the Peck apartment at 863 Park Avenue was spacious, one in a 22-unit cooperative building at 65th Street, where apartments today go for between $3 million and $4 million. In 1998, *The New York Times* described "863," as "one of the oldest luxury apartment houses on the park." It was built as a residence for the exclusive wealthy—the cooperative's board could vet who was permitted to buy, and who was not. When it opened, more than one-third of the resident-owners lived off private income.

Peck's father, David Warner Peck, Sr., was an ambitious and a brilliant lawyer. He entered Wabash College at sixteen, graduated from Harvard Law School at twenty-three—two years younger than his classmates. When he was brought into New York's Sullivan & Cromwell, Wall Street's most prestigious international firm, he had already worked for the U.S. Attorney General in New York, and as part of an international cartel arbitration legal team in London. His Sullivan and Cromwell assignment was to build up the firm's litigation department. The firm's style matched Peck Senior's tastes and ambitions as comfortably as did his Park Avenue address.

Sullivan & Cromwell was ruled by John Foster Dulles, named managing partner in 1926 at the age of 38, a remarkably young age at which to head the premier New York "white shoe" law firm. Leonard Mosley, Dulles' family biographer, wrote that when Foster brought his brother, Allen, into S&C, "It was a time to count blessings, and to be grateful to Foster, and Sullivan & Cromwell from whom all blessings flowed." A similar sentiment guided the head of the Peck family.

Scott's mother, Elizabeth Saville Templeton Getty Peck, easily handled cocktail hours and dinners for guests such as John Foster Dulles, Allen Dulles, and Tom Dewey, and their ladies. John Foster Dulles was not only Sullivan & Cromwell's senior partner, he became President Eisenhower's Secretary of State, the second most powerful person in the Administration.

Allen Dulles, also an S&C partner, was an Office of Strategic Services (OSS) operative in Switzerland during World War II, and when the Central Intelligence Agency (CIA) was formed, he was eventually named its chief. Thomas Dewey was a "Murder Inc." crime-busting district attorney, later New York governor and unsuccessful presidential candidate against President Harry Truman. Dewey was famed as the man in the *Chicago Tribune* headline who declared, the morning after the voting closed, "Dewey Wins." Dewey lost.

In the Park Avenue Peck's kitchen, "Aunt Sally," Sally Hooten, wife of Adolphus Hooten, came in daily from Harlem. The Hootens had no children. The Peck boys were her boys.

The courtship of Scott's attractive young parents in the ebbing years of the Roaring Twenties could have been scripted by F. Scott Fitzgerald. They were in their mid-twenties, Elizabeth a few months older than David. The two were introduced to each other in 1928, in the leisurely ambience of the first-class lounge of a New York-bound ocean liner out of Southampton. Peck had been head-hunted by Sullivan & Cromwell and was headed home. David and Elizabeth courted in New York, and were wed in 1929, just after the Wall Street Crash, herald of the Great Depression.

Scott Peck believed his father married Elizabeth because she was "very beautiful, and a very beautiful WASP," with the style, grace and antecedents his go-getting father admired. Three years after they were wed, their first child, David, was born. And three years and 10 months after David, on May 22, 1936, came Morgan Scott Peck. The "Morgan," for his paternal grandfather, was dropped in favor of "Scotty."

In the family, there was not only a profusion of Pecks, but a confusion of David Pecks, three Davids across three generations. For easy identification, Scott's father is referred to as "Peck Senior" until the point he is named a judge; thereafter he is "Judge Peck." Scott's brother David is "brother David," even though the term sounds slightly monastic. Scott's nephew, the Rev. David W. Peck, III, an Anglican priest and secretary to the Archbishop of Canterbury, was brother David's son. David number III was known to the family as "Tertius." After his initial introduction here he is referred to as "the Rev. Peck."

For a lad being groomed to take his place in the Eastern Establishment, Scott Peck had useful forebears. The Pecks had not come over on the Mayflower in 1620, but they weren't far behind. Deacon Paul Peck arrived in 1635 on the good ship "Resolution," to settle in Hartford, Connecticut. His brother, Joseph Peck, arrived three years later to settle in Milford, Connecticut. Practically all New England Pecks are descended from those two. New England offered only hardscrabble farming and a hardscrabble life. When the 19th century offered better lands, newly opened up in the Midwest, Scott Peck's great-grandfather, Egbert Peck, left the East Coast for opportunities in the richer soil of Indiana.

He settled in Goodland, Indiana and married Gertrude Morgan. Gertrude and Egbert had a son, Dumont Morgan Peck ("Pecky"), Scott's grandfather. Dumont remained in Crawfordsville after graduating from Wabash College in 1906. He became partner in a haberdashery with a man called Warner. Either before or after establishing that partnership, Dumont married Warner's daughter, Juliet, Scott Peck's grandmother. They had one son, David (Peck Senior), Scotty's father.

Dumont Peck owned one of the first automobiles in Indiana, and as there were no driver licenses in those days, David was permitted to drive the family car at about the age he could first see over the steering wheel. Family trips were not always a joy. Rough roads meant regular stops to fix flat tires. Nonetheless, Dumont, Juliet and David annually drove the thousand miles from Indianapolis to visit the Morgan family homestead in Vermont. There was always a side trip to Buffalo, to visit Juliet's relatives.

The Peck generations, from grandfather Dumont to Scott, were golfers. (Scott Peck's book, *Golf and the Spirit: Lessons for the Journey*. 1999, received good reviews and modest sales.) Peck was never on the links with his grandfather, whom he called "Pecky."

"Pecky was good fun," said Peck, whereas "my grandmother, a

tiny woman, was very smart and kind of tart-tongued. She and my grandfather would argue about bridge hands they'd played thirty years earlier. She was also a bit of a disciplinarian. I never felt she liked children much." In retirement, the Peck grandparents moved from Indiana to a small apartment on New York's Lower East Side, and they wintered in Florida.

At age eleven Peck, who suffered from eye infections, was sent to Florida where, it was thought, the change of climate might be good for his eyes. When his visit ended, but before he was put on the train for the one thousand mile trip back to New York, Scott stole a block of hard maple rock sugar from his grandmother's sugar box. Like a breadbox, it was a ventilated storage chest still common in some homes of the time. He wanted the maple sugar to munch on the train. "And thereafter, boy! did my grandmother give me holy hell, which I deserved," he said. By contrast, "my grandfather, who never seemed to be a very smart man, was extraordinarily loving." Juliet the haberdasher's daughter apparently was the business brains in the family.

Young Peck adored his grandfather. They spent much private time together, in the toilet and at the movies. His grandfather sat on the toilet for three hours a day, said Peck. "He claimed it was constipation. My surmise is that it was the best way of getting away from his wife and her arguing. He used to unlock the door and let me in. And so, while he was sitting on the toilet, with nothing happening, really, me sitting on the edge of the bathtub, we'd have these three-hour conversations." Movie marathons occurred once a month; from the time Scott was eight until he was about thirteen. On a Saturday morning once a month, Scott took the subway from plush Park Avenue to the slummy East Side to have lunch in his grandparents' cramped little apartment. Within the family, he said, his grandmother was renowned for her cooking.

On the Saturday afternoon, he and his grandfather went to a matinee double feature movie. They'd return home, have dinner, and attend a second double feature in the evening. On Sunday mornings, the movies were closed, but on Sunday afternoon they'd take in a third double feature before his grandfather sent him home. Scott Peck contended there wasn't a Hollywood movie made between 1944 and 1950 that he hadn't seen. "That's love," he said, "six hours of movies." Dumont had six hours away from Juliet, with a good excuse into the bargain.

A half-century later, when Scott Peck reflected on his

grandfather, he said, "Pecky was a wonderful man, but a kind of *species Americanus*. A conventional thinker, he was filled with clichés and proverbs. On our walks to and from the movies, he had all these corny proverbs: 'All work and no play makes Jack a dull boy,' 'Don't put all your eggs in one basket,' 'If wishes were horses beggars would ride,' 'A spoonful of sugar makes the medicine go down.' He gave me a lot of sugar along with the proverbs." A grandfather himself by that time, Scott Peck mused that perhaps it was a pity that today's children didn't know any of the old proverbs. He speculated that the proverbs played a role in his success. It was a pious thought.

On his mother's side, the Savilles and Templetons were WASP families that had known wealth. Scott's grandmother, Lavinia Saville Templeton was widowed early. Her husband died when Elizabeth was six months old. Some time later, Lavinia married a man called Getty, who owned a fleet of tug boats in New York harbor. At times, as a young woman, Scott's mother would call herself Elizabeth Getty rather than Elizabeth Templeton so she could say she was "Betty Getty." The Getty relatives were never close to Scott's family, and there was a sense in interviews with Peck that perhaps socially, they weren't quite considered "the right sort." Scott once commented that though his mother was a great storyteller she never talked about Getty or the Gettys.

"Betty Getty," with her mother, stepfather, and brother, George, grew up in Little Silver, New Jersey, just across the Hudson River from New York City. There's a poem, "Uncle George's Visit," in Scott Peck's *Golf* book. George married Madeline, who Peck described as "dumpy and unattractive, though George was very, very attractive." The family always referred to him as "poor Uncle George;" Scott Peck thought his uncle far smarter than the family allowed.

Elizabeth's background was American and English: the Savilles arrived in Virginia in 1652, seventeen years later than the first Pecks in Connecticut. Six centuries earlier, Savilles had accompanied William the Conqueror in 1066 when he successfully invaded England. The Templetons were Scots who settled in the North American colonies prior to the American Revolution, which they vigorously supported. Scott's grandmother, Lavinia, had a brother, Herbert, a lifelong bachelor, and a sister, Victoria. "Uncle Herbie," was Scott's favorite uncle. Victoria married a Brooklyn banker, Al Taber. "Al was a strange sort of guy, cigar chomping, squat. Al was as ugly as Vickie was beautiful. I used to visit them, and liked them very much," said Peck, "but Uncle Herbie was my favorite. He was elegant."

Peck described his mother "as a very beautiful woman as well as a very loving one. She had a conventional kind of mind. Compared to my father, she was not particularly bright in terms of IQ, but she'd tell about the wonderful adventures she'd get into as a girl." These were with two friends who remained friends for life, Edie Hazard and Dorothy McClave. "Edie's husband," said Peck, "was the first house-husband I ever came across. He kept the home and she worked as a secretary at Riverside Church." Edie was very religious, he said, and corresponded regularly with Scott until her death. She read all his books, and "gave me hell" for his tell-all book, *In Search of Stones: A Pilgrimage of Faith, Reason and Discovery*, published in 1995.

He described early memories of his mother. "She was very patient. When I was ill, which was frequent, she would sit with me for hours on end. She was mildly obsessive-compulsive when it came to child-raising. She was obsessed about my bowels; one of my unfortunate memories of my childhood was rather frequent enemas. But she could get angry." When Scott Peck was about four she collected him from a summer day camp and as she drove home, "she bawled me out for peeing on a toilet seat at camp. She was so angry she drove the car off the road and had to get a farmer to tow it out of the field. She had strange ideas about what kinds of food were good for children, particularly for the bowels. We were always in a battle over food." Scott's favorite was chocolate cake. When quite young he'd wake up early, before the household was awake, to climb on to the kitchen counters to search through cupboards to find some.

Baby Scott Peck was not baptized. The senior Pecks attended Christ Church on Park Avenue several times a year, "for appearances' sake," said Scott Peck, a remark that could be interpreted as both accurate and snide. There were no Peck family religious observances. God, family prayers, nominal Christianity, was never mentioned in the home. In his mother's old age he learned she was in fact a "crypto-Presbyterian," and had been all her life. Scott Peck had no religion, but retained a hazy memory from very early in his childhood of an Irish Catholic nanny. He was perhaps three or four, when she took him to Catholic weddings or church services. Were she typical of the influx of Irish nannies into

New York in the 1920s and 1930s, the nanny would have talked fairly constantly to Scott about God and Jesus, and the Virgin Mary. Of those possibilities Scott Peck had no recollection whatsoever, though he said that from the Irish nanny he received "the Catholic corpuscles" in his spiritual blood stream. On his deathbed he announced he wanted to become a Catholic, but then back-tracked.

Nanny-care was the Park Avenue norm. The Peck parents were great travelers and, given their culture and class, would have had no objection to leaving their young children with nannies as they sailed for Europe on vacation. In the first half of the 20th century, Irish nannies were so prevalent in Manhattan they even gave their name to a room, the "biddy" room. "Biddy" made it into song as the diminutive for "Bridget," a common Irish name. In popular parlance, a "biddy" meant a low-grade domestic servant. New Yorker's understood perfectly when Rodgers and Hart, in *The Girlfriend of 1926*, wrote a verse for "The Blue Room," it included, "… here's the kiddies room, here's the biddy's room." In the Peck apartment at 863 Park Avenue there were two biddy rooms off the spacious kitchen. Generally, they were only occupied overnight as last minute bedrooms for guests when the others were taken.

As a young boy Peck had a child's vivid imagination that included a not rare phobia about being lost, or deliberately abandoned. Otherwise, despite living in a household dominated by two ambitious and sports-minded macho males, his father, and brother David, Peck's early Park Avenue world was, essentially, reassuringly pleasant. David was an outgoing, highly energetic and athletic, physically brave and strong, though at times a bullying, older brother. His character was in stark contrast to Scott Peck's own introspective, more coddled temperament. Fortunately, Aunt Sally was good at drying tears for, unfortunately, Scott Peck frequently needed his eyes wiped.

For the eight-year-old Scott, two incidents in one week induced the three-decade no-crying trauma. Scott and brother David attended a private middle school in Manhattan. For reasons undisclosed to history, David, at age twelve, was asked to leave. The Peck parents immediately placed David and Scott in another private school, St. Bernard's, but again for reasons never explained, Scott Peck skipped a grade. Instead of going into third grade, he entered fourth grade—a year younger than everyone in his class. St. Bernard's he described as "a decidedly British-style private grammar school with a fairly harsh regimen." It possibly needed a harsh regimen to cope with David. Scott was a different child.

On his first day in class he was no sooner seated than the teacher, a Mr. Spicer, began to slowly read the story of Robert Bruce and the spider. The tale deals with how, under the watchful eye of the Scottish king, the spider continually tried yet failed to start its web. The story describes how the spider tried and tried again until it was successful. Because the spider did not give up, Bruce decided he must not either, but must return to battle and gain his rightful throne. Scott Peck was fascinated, and enjoyed the tale. He had noticed his classmates taking notes. When Mr. Spicer finished, they were "still scribbling frantically," he recalled. "I looked over at the little red-haired boy to the left of me to try to figure out why. When he finished, he saw me peering at his paper, raised his hand, and exclaimed in a loud voice, 'Mr. Spicer, sir, the new boy next to me is cheating.' The teacher arrived from his desk at Peck's, snatched up the paper and said, 'Why, this paper is empty.' They stared at each other, he with astonishment, me with dawning horror. 'There isn't anything on it,' the teacher said. It had been a dictation class," said Peck. "I began to cry, which was hardly the thing for a boy to do on his first day in fourth grade in a new school."

An evening or two later, his parents, walking along Broadway, saw a novelty store which printed mock front-pages of newspapers. The next day they presented the newspaper to Scotty. The headline stated: "Scott Peck Hired by Circus as World's Greatest Crybaby." This was the parental prank—Peck described it as "sadism"—that so stung him he vowed never to cry again. When Peck had children of his own, they became so tired of hearing this tale they had a facsimile of the newspaper headline made and stuck it in their father's Christmas stocking.

When describing his life, Peck's litany of complaints against his father, could surface in an instant. Judge Peck didn't stand a chance if he suddenly came under Scott's baleful glare. On ethics: "My father, despite being a judge of repute, had very little understanding of ethics—a brilliant capacity to find holes in other people's arguments and absolutely none to find any in his own. He was a very powerful man, in bearing, appearance and manner. He had a capacity to block out the stuff that he wanted to block out." Of his father's spiritual life: "My father purported to have had in his teenage years some kind of 'altar call' experience [an open admission of being a follower of Christ]. It never rang quite true with me. He was probably the most secular person in the world."

Peck Senior had a stellar legal reputation. A liberal Republican, he worked to reform the New York State Republican Party as vigorously as he reformed the New York Appellate Court system, to which he had been appointed from Sullivan & Cromwell. When he retired as a judge, he returned to the law firm. But he could do little right in his son's eyes, for Scott Peck damned his father with the faintest possible praise. Not least as a parent: "He was at least as good a father as I," said Peck, "though there were times I felt I did not get enough from him—though he gave as much as I gave my children."

During the taped interviews and casual conversations that shaped this book, a competitive father-son spirit could surface in an instant, and on almost any topic. For example, Scott Peck pointedly noted that no one had ever written a biography of his father. That was true enough, though Judge Peck himself, in a brief memoir, noted it first, "If my biography were ever written, which thankfully will not happen ...." Then, almost immediately, Scott Peck, as if suddenly aware he was slighting his parent again, and as if in recompense, spoke highly of his father's two books. They were *The Greer Case: A True Court Drama* (Simon and Schuster, 1955), and *Decision at Law* (Dodd, 1961). The father could have engaged in a brisk one-upmanship with Scott by remarking that no one had ever made a movie of one of Scott Peck's books, whereas, Judge Peck's *The Greer Case,* was a 1957 made-for-television movie. It starred Raymond Burr and Zsa Zsa Gabor.

So much about Scott Peck spoke to insecurities. Each summer of his childhood, before going to their summer home, the family first went out to East Hampton, Long Island for a couple of weeks at the shore. At East Hampton, they stayed in "The 1770 House" operated by a Mr. and Mrs. John Williams, the nine-year-old Peck wrote to his mother: *Dear Mom, I'm out to supper. Will be back for 90 cents at 6.40. If not in leave it with Williams. I still love you and hope that my manner hasn't changed so much that you don't love me. Much love, Scotty.*

The major portion of each summer, however, was spent in rural Western Connecticut, a summer gathering place on manicured estates for Manhattan's Establishment wealthy. During the years Scott was three to five years old, the family rented "the magic house, Hooper House, near Sharon." When the time came for Scott Peck, a married man with three children, to settle down, it was in rural Connecticut that he and his wife Lily found their home, not 30 miles from that first boyhood summer "magic house."

"The Hooper House was magical for there were sheep in a pasture beyond the gate," Peck reminisced. "There was an icehouse in the back. It was just magical. Lily thought so, too. It's all changed now. I have a hundred memories of the Hooper House. Years later, when we discussed it, my brother couldn't remember anything about the place."

Among his countryside memories, Scott Peck said as a three-year-old, he recalled being awakened by his mother and carried outside to see the Northern Lights "dancing in the sky." The impression was so vivid that as an adult he checked with his mother to see whether it had happened. She remembered it as September 1939. Europe was already at war. A year later he stood at the top of the stairs in Hooper House and watched his mother and a group of neighbor women knitting "Bundles for Britain," warm clothes for the war-torn British.

Even discussing Hooper House, Peck took the opportunity to take a dig at his father. "The Hooper House," he said, "was the only time my father ever lived in a valley. Otherwise he always lived on mountaintops, as befitted his image of himself." The year Scott was five Peck Senior built his own "mountaintop" house, on a hill in the Sharon area. (Judge Peck's final summer home, not this one, was called "The Schloss," German for castle.)

The year the Pecks spent their first summer in the Sharon house, Scott was a would-be Boy Scout, but was too young to join. He saw an advertisement for the official Scout hatchet, however, and asked for a similar one for Christmas—wish granted, it was under the Christmas tree. In the countryside with his axe, he found a sapling to hack away at, and instead cut open his knee. His first true experience of physical pain was not the injury, he said, it was being stitched up without anesthetic. His father took away the hatchet.

In his everyday New York experience, schoolboy Peck was a typical subway-using Manhattan "tunnel rat." In those days, however, it was children not adults who were mugged in New York—by other kids robbing them for their school money. Little wonder Peck preferred to think of himself as "a country boy." Not until he was fifteen and had to work on a farm did he find out that country life was more than sheep in the meadow. As a ten-year-old in the Sharon countryside there was time to experiment. There was a farmer's hay-rake parked in a field behind his parents' house. One day Peck decided it was no more than a giant Erector set put together with nuts and bolts and so, armed with a supply of wrenches, and accompanied by a summer pal his age, Scott methodically dismantled the hay-rake into its component parts and left them scattered across several acres, which, once the farmer discovered the damage, is probably what he would have liked to have done to Scott Peck.

Something happened of 1946 when Scott was ten that haunted him emotionally. He described his parents having "fierce quarrels;" his mother talked about getting a divorce. These conversations did not take place in front of her sons. Scott was eavesdropping. He would listen, he said, through "an adjoining window. I didn't really know anything about what divorce meant at the age of ten. But I don't think a woman in her mid-30s could, with two children, have divorced a wealthy, successful lawyer. What happened after that summer, after that period of arguing, was that my mother totally capitulated for the rest of her life. She just sort of gave up the ghost of her individuality, with the exception of a few rare moments of courage."

Though obviously riveted by the arguments that threatened the breakup of the family, Peck held back on the details—he would go no further in providing information of the parental disagreements, or the ensuing détente, of that summer. However, what statements he made as to what he'd heard through his parents' window did not stand the test of commonsense. Peck insisted that the bone of contention between the parents rested in what Mrs. Peck regarded as her husband's lack of integrity as a lawyer. It is wrong to try to second-guess history, nonetheless, the idea of a ten-year-old taking umbrage over his father's ethical choices as a lawyer tests credulity. Even if parents took different sides on ethical issues it would be highly rarefied grounds for contemplating divorce. At the very least, a ten-year-old suffering from hearing, perhaps seeing, his mother in tears during furious arguments, may have further turned Peck against his father, her tormentor.

In refusing to delve further, Peck instead essayed into an example of his father's ethical lapses. When Scott was eleven, the family took a two-month vacation at a Montana dude ranch. The parents didn't like ranch life, it was too rough and ready for them, but David, who was fifteen, loved it and wanted to go back the next year. Judge Peck said yes, provided David earned half the cost of $400 by working on a farm near the family's summer home. The bargain was struck.

In Sharon, the Pecks belonged "to a very WASP country club with the customary golf course and tennis court," said Scott. There was an annual Labor Day tennis tournament for which partners were drawn out of a hat. David and Scott were tennis players on a par with the average adult. Scott said that one boy, Donny Green, who always played in the tournament, was a terrible tennis player. For two years back-to-back, when tournament partners were drawn from the hat, "David was paired with Donny." The third year a drawing was made—the year of the dude ranch trip after their return—David was once again was paired with Donny Green.

When David saw the result, and given there were more than a hundred participants, he claimed the tournament drawing was obviously rigged. No one wanted to play with Donny Green; so he was palmed off on the other children. David decided to make a formal complaint to the tournament committee. His father was appalled and told David that if he didn't complain, he would be released from his debt for his return trip to the Montana ranch.

As Scott Peck described it, "David said, 'That's a bribe,' and I sat there and said, 'Certainly seems like a bribe to me.'" David did complain to the tournament committee and the tournament match-up was redrawn. For Scott, however, the lesson was elsewhere. "It was a very powerful experience for me to see my father, a powerful judge, who had this huge reputation for honesty and probity, make a bribe. It was my father's desire not to make any waves when he was in WASP heaven."

Peck had another tennis tale. In Sharon, he made friends with a couple of children, last name, Piel, whose father was Scott's father's protégé, a litigation specialist at Sullivan & Cromwell. At tennis, "Mrs. Piel was one of the few adults who would take some time out when I was ten years old to rally with me. She gave me the most important point in playing tennis that I ever got. She'd say, 'You're rushing the ball. Just remember you've got plenty of time to hit the ball.' I started saying to myself, every shot, remember to take the time and my game suddenly, dramatically improved."

Years later, Scott and Lily met the youngest of the Piel children, Tom, a Green Beret, and invited him to dinner. Tom Piel mentioned it to his mother and asked her if she remembered Scott Peck from Sharon days. "This was before I'd written *The Road Less Traveled*," said Peck. "And she said, 'Oh, yes, he was the little boy who was always talking about the kind of things that people shouldn't talk about.' It was an affirming kind of comment," Peck remarked.

That 1947 journey out West was Scott's last clutch at childhood. "I don't think I ever had an Oedipus complex, but during that trip I had practically an uncontrollable, very intense, desire and need to cuddle with my mother. She allowed this. I sat for significant periods during that trip on my mother's lap, cuddling her. My brother teased me like crazy about it. But that was what I wanted to do and my mother seemed accepting of it. That was the only time I remember that. I remember by the time I was twelve I no longer had that need or desire. I never consciously had any sexual thoughts about my mother." Montana was also the first summer after whatever Scott had heard and/or seen the previous summer during the "fierce quarrels" between his parents.

Sexual knowledge and awakening came a little late to Peck, but he caught up quickly. "I was relatively late in learning the facts of life—from that guy, Donny Green, riding our bikes back from the tennis club. I was horrified at the thought you would take your penis and put it inside a woman's bottom. I thought I'm never going to have sex." Later, he apparently had more than most men of his generation.

He became a smoker at thirteen when on vacation at Fire Island "long before it became a gay community," he said. He never lost the habit. "Some fifteen-year-old little bastard taught me to inhale. He smoked Camels." So did Peck, three packs a day, for the rest of his life up to within a year or so of his death. Even on his sick bed he'd take an occasional puff if his wife held the cigarette. He did stop smoking a couple times, he said, once for two days. He was in his 40s and staying in a convent.

"David smoked and drank like I did," said Scott. "He was a great believer in [the organization] Smoke-enders, which he went to twice. He said he was the only member of his group that didn't quit. My father, though not frequently, smoked cigars, which he loved. He always chided my mother rather nastily for smoking cigarettes."

Undoubtedly, Scott Peck was a deeply introspective child. Over the years he penned poetry that varied in quality but was usually revelatory. A few lines of his "A Star in the East," offer a glimpse of him in adulthood interpreting his childhood:

A Star in the East

Two nights before Christmas
In the year of Our Lord nineteen hundred and forty-three,
My earthly Father and I drove to the train station
Through bitter cold and darkness to meet my two great
Uncles and one great aunt.
I looked through one of the windows,
Frosty with our combined breaths,
And saw the hugest star I had ever seen.
None of the adults seemed to notice.
I checked to be sure;
There was no doubt,
The star was definitely in the East.
My roaring inclination was to scream,
"Look there's the star in the East!"
But in that moment, I took a step out of innocence.
Somehow I knew that their response would be, "Oh,
Isn't he cute?"
So with my new found wisdom,
For perhaps the first time in my seven years,
I held my tongue.

His newfound wisdom about holding his tongue didn't last long. The next year, at age eight, he attended a wedding in Lakeville, Connecticut with his mother. He had a glass of champagne. He called down the table across three people, not realizing that one was the bride's mother, "Hey Mom, it's a lousy wine, isn't it?" His mother, extremely embarrassed, quickly silenced him. In the car later, she more soundly rebuked him. She was not disciplining him for drinking, but for rudeness. Scott continued to insist that the wine was of poor quality. They went around and around on the incident, he said. Finally his mother admitted, "Yes, it was a rather poor wine."

The household mores were clear. Scott at eight could knock back champagne, but not transgress the WASP social code.

CHAPTER TWO

Father Knows Best

Three torments conspired to gradually come together to govern Scott Peck's life during the period between entering elementary school and his college graduation: his overbearing father, sibling rivalry, and sexual awakening. Each spelled trouble in a different way.

When Peck discussed his relationship with his brother, David, it had elements of a re-run of the difficulties with his father. Scott's choice of words suggests he did not have much by way of emotional filters when it came to dealing with either of them. He could declare, "David was very bright but for much of my life, certainly during my twenties and thirties, I hated him." "Hate" is pretty strong, but everything with Scott Peck came out as either light or dark. There were never any grays, little nuance in his observations. Peck's mother died in 1980, and his father subsequently remarried—a high school sweetheart from Crawfordsville, Indiana. Scott liked her at first, but later declared her the "most evil person" he'd ever met. Peck's judgmental pendulum was given to wide sweeps.

Though he found David "a very confusing character," Peck said, "We had a lot of fun playing together. I looked up to him and admired him, but then at other times he would treat me really shittily. He would jump on top of me, hold me down on the bed, put his finger up his ass and then take it out and put it under my nose. That's a little sadistic. He used to be sadistic with other people, too."

In most families with a couple of boys, the brothers have spells of major cooperation, as well as moments of almost brutal discord. In the brothers' case, four years was a wide age span in the pre-teen and teenage years. Psychiatrist Peck speculated, "Adlerians believe that siblings tend to define themselves off each other. Whether this happened or not, I don't know. My brother became a rabid Republican. I've been a lifelong Democrat." David was gregarious, Scott introspective with little small talk and no time for cocktail parties.

Speaking of his self-centeredness, Scott Peck's second wife, Kathy, said Scott "was so hurt because people in that family didn't know how to love. This is just my pop-psychology, but I think he developed a coping mechanism, and that was the narcissism. I really think that the damage was done in childhood. It was from a bullying father, a bullying brother and a mother that went along because she just succumbed to the situation she was in." Kathy Peck had some supporting evidence for that latter remark. Scott's son, Christopher, said his Aunt Greg (brother David's first wife, mother of their three children) had told him of a time when Scotty's mother admitted she was "just a terrible mother because she didn't keep Scotty and David from fighting." Fighting was not something David was afraid of.

Said Scott, "David had lots of fights as a kid, fights as an adult, In New York City he was ganged up on by some people who wanted money. He was 50 or 55 and tried to fight them off. That was my brother. I would have run, or given my money and run. We were totally opposite in personality. I admired him. He went from Princeton, where he majored in Arabic studies, to Arabia with Aramco, and was kicked out after two years for reasons never made clear. My brother had a way of doing atrocious sorts of things. It was after Arabia he went to Harvard Law, flunked out, but went across the river to Harvard Business School and did wonderfully. He was a Republican, he was in business, he talked my father's language. So, from adolescence on, my brother seemed to be the favored one, while I was doing flaky things like dropping out of Exeter, and refusing to take ROTC."

If Scott Peck felt bullied and put upon, there must have been times David felt put upon in a different way, from having to keep an eye on a much younger brother. When the younger brother got the better breaks that could really hurt. The lawn at the Sharon summer home was the thin end of one such wedge between Scott and David.

"My father, the perfectionist, wanted the finest lawn in all of Connecticut," explained Scott Peck, "so he consulted with the Department of Agriculture. He planted something, didn't like the result, rolled it over the next year, then replanted it with something better. Sure enough, by the time I was eight and David twelve, he had the finest lawn in the state. The lawn by then was so thick it was nearly impossible to mow—and that was David's job, with a hand mower. David was mollified only by the fact that when I became twelve it would be my job to do the mowing. That was the summer my parents bought the power mower."

Scott said David was furious and held it against him that he'd gotten a reprieve. "I used to refer to David as having a lawn mower neurosis. But there was a reason for his neurosis."

David's son, the Rev. Peck, comparing and contrasting his father with his uncle Scott, suggested that "one thing Scotty despised, I think, was charm and superficiality," and "as he lived in a world that valued these things over the gifts he had, his life resulted in his adolescent martyrdom. My father was 'winning' in a crowd, as an athlete, a joker, and one who rarely thought too much! So [Scotty] must have felt badly under-rated as a small, bright and sensitive boy in a world of boisterous charm. No doubt he [also] internalized the insecurity that I think my father and grandfather would have felt in their own social aspirations—as relatively new and poor comers to the world of serious old money they inhabited—and in my father's case, married into through my mother."

"Despite every cultural advantage," said the Rev. Peck, "my father never reached his peak. He always said that Scotty walked to the sound of a different drum, long before Scotty wrote a book of that title, but my father never had a killer business instinct, great brains, or great drive. He liked a party; was fun and charming; relatively successful, but never seriously so. He lacked or recoiled from the risk-taking and strategic thinking one needs in the world. He was supremely clubbable. Scotty was the earnest, the sincere, the driven and sensitive one—the suffering poet as opposed to the party-boy. He was far more attractive to me than my own father. But that is what uncles are for!"

In a sense, said Scott Peck, brother David was "totally unadventurous, never introspective. He was one of those guys where the peak of his life was at Exeter. He died at 66—I outlived him. He was much older and bigger and he'd beat up on me, but on one occasion, I don't know what happened, I was suddenly tossing him to the other side of the room. Other than that, when I was in a fight I'd just curl up and protect my testicles, whereas he, after rotator-cuff surgery on his shoulder, was white-water rafting two weeks later. I was a better tennis player, but sometimes he would beat me because, when he went for the ball, he didn't care whether he'd hit the fence, or how hard. Later, I thought my brother had been the sacrificial lamb—sacrificed to the WASP cause—the family scapegoat."

Scott loved his first summer as a teenager. It was fun because in his class at St. Bernard's was a boy called Carl Brandt, Jr., whose mother was a top literary agent of the day. On a temporary basis she was also a vice president of MGM in charge of selecting books with potential as movies. "Carl, her son, and I were both going to attend Exeter," said Peck. "Mrs. Brandt thought it would be a good idea for the two of us to establish some friendship so that we would be able to support each other at Exeter. So she invited me for a week up to the mansion she and her husband were renting on Long Island. She and I became very fond of each other. It was not a romantic kind of love, me at thirteen and she in her mid-forties, but this very important powerful woman cared for me greatly. Every vacation we used to meet and she would take me to '21,' and supply me with cigarettes, caviar and champagne, much to my parents' horror and chagrin. She'd invite me to quite a fair number of her parties in Manhattan. There were no artistic people in parties at my house, but there were indeed at her house, so I met a number of the great authors of the day. She never really told me anything about writing but encouraged just by her interest in me. The only thing she did give me were little tips, terribly important, like save all your typewriter paper boxes because you'll want those to send the manuscript to publishers, and always have a duplicate copy of anything you're working on lest you lose the original. She encouraged me in bigger ways than just writing."

Summer's pleasures ended abruptly. His parents drove up to New Hampshire, to Exeter, to drop him off at Phillips Academy, perhaps the top-rated boys' prep school. The emotional trauma of being sent to boarding school is a stock feature of early 20th century English autobiographies and biographies. It is not prominent in American literature, mainly because most American boys enter prep school in their early teens, where in Britain it could mean being sent away from home as young as six or seven. Peck, however, made his Exeter trauma one of his life themes. Given his relationship with his father. When he left Exeter halfway through high school it was a clear display of despair-driven courage.

Scott arrived in Exeter well aware David had enjoyed Phillips Exeter Academy, for he'd been a brilliant success, at least in sports. He was the only Exeter student, Scott said proudly, to ever gain three letters—as a goalie in varsity soccer, varsity hockey and varsity lacrosse. Scott understood what Exeter was ordained to mean in the WASP ascendancy of the day: he was in no doubt that he was genuinely fortunate to have been accepted at Exeter. He understood he was set on the rails of WASP success, hooked to a career locomotive that would pull him on to the best of the Ivy League universities, in the company of boys soon men, whose careers in high finance and government and the professions were as guaranteed as his own. It was how aspirants to the Establishment lived out their aspirations. Fifty-plus years on, Peck mused that he felt embraced by the "security which came from being a part of what was so obviously a proper pattern." He could revel in the fact that "there are a whole number of prestigious WASP prep schools—though if one is more prestigious than any other it would be Exeter." He could conclude he was "ready for the intellectual stuff," for he went in as a freshman taking sophomore level courses; while emotionally, he was little boy lost. "I felt horrible there right from the start because I was so depressed and miserable. Right from the start, even before classes began. I can remember sitting around with a bunch of kids. A kid asked me, 'Hey, you ever been laid?' I didn't know what being laid was. I was thirteen. I knew it was something good, so I said, 'Sure, sure.'" Peck was bobbing in currents over which he had no control.

Exeter was a "culture totally dictated by kids between the ages of thirteen and eighteen," contended Peck. "It was like the book, *The Lord of the Flies*. That could have been written by an Exeter graduate. There was no interaction between the faculty and the students. You were appointed a faculty advisor. The entirety of my first year I never once met with my faculty advisor. The faculty had no real contact with the students." Another "big thing at Exeter," he said, "was tremendous homophobia where all the worst people in the 'out group' were called 'Fairies,' or, 'Zoom! There goes a fairy.' The living environment was deliberately harsh. You weren't really allowed any decorations in the room or anything to make your room comfortable. The only respite, the only touch of home, was that every Sunday evening someone prominent would travel to Exeter to lecture. It was a voluntary kind of thing to go to, but after the lecture, those who wanted to could go to a large faculty home. In the living room they would gather around and talk with this famous lecturer. I would go faithfully, not because I was particularly interested in the subject or the person, but for the opportunity to go this house that had sofas decently upholstered, curtains, warm and soft and gentle. I would go just for the opportunity of going into a real living room. Exeter took, and as far as I understand still takes great pride in being harsh. The race is won by the swift and hardship will teach you to be swift. If you can't deal with this kind of hardship then you better get out. It was the most un-nurturing place that I have ever seen."

Exeter's "in-group" had immediately pegged Peck firmly in the "out-group." He hated his general predicament and despaired further in being among the "outs." When his parents came to visit during the first Thanksgiving they saw he was depressed. They asked why. Peck denied it was so and said he was getting along fine. Later he said that he felt so much pressure to succeed at Exeter he couldn't acknowledge his depression to his parents. He endured the first year and "went back for the second year because I was expected to. It was what I was supposed to do. Here was this great school with a great reputation and I was supposed to tough it out." In fact, he was doing poorly academically and lived for the vacations.

During vacations and away from Exeter, at ages thirteen, fourteen and fifteen, he said he was becoming critically aware of the world around him. He was already well along the road to holding strong opinions based solely on personal reaction to his parents' preferences. His parents occasionally attended Christ Church on Park Avenue, "a weird church that was built around one guy [the Rev. Ralph Sockman], *the* minister for the upper crust Park Avenue types. He was smooth, he was oily." At fourteen, Peck struck out on his own and several times attended the Madison Avenue Presbyterian Church, presided over by the Rev. George Buttrick, a famed preacher, and later "Preacher to the University" at Harvard. "Buttrick would weep during his sermons, I remember one was 'come with me and I'll make you fishers of men.' I decided that sounded like a good idea, to become fishers of men." Spiritually marooned somewhere between Sockman and Buttrick, Peck found only confusion in religion. "The reason Christianity made no sense to me," he said, was here were "two famous ministers. One, I knew, I was spiritually ahead of, while the other, slightly less famous, was light years ahead of me spiritually. It just didn't compute." On the religious front at Exeter he paid "no attention to God." His best friend at the school, he said, was Rene Tillich, son of the noted U.S. theologian Paul Tillich, and he and Rene had "great intellectual discussions late into the night."

Peck said he found himself reacting to ethical issues that ranged from his adverse reaction to hearing Senator Joseph McCarthy on the radio, to suspicions about his father's home away from home,

Sullivan & Cromwell. During Peck's first summer break from Exeter, he said, he was ill and bored. He rarely listened to the radio but turned it on and "heard someone by the name of Joseph McCarthy speaking. I didn't know who he was, or anything about the issues of communism or what not. I just caught about 30-45 seconds of a speech he was giving. The voice was so ugly," he said. "I turned it off and I remember going down the hall from the bedroom thinking, 'That was the voice of evil.'"

Sullivan & Cromwell was prominent in his musing as he began to follow the Korean War, which was just in its early stages. "The accounts in *The New York Times* as to why we were there did not add up," Peck said. "Earlier than this, John Foster Dulles and Allen Dulles used to inhabit our living room from time to time, and these guys were, to me, by and large, baddies. Certainly, later, the Vietnam War would be waged according to something called the 'Dulles Doctrine,' which was an unethical doctrine. It was a very clear kind of 'the end justifies the means.' Korea seemed to be the same." When Peck mentally lumped his father in with the Dulleses this was not just abstract, knee-jerk teenage reaction. His father, through the Dulles and Sullivan & Cromwell, and especially through the Peck Panel, was deeply immersed in the deepening Korean War.

On June 25, 1950, North Korea brought its tanks down to the 38th parallel, the standoff line with South Korea. The move sent shock waves through the U.S. government. The United States was already faced with a deepening Cold War in Europe and potential conflict with the Soviet Union. War-torn Europe still needed rebuilding. The once industrially mighty West Germany was in ruins. Germany, the war-torn leading "sick man of Europe," needed rapid revitalization. The Cold War made it a necessity, the Korea War an imperative.

The New York Times regarded North Atlantic Treaty Organization (NATO) policy as contradictory, for the Western Allies wanted to revive Germany's heavy industry capabilities while "holding down the industrialists." One of those industrialists was Alfried Krupp. The Nuremberg Trials judges had imprisoned Krupp for using forced labor. He still headed the centuries-old Krupp armaments maker which controlled vast resources of iron and coal. Sullivan & Cromwell knew that terrain well from its considerable involvement in German commerce almost up to the start of World War II. In the 1930s, when Judge Peck joined the

Sullivan & Cromwell firm, Hitler was transforming Germany into Nazi Germany. The fact that Sullivan & Cromwell, late in the 30s, still had an extensive manufacturing, financial and commercial clientele, both German and American, doing business in Nazi Germany, led to complaints from many of S&C's own lawyers.

Sullivan & Cromwell's principals were on friendly terms with the pro-German John J. McCloy, the U.S. High Commissioner based in Frankfurt. McCloy was a major figure in U.S. political and financial circles where he was known as "the Chairman of the Establishment." Prior to the war he had been legal counsel to the German chemical combine, I. G. Farben. That was the time Sullivan & Cromwell was drawing a significant part of its income from its work in Germany with similar corporations. McCloy also had a World War II reputation tarnished at the edges. There were charges he'd prevented the United States from bombing particular German targets.

Nonetheless, in 1950, he was High Commissioner in Germany. McCloy was considering establishing The Advisory Board on Clemency for War Criminals—a review board for Nazis, Nazi-sympathizers and their supporters—who had been imprisoned by the Nuremberg Trials.

Spurred by the Korean War outbreak, McCloy established his Advisory Board on Clemency for War Criminals; its short form tag was "the Peck Panel," for Judge Peck chaired the three-member commission. This much-reduced follow-up to the Nuremburg Trials had a purpose—to establish whether certain war criminals should be released. It could reduce sentences, it could not inquire into findings of guilt. The Peck Commission studied the war criminals' trial records and within 40 days, in August 1950, issued its report recommending clemency. That suited the many pro-German sympathizers in Congress. As high commissioner, McCloy ruled that Alfried Krupp, though still a war criminal, could resume leadership of the decartelized Krupp empire. As William Manchester noted in his book *The Arms of Krupp*, Eleanor Roosevelt wrote to McCloy to ask, "Why are we freeing so many Nazis?" McCloy's reply was evasive, rather than persuasive.

This era is an extremely murky period of U.S. history. In the late 1940s, certain circles still warmed themselves from the dying embers of the (pro-Hitler) American-German Bund. These Members of Congress and their supporters' language was Cold War rhetoric and what blossomed into the viciousness of the

"McCarthy era." Indeed, Manchester quotes Senator Joseph McCarthy's reaction to McCloy's decision to release Krupp: "Extremely wise."

Scott Peck was 28 and his father was 62 when Manchester's *The Arms of Krupp* was published. And while Manchester explicitly refers to Judge Peck's probity, the overall tone of Manchester's reporting is that at the highest levels of the U.S. government and Administration, the fix was in. "The Peck Panel" was simply a variation on an earlier theme, when the United States had siphoned off Nazi Germany's rocket scientists and others for its own development programs without holding them responsible for their actions supporting Nazism and Hitler's genocide policy.

"To give my father some room, at least," said Scott Peck, "I have my own suspicion that [the decision] was ordered by John McCloy, and hence probably by [President Harry] Truman and [General George] Marshall. That's my suspicion. It doesn't let my father entirely off the hook." Peck "vaguely remembered" his father was angered by the Manchester book.

The summer Scott was fifteen, he briefly played competitive tennis. More lastingly, he discovered girls. "One of the reasons I was never a better tennis player, never a great tennis player, was I went on a tournament tour that summer. But I hated the tournament circuit and I hated the kids, stuck up. I'm very competitive, but I had none of the killer instincts the great tennis players have. There were no ball boys or lines people, you had to make your own call. Whenever I called a ball and was questioned did I really see it, I'd wonder could it have been my imagination that it went out. And I would invariably lose the next point."

That same summer, staying on Long Island, he French-kissed a girl and decided he had met the love of his life. She ditched him and dated all the other boys. "I spent much of the summer watching the waves come in from the ocean and pondering the mystery of it all." When, towards the end of the summer, she'd run through all the boys in town and asked if they might not date again, he took her out. They necked and kissed. "She said, 'You're distant, don't you love me any more?' And I said, 'No, I don't. Frankly, my dear, I don't give a damn.'" But he was not unmoved. He later memorialized that summer by writing two poems, one on death called, *Life Wish,* and one on sex called, *Death Wish.*

Back at school in the Fall of 1951, the lonely confines of Exeter gave Peck more time than usual to brood about his father's shortcomings, and on his father's reaction to what Peck felt was an inevitability—his need to leave Exeter as an act of personal survival. "My lungs were hurting. I'd no idea how my father would respond. I was depressed. I felt I was a failure. It wasn't any of the masochism of rebellion." Leaving would be an act that "almost confirmed that my father should respond that way because I was such a *failure*." But as a thirteen to fifteen year-old at Exeter he daily felt "my life appeared meaningless and I felt more wretched. The last year I did little but sleep, for only in sleep could I find any comfort. In retrospect I think perhaps I was resting and unconsciously preparing myself for the leap I was about to take."

He was more than despairing, though, he was angry. "I may not seem it, but under the surface I'm potentially a very angry man, as was my father. And it comes, maybe it comes, from my father." Decades after Exeter, he'd decided his malaise at the school was a "heritage from father's deepest motive life in life, to look like a WASP and to raise his children to be the ultimate WASPs. Father succeeded in David. In retrospect I was walking out of the WASP culture into the absolute unknown."

Unexpectedly that semester, Peck's situation at Exeter brightened. He entered the "in-group" through being cast for a small part in *Billy Budd,* the school play. It was a minor role but he enjoyed it. One of the co-authors of the play was John Chapman, drama critic for *The New York Times*. Chapman, a friend of one of Exeter's teachers, came up to see the production; then he reviewed it for the *Exonian,* Exeter's newspaper. "The review was full of kind praise," said Peck. Peck's eyes raced down Chapman's column searching for his own name, he said, but Chapman "mentioned everybody in the play in his review, everybody but me. As I kept reading I wasn't there, I wasn't there, I wasn't there. Then I came to the last paragraph, which I thought he would use for summation. Instead he wrote, 'I would like to end by making special mention of Scott Peck, who although in a minor role as Lt. Radcliffe, as far as I'm concerned, played that role better than it was played on Broadway.' That helped me get into the in-crowd."

Peck wrote home, *"How did you like my reviews? They were pretty great. Did you save the Exonian?"* Despite his relentless disparagement of Exeter, Peck had his achievements, and writing was one of them. *"I have got a swelled head,"* he wrote home. *"My English teacher thinks I am a genius as a writer. We had to write a description and I wrote about the reflections of the headlights of cars on the walls of my room at night.*

He read it to the class saying the paper showed genius and compared me rather favorably to John Steinbeck. Now he is keeping it to read to the English department."

Peck's acting helped him develop his fledgling hypochondria into a minor art form. One way to get a break from the school milieu he hated was to talk his way into bed at the school infirmary. His illnesses, real and feigned, provided respite, a time to read. To his parents he wrote from the school infirmary, *"All Sunday night I had a beautiful headache so I came in Monday morning to make my weekend a long one. I have just finished having the first of fourteen nice penicillin shots. I just have a little sinus problem, it is nothing to worry about and I will soon be out."* Within weeks he was writing, *"Life is just about the same as usual, not depressing, but frustrating because I cannot read English all the time. Probably I will zip off to the infirmary and read a couple of books sometime soon."*

Peck's triumphant acceptance into the ruling elite did not play out the way one might expect. Rather than his new status making his continuance at Exeter likely, he felt that being accepted into the in-group gave him the emotional freedom to pursue his plan to quit the place. "When I got into the in-group I felt I could leave as a success. I couldn't have left as an out-group failure." Peck's second stroke of good fortune in the in-crowd was making friends with Tim Childs, "a very eccentric and wonderful man, quite potent in the intellectual circle of the in-crowd."

Childs and Peck were in the same class, and he took Peck under his wing and let it be known they were friends. "We remained good friends for a half century until Tim's death," he said. In fact it was more than "good friends"—Peck was in awe of Tim Childs. Down the years Peck would periodically befriend or be befriended by a strong, father-figure type he could admire, look up to, and indeed depend on. In turn, Peck was known as a good friend to have.

Determined to leave Exeter, Peck first went to see his advisor, Mr. Lynch, "a kindly person who had barely spoken to me in the previous two and a half years." At that meeting, Peck had barely begun speaking when Lynch broke in and told him it would be preferable to graduate from a superior school like Exeter with lesser grades than from a lesser school with better grades. "And your parents would be quite upset, just go along and do the best you can." Peck was totally dissatisfied with that response and met next with "the crusty old dean of the school who cut me off straightaway. He told me Exeter was the best school in the world and I was a damn fool for thinking of quitting." Finally Peck went to see his math teacher, a somewhat younger man. "I chose him not because we had any relationship or because he seemed to be a particularly warm sort of person—indeed I found him a rather cold mathematical kind of fish—but because he had a reputation for being the faculty genius."

The math teacher let Peck talk for five minutes then asked him questions for three-quarters of an hour. Then the teacher leaned back in his chair, and with a pained expression on his face, told Peck, "I'm sorry. I can't help you. I don't have any advice to give you. You know, it's impossible for one person to ever completely put himself in another person's shoes. But insofar as I can put myself in your shoes—and I'm glad I'm not there—I don't know what I would do if I were you. So, you see, I don't know how to advise you. I'm sorry that I've been unable to help." Five decades later, Peck said, "It is just possible that the man saved my life. I was close to suicidal, but when I left his office I felt as if a thousand pounds had been taken off my back. Because, if a genius didn't know what to do, then it was all right for me not to know what to do."

It was a fine rationalization. Peck had been desperately trying to survive at Exeter on his own terms. Now, headed home for the Christmas vacation, he was prepared to leave on his own terms. Back home in Park Avenue he told his parents he hated Exeter and wanted to quit. His parents asked him why he hated it so; he could give them no rational answer. When they asked which school he wanted to attend, he said he didn't know. "They worked on me and convinced me to stick it out for at least one more semester and if, at the end of another semester, I still wanted to quit, well, then I could."

The adult Peck said his Exeter problem was his reaction "against the WASP culture so cherished by my father, Exeter was one of White Anglo-Saxon Protestantism's formation centers." Possibly so, though the WASP bogeyman may have been a handy scapegoat for a Scott Peck who was genuinely unhappy away from the familiar and comfortable. He made it through Exeter's winter semester, had a small role in the winter play and was cast as lead for the spring play. Nonetheless, although he hated letting the school and the play down, when he came home for the spring break, he told his parents, "You said I could leave Exeter and quit if I wanted to, and I still want to." They asked him again where, instead, he wanted to go to school. He could give them no answer. They told him he must be crazy not wanting to go to Exeter, and ought to see a psychiatrist. No sooner said than done.

Judge Peck had a classmate from Wabash who was a psychiatrist with a posh residential treatment clinic, Silver Hill, in New Canaan, Connecticut, well-known as a place where the addicted rich and famous dried out. So, at his father's behest, Scott Peck went to see the man. He took an instant liking to him, despite being told, "You're depressed and I think you ought to come into hospital here." The doctor informed Scott he was not so depressed he could be committed, that Scott had to admit himself. "It's your choice, but my advice would be that you come into the hospital." That night, said Peck, "the doctor made an appointment to see me again the next morning for my decision." As with several of Scott Peck's life stories, delivered almost rote, when he repeated the Exeter tale he would contend again that leaving Exeter was "the bravest thing I ever did, while making the decision that night to enter Silver Hill, the hardest."

If standing up to his father on quitting Exeter was courageous so was his Silver Hill decision. Mulling it over, Scott said, he again had thoughts of suicide. "I couldn't sleep until, finally, as I recounted in *The Road Less Traveled*, these words came to me, that 'the only true security in life lies in relishing life's insecurity.'" He told himself he would go into the unknown. He went into Silver Hill and stayed for five weeks.

Peck said that the major discovery in his therapy centered on the psychiatrist pushing him to answer what, in relation to Exeter, he was most angry about. He was angry at Exeter, said Peck. The psychiatrist asked him to think about the question and arrive at a different answer for their next meeting. The next day, Peck said, "I told him, 'Well, I guess what I was angriest about was not Exeter but angriest about myself for being a failure at Exeter.' The psychiatrist said, 'Well, I think that's correct.'"

At Silver Hill, Peck had been given psychological testing. The only thing the psychiatrist said was it indicated Peck had a certain fear of sex. "He asked did I masturbate and I said no. And he said, 'Well, you know it's perfectly normal to masturbate.' So, having gotten permission, I went off and immediately started masturbating." He was not quite sixteen. He'd also gotten permission to leave Exeter. But was Exeter leaving him? In one sense—according to his nephew, the Rev. Peck—Judge Peck,

Sullivan & Cromwell, Park Avenue and Exeter prevailed, for "Scotty," the Rev. Peck said, "has a real snobbishness that is straight from the same flask as my father and his father." The WASP culture had enfolded him. He could poke holes through it, but he never escaped it.

Scott Peck left Silver Hill shortly before his sixteenth birthday. Early that summer he went to work on a farm attached to a school out near Sharon, work for which he was paid. He was living at the school. There were other people his age as friends with whom to spend the evenings and weekends. He worked what he regarded as a grueling 40-to-50 hours a week on the farm. "That's how I became familiar with what it's like to get the stones out of the field," he said. The only thing that upset him was that two or three weeks before the end of summer, he learned his father was paying the school "to have this position where I was working my balls off. I got furious at my father, furious at the school," but not at the farmer he worked for.

"The farmer was close to a mentor to me, a beautiful sort of gnarled, weather-beaten huge man, strong as an ox." Peck's gentle nostalgic tone was a rare poignant moment in our hours of interviews as he spoke of the farmer's love for his son. "He had a son about seven or eight. I used to be impressed by how he always called his son 'dear,' or 'sweetie.' He obviously just loved his son. He was also very good to me. He was always clapping me on the back and saying, 'You've got to know your business. You've got to know your business.'"

By the time Scott left Exeter, David was already half way through college. "My brother and Timmy Childs [from Peck's in-group]—who loved Exeter—would go back for reunions, and whatnot. I never would." That adamancy was bedrock, at one with two other "great ambitions of my life. That when my 25th college reunion rolled around, I'd be too busy doing more important things than attend. That was fulfilled. The other ambition, which looks like is going to be fulfilled, is that until the day I die I'll have someone like Gail [Puterbaugh, his executive secretary] filling out the insurance forms. I'll be unlike my father who was beginning to get confused and old and shaky. He spent hours over Medicare forms, and I'm damned if I'm going to spend the last few months of my life fussing over Medicare."

In the 1950s, both Peck sons were still very much dependent on their father, and their father's standards were high. The Rev. Peck said, "My father was certainly stunted by his need to perform according to certain [parental] norms—and by his inability to do so because his heart so often lay elsewhere. I see so much of my father in Scotty it is amazing, the man who Scotty must, in so many ways, feel unlike. I find it utterly uncanny when we are together." Both David and Scott had tales of their father's mischievous— Scott called it sadistic—streak. Scott had the "crybaby" newspaper headline to haunt him. David had the sweetheart ring. Judge Peck usually played a joke on one of his sons at Christmas in a Christmas stocking gift. Scott said that when David had a crush on a local girl called Josie, there was a little present from her in his stocking. "It had a card, signed Josie, that read, 'David, here's a ring, love Josie.'" David opened up the present and it was a tiny bathtub with a ring around it.

The Fall of the year he left Exeter, Peck was admitted to Friends Seminary, a day school on the border of Greenwich Village. It is the oldest Quaker school in the New York City. He repeated his junior year, 11th grade. In conversation both his eyes and his voice lit up when he talked about the school. "Friends Seminary was an extraordinary place. I'm sure it had something to do with the Quaker Meeting House and Quaker background. It was the opposite of Exeter," he said. A day school, small and co-educational (Exeter was not during Peck's years). "It was liberal and loving where Exeter was conservative, and I just blossomed. Part of my guilt at leaving Exeter the last semester was that I had to write a 10-page paper for American history, fully annotated with bibliography, endnotes and footnotes. I was aghast at the prospect. I just didn't feel I could do it and I wondered if I quit Exeter just because I didn't want to write that paper. Then I repeated the American history course in 11th grade at Friends and sailed effortlessly through full 40-page papers, fully annotated, all of them about religion. They particularly specialized in Jonathan Edwards and the Great Awakening. Now I was not a Christian and I was approaching this as a historian or sociologist, but it's still interesting that I chose to write about religious history."

There was also something in the Quaker approach to religion that Peck responded to. "Once or twice a week we had meetings in the Meeting House. Once or twice a month those meetings were traditional Quaker silent meetings. It wasn't that you couldn't speak, but you could only speak if you felt moved. It was there I had my first experiences of being moved by something that the

Quaker would call the 'inner light,' which today I would call the Holy Spirit—to stand up and speak and say things that were wiser than I even knew I had to say. That was a very powerful spiritual experience and indeed became a foundation of FCE [Scott and Lily Peck's Foundation for Community Encouragement]."

In his senior year at Friends Seminary, Peck would have described himself as an agnostic. He found the religious studies textbook a problem, so much so that "the stuff about Christianity, Judaism and Confucianism made absolutely no sense to me." What did make sense were some of the Hindu and Buddhists and Taoist mystical writings. "I felt that I had intellectually come home," he said, "and of course, they're filled with paradox. It wasn't that I discovered paradox through them, but I discovered I wasn't the only person that ever thought about paradox, and I was really turned on. If you'd have asked me at 19 or 20 what I was, I would have told you then I was a Zen Buddhist. That's very fashionable now. But back then, in the 1950s, if you told people you were a Zen Buddhist they'd think you were either queer or pinko. But I just found it very, very exciting stuff."

At sixteen he'd also discovered something equally exciting—sex. There had been no sex play of any kind among Exeter boys, he said; homosexuality was the great taboo. He may have made a pass at a boy, on one occasion, he thought, but he wasn't sure what he had in mind, and nothing came of it. The incident was not repeated. Peck was sixteen-and-a-half when he fell deeply in love with a girl he referred to only as "Q." He felt then, and still felt a half century later when he spoke of it, that he had treated her shabbily. It was the only time Peck expressed feelings of remorse. The same depth of feeling was not present regarding his marital infidelities, or his divorce from Lily.

Q was spoken for—she had a boyfriend in some distant state and wore his ring on a chain around her neck. Peck initially kept his distance. In late 1952 they were together in a library. "I was looking at her and I said, 'God, I'd really like to date her.'" He passed her a note asking her for a date that weekend. Her note back said yes, and they had their first date, with follow-ups the two following weekends. A couple of nights after the third date, "I came to the sudden realization I had fallen hopelessly in love. I called her and said, 'I've got to talk to you,' and went down to see her." She reminded him she was still in love with the other man. Even so, she and Peck continued to date and she gave up the other fellow. "She

31

taught me about half of what I needed to learn about sex. I was a slow learner. I don't know, maybe it was Oedipal stuff with my mother, that I somehow thought women were off-limits, or untouchable, or that they didn't like sex. I don't know. Part of it, too, was about the holiness of sex. The first time she touched my penis it was like my experience of French kissing—I mean I just never dreamed that a woman would have any interest in touching it. So that became a ritual and, eventually, it went all the way to intercourse."

Then came the incident of the "biddy room." Peck said, "I perpetrated this terrible lie on my parents that, because New York subways were dangerous, it was dangerous for me to take Q back home at night and return alone. I might get hurt. It would be nicer if Q could stay the night at our apartment." His parents agreed. Q slept in what had been David's room. "Until one day my mother had a friend who was staying in my bedroom and I was relegated to one of the tiny maids' rooms [a biddy room]. Early the next morning, my mother and her friend were in the kitchen, about 7 a.m., banging pots and pans around. I stumbled out, all rumpled, in my pajamas and my mother's friend said, 'Oh, Scotty, I'm sorry we're making so much noise. Go sleep in my room if you want.' I said, 'Oh, that's all right,' and stumbled into David's room where Q was and crawled into bed with her. And that's how my mother found out. My mother was furious that I'd done that in front of her close friend. 'How could you that?' she kept saying. 'How could you do that to my friend, my close friend?'"

Peck's regrets regarding Q, whom "I loved as deeply as I've ever loved anyone," were several. They dated for two years, but there was "nowhere for our relationship to go except to get married, and it was not necessarily a neat idea to get married at eighteen." Even so, he would have considered it, he said, had there not been some major differences between him and the girl that convinced him it was a marriage that would never work. They broke up. Six months later, when they met again at a dance, the relationship resumed. "I was still desperately in love with her," but nothing had changed, he said. After a year, the relationship faltered on the same grounds as earlier. He declined to say what those grounds were. "I feel badly," Peck said. "I'd stolen her from this guy—although I don't know who the hell he was. But the big point was she was deeply in love with me and deeply caring. I had the experience of twice ending a relationship with a woman who I know loved me to the hilt and who I loved as deeply as I've loved anyone. The only time I ever cried between the age of eight and the age or 32 was those two times when I broke off with her. Lily [his wife at the time], to this day, thinks I carry a torch for Q." Even in the 1990s, Peck could say that besides his wife, Lily, "she's the only woman that I love until this day."

Once he'd become famous, he said, "all my old girlfriends, including the one I French-kissed, made contact. Except Q. I'm glad I didn't marry Q, but it wasn't for lack of love."

There was another side to his sex life. From the age of sixteen onwards until his marriage, Peck had casual homosexual encounters. He got the idea after an incident he witnessed in the men's toilets at Grand Central Station. After that he picked men up in the streets and went back to their place. "It's the easiest way to get it off in the world. They don't want any responsibility. You don't want any responsibility, and you can just arrange it with your eyes. When I was feeling horny, I'd go out and do that. But there was never any romance associated with it. It was a turn on." He never paid for sex: "I was too cheap. For a few years I wondered whether I was a homosexual or heterosexual." That issue was resolved with Q, he said, he was heterosexual. But whenever he was horny and girls were unavailable, he said, he'd cruise, pick up a man, and go back to his place. "There was nothing either emotional or romantic about my hour-long homosexual contacts," he said. Later, "stopping cruising was easy because sex was available with marriage, and Lily was never one to say, 'Oh, I've got a headache tonight, dear.'"

He and Q had avoided pregnancy, he said, by using *coitus interruptus*. He hadn't begun using condoms. That started the following summer when his father said he was taking him to Europe. "I knew I was going to get laid in Europe," Scott Peck said, "and that I'd better have some condoms." When he went to his father to inquire about the best brand, his father gave him a lecture about not doing anything that would require condoms. "By that time," said Peck, "I'd learned how to stand up to him. I said, 'Listen, I came to you for advice, not for some kind of moral lecture. Answer my question about what's the best condom or it's the end of the conversation.'" His father replied, "Well, probably Ramses."

How was it that Peck could tackle his father on brands of condoms, yet quail before him on so many other fronts? Possibly because it was an all-men-together-thing, not a father-and-son-thing.

The word Ramses may have solved Scott Peck's immediate quest, but it didn't prevent some subsequent embarrassment. Buying condoms in the sex-doesn't-exist 1950s was a blush-producing venture, plus not all pharmacies stocked them. Peck decided to seek a pharmacy far from the one nearest home. There was one about a mile away that looked sufficiently disreputable to stock condoms. He stood on the opposite side of the street waiting for the light to change. When it did he went charging across the road, eyes downcast, straight into the store and up to the counter. Embarrassed, he raised his eyes. He was face-to-face with one of the few female pharmacists in New York City.

At Friends Seminary, small and co-ed, and with college looming, Peck decided on a larger version of the same thing, Middlebury College in Vermont. His summary, "It was dull, dull, dull," said Peck. "The faculty were terrific but the students were mostly there just to get their degrees so they could buy what was then the ideal house, $60,000 [probably $600,000 today]. Drinking and fraternity life was the big thing. I was involved in that but took no joy in it. I also felt that the women were dull. Every weekend I went down to date Smithies [at Smith College, North Hampton, Massachusetts], a considerable drive."

During a break in his sophomore year, when Peck went home to New York City, he called Carol Brandt and asked her if he could take her out for lunch. "In her typical commandeering way she said, 'Oh, I'll take care of it all.'" The result of that lunch for Peck was an apprenticeship under John P. Marquand, one of the most prominent and successful writers of the day. Brandt told Peck the name of the restaurant, he was there a little early and there were three chairs. "When she showed up, it was with Marquand. They were in the process of trying to make a movie out of Marquand's *Sincerely, Willis Wayde*." He later surmised that Brandt was having an affair with Marquand and his presence provided good "cover" for their public meeting.

Peck said the couple seemed "stymied" in how to approach the book as a screenplay. "I'd had about three martinis and Marquand had about five, and I don't know what I said but suddenly they were both clapping me on the back, saying, 'You've got it, you've got it.'" Apparently he'd come up with a screenplay outline plan for the plot. The next thing Marquand said was, "Well, young man, if you want to write, why don't you come live with me this summer?" Peck thanked him and returned to college, presuming it was something of a five-martini invitation. "Two days later in the mail comes a letter saying, 'I'm quite serious about wishing that you would come live with me this summer.'" It was a two-and-a-half month apprenticeship under a master. "The only thing I wrote," said Peck, "was a romantic sort of thing set in Mexico, which I didn't know anything about. He thought it was pretty terrible."

Peck regarded Carol Brandt as the first adult to take him seriously. Marquand was the second. Among other things, Marquand taught Peck about the discipline of writing. Marquand left his house at 9 a.m. each morning, walked a hundred yards to his study in a little barn where his secretary waited. He'd dictate until 1 p.m. on the dot and then go to play golf or bridge. Said Peck, "I realized that if you're going to be a professional writer, you don't write just when the spirit moves you." Peck decided to become a professional writer.

Undergraduate Peck stayed only two years at Middlebury College before transferring to Harvard. What put the finishing touches on the Vermont college stay, he contended, was that the college couldn't produce enough volunteer students to make a Reserve Office Training Corps unit viable. So Middlebury mandated attendance at ROTC parade for all freshmen and sophomores. "They left that out of the college catalogue," Peck said. The requirement infuriated Peck and never more so than when, in his second year, there was to be a parade that conflicted with his favorite course, an advanced seminar on modern British poetry. He went to the dean to explain the conflict. The dean listened and said come back in a day or so. When Peck returned, the dean said he'd have to relinquish the seminar and go on parade. Peck disputed the decision, the dean wouldn't budge. Peck said he was quitting ROTC, and refused to attend. Middlebury docked him one-third of an academic credit for each missed ROTC parade or class. By the end of the year he'd lost most of his academic credits. He'd also become much loved by the faculty, who hate the ROTC-canceled academic classes as much as he did. Later, Peck would make it appear that his ROTC protests were in some way an anti-militarist stance. Nothing of the sort. He objected to ROTC interfering with a course he wanted to take.

Peck's application to Harvard was accepted, most probably because his father was active on Harvard alumni committees.

"Anyway, Harvard restored all my academic credits [dropped by Middlebury]. I mostly loved Harvard. It's just a magnificent college and university, the exception being the teaching. The teaching is terrible. I was in the department of social relations. It included psychology. One semester, there was a mandatory statistics course taught by a German statistician who Harvard had gotten for a year because he had some new statistical technique they wanted to use. He barely spoke English and during the entire semester never changed his shirt. Today, students wouldn't put up with that. We were part of the silent generation.

"Going to class was ridiculous. I just read the book as best I could and got a passing grade. Not all the teaching was that bad, but the teaching at Middlebury was far finer than Harvard's. What makes Harvard so distinctive is not its teaching but its location, ambiance and the student body. In Middlebury hardly anybody was interested in intellectual stuff, whereas at Harvard, everybody was. That was a great plus. It didn't matter whether you were in class or sitting out on the campus, everybody wanted to talk."

Peck did volunteer work in prisons and, for his first Harvard summer, and admittedly using his father's name as entree with the head of the department, he worked himself into a summer job. It was with the New York State Department of Corrections. "I proudly came home to announce to my father I had gotten a job working in New York jails for the summer. He threw a quiet kind of fit. I knew something would happen. Three days later he came to me and said, 'I know you got this job, and I'm very proud of you, my boy, that you got it. But I just happened to have found a job that might interest you more.'" It was in Geneva, Switzerland with the International Labor Organization, run by David Morse, ILO Director.

General Morse was an old political pal of Judge Peck's from their U.S. Attorney General's office days. During Morse's tenure, the ILO, the United Nations agency that promotes human rights and justice for workers, was awarded a Nobel Peace Prize. Scott Peck was encouraged, envisioning he'd be shifted around from department to department as training in organization and management.

Not at all. He traveled to Switzerland to find himself in an office in the bowels of the ILO building. There were twenty-five women to the right of him, twenty-five women to the left, collating papers for reports. He was in the "one thousands" division—pages

1001, 1002, 1003, 1004, 1005, which he fastened with a rubber tie. He then passed on the pages to the next collator. There was little conversation. Peck could not speak French beyond a few halting phrases. When there were no pages to collate, Scott operated the Roneo, a messy duplicating machine, to spin off thousands more copies of the pages. After six weeks he asked Morse for something more challenging. Morse said he didn't have anything. Peck's parents were arriving in London on vacation. He handed his resignation to Morse and left for Britain. "I figured my father owed me a substantial living for having given up the Department of Corrections job, and could fork up for me to live a good life in England for the rest of the summer." Then it was back to Cambridge, Massachusetts, and Harvard.

Harvard made Peck. He took an honors program that required a thesis, and in key ways the final result was a precursor to *The Road Less Traveled*. Peck was much taken with the poet W. H. Auden noting that the West was mired in the Age of Anxiety, so he decided to explore Auden's assertion.

In his thesis he developed three neologisms on the grounds that everybody who tried to explain society and the way it worked fell into one of three camps. One camp believed in *intra-organismic* theory, that the impulses that govern the behavior of the organism rise from within the organism. The second group believed in *extra-organismic* theory, that the organism's behavior is governed by external forces, like God or one's upbringing. The third camp, which Peck liked the most but still had problems with, was the *inter-organismic* theory, which said that the nature of things is dictated by the relationships between organisms. Peck argued out that in the age of modern science none of these theories work, that when human beings realize they don't know something that knowledge produces anxiety. Twenty years later, *The Road Less Traveled* was his answer to the Anxiety that fascinated Auden.

Peck spent a great deal of time and energy on *Anxiety, Modern Science and the Epistemological Problem,* but, as he hated academic writing and was too lazy and uncaring to be bothered with bibliographies and footnotes, it was a total armchair thesis. Jake Severance was Peck's roommate at Harvard during his senior year—because Judge Peck and Jake's father, who was in the New York District Attorney's office, were acquainted. Judge Peck arranged the room-share. Hope Childs, the wife of Peck's friend from Exeter, Tim Childs, recalled that she and her husband visited

Scotty in that room. Everything was painted red, she said, and it looked dreadful.

Severance had no later comments about the room, but he did provide a description of Peck as a young man. "At six-foot he'd attained his full height and even then wore the round lens glasses that are his trademark, the ones he seems to have worn all his life. He didn't party. He dated at least two different women, but he was very, very serious about the work he was doing. He would stay up until three or four in the morning writing on his yellow legal pad. In wintertime there was usually a six-pack of beer sitting on the windowsill outside, keeping cool. That was the extent of his partyness. Every now and then you'd hear a little 'pop!' that meant he was having another beer to help him think."

Peck had a couple of habits that irritated Severance. Severance had a bridge lamp next to Peck's chair and Scott would keep sliding its adjustable arm up and down the pole. Severance told him, "Scotty, I spent a lot of time trying to get that thing painted so it would look nice, and what you're doing is chipping the paint off. He'd say, 'Oh, sorry,' and promise not to do it again. Whereupon he'd start doing it again. I said, 'Please don't do that or there's going to be a catastrophic reaction.' 'Catastrophic reaction' was a term Scotty had taught me only the week before. It's a sociologist's term, I believe. It basically means a temper tantrum." Peck was so amused by Severance's use of the term he stopped fiddling with the lamp. It was scarcely surprising that in the dedication, Peck thanked Severance "who suffered admirably through this busy year when I have undoubtedly not been the easiest person to live with."

Severance said Peck was given to telling jokes, "usually rather erudite, usually to do with psychology or sociology. Occasionally quite bawdy. He had a wonderful sense of humor."

Peck's humor was not limited to telling jokes. That same year, Peck was a member of the Timothy and Hope Childs wedding party. Tim, later a Foreign Service officer, was always intensely keen on military history. Prior to the Childs' wedding, Severance said, Peck had acquired "a bunch of swords somewhere on Third Avenue," with which the wedding party formed an honor arch as the newlywed Childs emerged from the church. Hope Childs recalled shielding herself behind her husband when she saw the display.

Severance said Peck's thesis' fate was a story unto itself. A Harvard undergraduate thesis usually had only two readers, one of the student's choosing, and one chosen by the department. If there was a discrepancy of more than three grades, the department called in a third reader. Peck's choice of reader was a Charlie Slack. "He seemed to be a fun-loving guy and off the wall, so I selected him. Well, Charlie Slack, for some reason, designated my thesis to be 'unacceptable,' the worst you can get. The guy who I hadn't selected, don't even know who he was to this day, graded it *summa cum laude*, the highest grade you can get."

Severance said that created all kinds of problems in the department, "and not just for Scotty. He had to spend a week—or two weeks, I think—going to daily sessions to defend his thesis. It was too general."

The third reader called in was Gordon Allport, no small name in his field. He was an extremely well-known social psychologist with his doctorate from Harvard. Said Peck, "I knew mine was kind of a weird thesis. Gordon Allport gave it a *summa* and sent a letter congratulating me on it. They averaged it out and I graduated *magna*."

Peck had shown he was an able generalist who preferred to range across what he was thinking, someone who rarely relied on the informed opinion or the views of others except to further jog his own thoughts. Neither in his Harvard thesis, nor in any of his books, did Peck go the multiple footnote route. That had been a sticking point with the academic who would not accept the thesis. Some reviewers of his books noted it, too.

The newly graduated *magna cum laude* from Harvard had wanted to be The Great American Writer. To justify his decision not to go that route, Peck would offer, "I had absolutely nothing to write about." Rather than take the risk, he followed his father's suggestion he study medicine. Peck gave his decision a positive spin as "one of father's better suggestions. I gave up the dream of writing and thought I would do something responsible like my father advised." Not long before Peck died, however, he said that while he had never regretted becoming a medical doctor and psychiatrist, he had "copped out" by not pursuing the writer's life.

The writing bug had burrowed deeply but after Harvard went dormant. When it reawakened, Peck did have something to write about. It would be far removed from the Great American Novel he'd dreamed of producing, but likely far more successful.

CHAPTER THREE

Disowned

Peck's medical school years began badly. His father disowned him and withdrew all financial support. The saga began in an amphitheatre at Columbia University.

When Peck succumbed to his father's suggestion about becoming a physician, Scott had done no pre-med. It was 1958. For admission in 1959 he applied to both Cleveland's Western Reserve (later Case Western Reserve) and Harvard medical schools for admission. He went to Western Reserve for an interview with medical school associate dean John Caughey. The dean glanced at Peck's academic record and immediately accepted him. There was no word by then from Harvard Medical School, so Peck decided, "the hell with Harvard," and accepted Caughey's offer.

For the next academic year, he lived at home while he took pre-med courses at the School of General Studies in Columbia and worked 20 hours a week at Bellevue Psychiatric Hospital thinking he might want to be a psychiatrist. At Harvard he'd majored in social relations, which has a large psychology component, but Bellevue was "such a hopeless place," he concluded, a psychiatrist was the last thing he wanted to be.

At Columbia, said Peck, "We had one of the greatest teachers I ever experienced. He was a fascinating man on loan from the University of Buffalo. He began his first class by saying, 'My name is Dr. Payton. It rhymes with Satan. I have certain principles by which I teach, and one of them is that all students cheat. And so, henceforth, to remove you from this temptation, you're going to have assigned seats, three seats apart from each other in this much too large auditorium. In addition, on these hot summer mornings, it will help to circulate the gases amongst you.' And then he was off on the circulation of gases."

A young Chinese woman pre-med student, Lily Ho, was assigned to a spot three seats down from Scott. So he looked down on the nape of her neck. "I think I became a nape man," he said. "She was also working in the lab so she was always five minutes late. We palled around a bit that summer with a couple of other

40

people and then in the fall began to date."

During the summer he'd discovered he'd fallen in love with Lily. "She was lithe, beautiful in a Chinese way, intelligent and fun to be with," he said. What she wasn't, was a WASP. This was not the type of Establishment wife the Pecks wanted for their sons. After he'd taken Lily to his home several times for dinner, his father one day suggested he and Scott walk down to the 68th Street Bloomingdales department store. "I liked to walk with him," said Peck, "it was the only time we really got along well."

On that walk Judge Peck talked "about how wonderful it was to get to know people of different cultures. That it was broadening. But one should definitely not get too serious about it. That was the beginning," Peck said. "From the time we announced our engagement, from then on there were violent fights, both with Lily's parents and mine. Finally, I knew I was going to be disinherited. I was not looking forward to that fact in medical school."

To resolve the growing impasse, father and son met with the psychiatrist who had originally talked to Scott after he quit Exeter. "I was feeling vulnerable," said Scott Peck, "and agreed at that time to try to make it through medical school before marrying. Then, a month after I got to medical school, I felt I had sold out. I told my father that I felt it was a dishonorable agreement I had signed on to." Peck contended his father had earlier vacillated over his oft-repeated dictum to his sons that they shouldn't marry before the age of 30, a point at which they were able to support their wives. Despite that parental dictum, twice, even when Scott was "20 at most," he said, there were two girls among the several he brought home of whom the father said he'd be willing "to make an exception and support me if I chose to marry one of them." But not Lily Ho.

It was December 1959. Peck had just completed his first semester at medical school and was home for the vacation. Christmas was barely two weeks away. The scene at the senior Pecks household on Park Avenue brought no promise of Yuletide joy. Scott and Lily were at the apartment together to meet the Peck parents in yet another attempt to gain parental blessings for their forthcoming marriage. Instead, on hearing their voices, a visibly annoyed Judge Peck emerged from the bathroom wrapped in a bath towel. He wanted none of these wedding plans. When he saw Lily, he wagged his finger at her and roared, "You! You! You adventuress!" The pair left, defeated.

A day or two later, they girded themselves for a visit to Lily's equally hostile parents. In contrast to the high emotional drama on Park Avenue, the scene at the Ho family apartment in the modest high-rise on the edge of Chinatown played out like slapstick. On seeing Scott and Lily at their front door, the Reverend and Mrs. Ho, let them in but wouldn't let Lily leave. "They were clutching Lily," Peck said. "There was no way for me to get Lily out of the apartment without physically fighting with them." He went to another apartment where he used the telephone to call the police.

The Peck and Ho parents were responding to the same impetus—the emotional upheaval that can result when adult children who are not quite independent want to live their own lives. The Peck parents had made it quite clear they did not want Scott to marry a Chinese. Whether Judge Peck also knew that Lily was almost two years older than twenty-three-year-old Scott is uncertain. The judge thought he had a binding promise from Scott not to wed until he finished medical school. On the Ho side, Lily's parents were opposed to her marriage to a non-Chinese. Indeed they expected her to become a doctor—she, too, had been taking pre-med classes.

The Senior Hos were born in Canton, China, as was Lily's brother. The family moved to the British colony of Singapore, and Lily was born there. The family survived the Japanese World War II occupation. Ten years before Lily left Singapore, the Hos had sent their son to the United States to become a pharmacist. He'd switched to engineering without telling them, said Peck, and then, after about ten years in the United States, he informed his parents he was marrying an American woman.

Lily was fifteen when she went alone to the U.S. Embassy to apply for a visa to the United States. "She wanted to get the hell out of the traditional Chinese culture," he said. She arrived in the United States at age seventeen.

With her brother thoroughly Americanized and going his own way, the Hos were not about to let Lily choose her future, said Peck. According to him, they'd supported Lily's application to leave Singapore for the United States, dreaming that she'd become the doctor. "She'd been programmed for medical school. When we met she kept forgetting to take the medical aptitude test," Peck said. The senior Hos arrived in the United States several years after Lily, when pastor Ho took over a conservative Baptist church in Chinatown that needed a Chinese-speaking minister. The Ho parents' ambitions were further assaulted by Peck's spiritual interests. Lily knew of Scott's interest in Zen Buddhism, and for Christmas had bought two books on the topic. Her parents had seen the books. Pastor Ho was outraged. He railed at his daughter, "We have not been Christians for four generations for you to marry a Zen Buddhist!"

This was the backdrop, said Peck, as two New York policemen arrived, knocked on the Ho's apartment door and demanded they open it. The Hos complied. The police asked to see Lily. She came to the door. The police asked if she was being held against her will and wanted to leave. She said she was, and she did want to leave. The burly cop stood in the doorway with his arm against the doorjamb in such a way that Lily was able to quickly duck under it into the corridor, and race toward the elevator. Scott said he followed immediately behind her but then the Hos broke past the police. Lily and Scott ran into the stairwell, and headed down, seventeen floors ahead of them. The police, to keep her safe, came down behind Lily. Mrs. Ho, not to be deterred, joined in the descent while the Reverend rang for the elevator. If he intended to get there first, to catch Lily at street level to prevent her from leaving, it didn't quite work out that way. What happened instead, said Peck, was that Mrs. Ho caught up with a policeman and bit him. The Hos apparently then had to rely on a persuasive Peck— for the Hos did not have Peck's English fluency—to plead and reason with the cops to prevent Mrs. Ho being hauled off to the precinct house and charged with assault. The police agreed, and Scott and Lily were out of the door. The Hos gave no further pursuit. Nor, said Peck, did they speak to their daughter for the next six years, by which time Lily was a mother with daughters ages four and five.

All this time Scott was still living at home, and Lily would stop by to visit. During the uproar over the marriage plans, Aunt Sally in the kitchen would say to each of them "give me a hug," and console them. "Don't you worry, Miss Lily," she'd say. "It will all work out. Don't you worry, Miss Lily, I'll see to it. You're a dear girl. They'll realize it eventually."

Scott and Lily became Mr and Mrs M. Scott Peck on December 27, 1959 in a high Episcopal ceremony at Grace Episcopal Church. Lily was nominally a Methodist at the time. They chose Grace Episcopal because the minister had a brother who was married to a Filipina, so the minister was familiar with racially mixed marriages, still a rarity in the United States of the 1950s—and in some states, illegal. Among the few friends in attendance were Timothy and Hope Childs. The only parent to attend was Mrs. Peck. "It was an act of real courage," said Peck, "the only time my mother directly defied my father." None of Lily's family was present at the wedding. Among Lily's friends were the Grangers. Lester Granger was president of the National Urban League, the 1910-founded organization for African-Americans. "The Grangers were lovely people and had formed a friendship with Lily," said Scott Peck, "which gives an idea of her talents right from the early days. Lester said he would be happy to give her in marriage if her family did not attend." Judge Peck may have bridled further when he learned that his now daughter-in-law had been given in marriage by a black man.

With the wedding date set, Peck called a college friend whose family lived near the church. He asked, could the wedding group bring a couple of bottles of whiskey and have a celebratory gathering at the apartment. The friend checked with his parents, who said yes and donated a case of champagne. "They were Orthodox Jews. That wedding was about as ecumenical as you could get," said Peck. Scott's wedding gift from his father was that his father refused to speak to him, and cut him off financially.

Following the wedding, with the breach between Peck and his father complete, the not-so happy pair headed off to Cleveland. They were given to singing, "There's a place for us, somewhere a place for us"—the plaintive song from the musical, *West Side Story*, also an interracial tale. They headed West not quite broke. Scott had $800 in the bank, Lily had nothing. They bought a bed and a bureau. They had no food, no dishes, and no car. Lily worked full time as a lab technician at the university hospital. And three evenings a week they both worked as lab techs in the main laboratory. About a month and a half after his marriage, Scott Peck received a letter from his father. It read, "Scotty, if you send me the bill I will pay your tuition. And please find enclosed a check for $100 which I will remit same monthly 'til your graduation." It was signed, "Your father."

Scott wanted to tear it up, write back and say, "Take it and stuff it up your ass," he said. But the very day they received Judge Peck's letter, he and Lily had dinner "with an older and wiser couple." The couple pointed out the obvious, that not only did Scott desperately need the money, but at that point the money was the only real way his father could express his affection. By refusing it, Scott would be cutting off communication completely. Peck wrote back and said, "Dear Dad, I thank you very much for your generosity, and I accept it." Less than 18 months later, when their first child was born, Judge Peck increased the allowance to $200 a month. The father may have eased up on Scott, said Peck, but he didn't speak to Lily, "or even look at her directly," for the first five years of their marriage. "Then he started treating her like an ordinary human being—though he favored my brother's wife, Greg. Later, my father came around and would send Lily roses."

Scott and Lily were living in the attic of the Two Sisters Nursery School for $45 a month. It had a back yard with swings and slide, "which made for great parties," said Peck. As part of the rent Peck had to mow the lawn and shovel the walk. The walk was twenty yards long and the lawn was all of twenty yards square. "It wasn't much of a task," he said.

One hot summer evening under the eaves of the Two Sisters, sweating away in those pre-air-conditioned days, Peck said to Lily, "I don't believe there should be any secrets in a marriage." Lily replied, "Well, I do." On Peck's side, there wouldn't be any serious secrets to keep for a while yet. However, one Peck family secret was about to come out.

Close to Scott's 24th birthday, in May 1960, Elizabeth Peck traveled out to Cleveland to visit her son and his wife. They put her up in a nearby fashionable hotel. In Peck's words, "She immediately downed three martinis, one after another." Mrs. Peck acknowledged that the children were really ready to get married and said in these kinds of situations there were always upsetting moments. She even admitted that at one point she broke off her engagement to Peck's father. It was at that point, when Scott asked why she did that, she replied, "Well, you know that your grandmother is a Jew." "Daddy's Jewish?" said an astounded Scott. The senior Peck had never mentioned to David or Scott that their grandmother, Juliet, was Jewish. Scott's brother, David, was 23 and on the dance floor of the Nantucket Country Club when his fiancée asked, "David, why didn't you tell me your father was Jewish?" And in his protestations, David Jr. learned the facts.

Such was the chasm between father and sons that never once in the ensuing three decades did Scott or David raise the issue with their father.

Scott Peck said that once he was aware of the Jewish heritage in the family other things began to make sense. "At every family

45

celebration, there was always smoked salmon—I didn't know what lox was until I was in my 20s. When Dad celebrated it was always with his mother's bread, kneaded over and twirled with poppy seeds, and the lox." It was challah bread, the traditional braided or twisted white bread eaten by Jews on the Sabbath and holidays. "Now in my parents' defense," said Peck, "it was an anti-Semitic world in that day and age. Just up the road from here," referring to a village close to his Connecticut home, "there's a wonderful inn that well into the 1950s used to advertise itself in *The New York Times* as a 'gentile' inn."

Peck recalled another clue, unrecognized at the time, to the family's Jewish heritage. "One boring, long summer day, we were in the living room of our country house in Sharon. David and I were singing the St. Bernard school song. A chorus which goes, 'Come let us sing in a jubilant chorus / School days and college alike ...' but there's great emphasis on the word or symbol 'jubilant.' Well, my mother came running out of the kitchen, through the dinning room, into the living room and said, "Don't you boys talk about the Jews that way." And we said, "We weren't talking about the Jews." She said, "The Jews are ordinary people, just like us.". Scott also surmised something from the detour his paternal grandparents made during annual automobile pilgrimages from Indiana to Vermont—that the side trip they made with their young son David to Buffalo, was to the city's German-Jewish community of Scott's grandmother Juliet's family. When Peck Senior reminisced fondly of Buffalo, it was about the quality of the ice cream in his favorite shop there, never about his German-Jewish relatives.

Early in their marriage, when Lily asked Peck what she could make for him, he asked for bread like his grandmother's. As they were living in a primarily Jewish area of Cleveland, he spotted the bread one day in a Jewish bakery and said, "There, that's it. My grandmother's bread." It was Lily who informed him, "Well, it's challah." Unwittingly, challah was as close as Peck had ever come to connecting with his Jewish heritage.

By then the younger Pecks were living in Cleveland's Jewish area because they'd been evicted after a particularly rowdy party for adults on and around the nursery school's swings. Lily was pregnant with their second child. By that time, having scrimped and saved, the couple had $5,000, mainly from Lily's wages. She was no longer working, and there was just $200 a month coming in from Judge Peck. On the Western Reserve faculty was a medical doctor who, with his wife, had a thirty-room home in a prime part of Cleveland. They rented the Pecks seven rooms. The bonus, with two babies in diapers, was the use of a washing machine. On the off-chance there'd be future parties, there was a refrigerator, too.

The Pecks' first child, Belinda, was born in 1961, her name prompted by the movie *Johnny Belinda*, said Peck. Fifty-one weeks later, in 1962, Julia Alison was born. Her name, he said, was adapted from his maternal grandmother, Juliet, while Alison "was conjured up out of the stars." Possibly earth-bound movie stars, too—such as June Allison. Their third child, Christopher Scott, was born seven years later on Okinawa. Watching his daughters grow, said psychotherapist Peck, he never ceased to marvel that two girls, born so closely together to the same parents, could display such totally different personalities.

Peck said he'd chosen Western Reserve not only for its highly regarded medical school, one of the top ten in the country, but also because it was liberal and non-competitive. At most medical schools, he said, grades were posted each week along with class standings. At Western Reserve there were only 13 exams during four years of medical school. The grades were E for excellent, S for satisfactory or U for unsatisfactory. Peck said that generally, on any given exam in the class of eighty students, six or seven would get an E, five or six would get a U, and the middle sixty-five or so would get a S. During those three years Peck had thirteen Satisfactory, not one Excellent, not one Unsatisfactory. "I was obviously no medical genius," he remarked.

Until two or three months before the completion of medical school, Peck had proceeded "with the delusion that I was going to be a general practitioner, a missionary type, working in the Deep South or Burma." However, at the point in his clinical year when he was "doing a lot of emergency room work, I realized I didn't really like most medicine. It was cookbook kind of stuff—you followed the recipe. I realized that what I really liked to do was talk with people. So I revived my desire to become a psychiatrist."

Finances were an issue: how to afford to live during an internship and psychiatric residency? "At that time," said Peck, "all medical school graduates had to take what was called a rotating internship, to rotate amongst different specialties. Then they could become a general practitioner or go on to residency to become a specialist. At good hospitals they were paid nothing. At Brigham Hospital in Boston, as an intern, they got $13 a month. And it ranged from about $13 a month to $100 a month at other universities. The only place you could get high-class postgraduate medical training, and survive financially, was in the Army, Navy, Air Force medical corps, or public health services. And so with some misgivings, not knowing anything about Vietnam, except it was some place in the other hemisphere, I joined the Army where there was a livable wage. I could get by without being financially dependent upon my father—there were all kinds of strings attached to being so dependent."

When it came to his U.S. Army medical career, Peck never fared badly as far as location was concerned: Hawaii as an intern, San Francisco as a resident, Okinawa as a psychiatrist, and Washington, D.C. to conclude his service. In July 1963, the four-member family left for Hawaii and Tripler Army Medical Center, at Oahu. The huge medical building was known as the "Pink Palace." Medical corps officers did not participate in basic training. The closest Peck got to "boot camp" was two weeks learning how to salute and listening to some general rules concerning army life.

After Hawaii, Peck was posted to the Army's Letterman Psychiatric Hospital in San Francisco for three years of psychiatric residency. He worked rotating shifts at the military hospital, and was on hand for psychiatric emergencies. During interviews, when Letterman came up in his conversation, Peck had unstinting praise for the quality of the faculty during his years there. In his not unusual flights of hyperbole, the faculty members were "geniuses" and "giants."

There was no shortage of practical experience in the military psychiatric hospital and soon the fledgling psychiatrist was stretching his professional wings. At home in the Officers Married Quarters, the situation was somewhat different. He refused to have his wings clipped, and was less successful in applying his new psychological insights to himself and his family situation. During a medical residency, it is not abnormal for a doctor, military officer or otherwise, to work long shifts. Peck, however, was gone from home even more than most other residents, a clear indication he wasn't handling his workload well. He had something else to learn besides psychiatry—time management. Other residents were out of the office by 4 and 5 p.m., Peck wasn't getting home until 8 and 9 p.m. When he asked for fewer patients, on the grounds he spent more time with his patients than other residents did with theirs, Dr. "Mac" Badgely, director of the outpatient psychiatric clinic, simply replied Peck had a problem that Peck had to resolve himself. Peck stomped out of Badgely's office, he said, and it took him three months longer to see that Badgely was correct. The difficulty was his to solve.

He did, and though he may have learned to manage his time better to his own or the Army's satisfaction, it was never to Lily's. Peck knew what he should do to placate Lily. She was home alone with two very young children. But he couldn't or wouldn't or didn't change his work habits. It became a source of fairly constant friction in the household. Captain Peck was busy, he was also a male chauvinist, a man of his time, and he never achieved a work and family-life balance that met his wife's needs.

In his residency, Peck had a faculty member, a lieutenant colonel, he dubbed "Colonel Bumbles." To his delight, Peck contended, he saw that though Bumbles was a career psychiatrist, the lieutenant colonel's diagnosis was invariably incorrect. "If I thought a patient was schizophrenic—but I didn't have a diagnosis—and Colonel Bumbles said, 'Oh no, this person doesn't have schizophrenia,' I knew I was right to suspect schizophrenia." Later, in Washington, D.C., when Peck was a lieutenant colonel himself, he saw Colonel Bumbles, and admired him. "He might not have been a great psychiatrist," said Peck, "but he was a first-class hospital administrator."

Less delightful, though with a greater lasting benefit to Peck, was the fact that the Letterman experience propelled him into therapy during his final year of residency. A series of incidents in a single day led him to seek help. The day, as Peck recalled it, opened badly. It began at the reaction he experienced when, during an early morning seminar, he'd played for his peers and supervisor the tape of an interview he'd conducted with a patient. They "raked me over the coals for the clumsy way I'd handled it." He took his lumps, he said, and rationalized the incident out of the way, though it still rankled. He told himself, "Well, they always rake you over the coals, that's standard operating procedure.'"

After the seminar he had some free time. "I thought I'd use it to get a haircut. I didn't feel I needed one, but I knew General Jingles would think I needed one. Off I went. As I had to pass the post office I thought I'd check my box. And there, to my dismay, I found a traffic ticket." The ticket dated back many weeks earlier to an afternoon when Peck ran a stop sign on post on the way to play tennis with his commander, a Colonel Connor.

Normally General "Jingles," the commanding officer, fixed the tickets. Peck was loath to approach the General. Post commander Connor said he'd fix the ticket with the Military Police's Provost Marshall.

Six weeks later, however, the Provost Marshall was fired without time to clean out his desk. In one drawer there was a stack of fixed tickets. The authorities "unfixed" the tickets and the miscreants were now being held liable. Feeling "worse and worse"—raked over the coals and with an unfixed ticket surfacing—Peck went for his haircut.

Peck was in the barber's chair, halfway through the haircut, "when in walked General Jingles to have his hair trimmed. In that situation," said Peck, "even a general has to wait his turn. To show you what bad shape I was in, the last minute or two of my haircut all I could think about was 'Should I say hello to the bastard, or shouldn't I?' When my haircut was finished, with great aplomb I passed by General Jingles and said, 'Good morning, General Jingles,' and went straight out of the barber shop."

Peck hadn't paid for his haircut. "The barber came running out after me, 'Doctor, doctor, you no pay for your haircut. You no pay for haircut.'" Peck returned to the shop, but he was so unnerved by Jingles' presence "I dropped all my change on the floor, right at General Jingles' feet. So there I was, kneeling at his feet while he was laughing uproariously at my predicament. When I finally got out of the barbershop my hands were shaking like crazy. I said to myself, 'Peck,' I said, 'you're not okay. You need help.' It was one reason I always disliked the title of that book, *I'm Okay, You're Okay*. That's because one of my finest hours was when I could say—painful as it was as a breaking moment for me—'Peck, you're not okay. You need help.'"

Reflecting four decades later on his therapy, Peck said what he was suffering from at the time was an authority problem. "In every job I'd had, for years, college, or General Jingles, there was always some son-of-a-bitch in charge of me whose guts I absolutely hated. Always a male, always an older male. So that's how I went into therapy." It was a one-year, three times a week therapy program with a Dr. Aikers. It proceeded well. The therapist accepted "all of my stuff that my parents didn't accept, my weirdness and uniqueness and whatnot, and I just felt less and less anxious." At about the ten-and-a-half month mark, said Peck, he was feeling so good he talked to Aikers about stopping.

"You know, I feel so much better. You've been such a great help to me that I've been thinking maybe we really don't have any more work to do."

Aikers said, "I wonder if you're not angry at me."

Peck said, "No, I'm not angry at you. I told you that. Actually it's because you've been so kind to me and the excellent work has made me feel so much better. I'm not angry at all."

The therapist continued, "Maybe you're angry at something that happened last session?"

Peck denied it. "As a matter of fact, it was such a dull session that I was writing a paper for this course I was taking—an evening course on Buddhism—and asked you if you knew anything about Buddhism and you said you didn't. So I spent the whole hour talking to you about Buddhism, and actually it was kind of a wasted hour. As a matter of fact, come to think of it, for somebody who has been to the Jungian Institute in Zurich, it's a little hard for me to believe the fact when you said you didn't know anything about Buddhism. I'm not sure you weren't withholding from me. Matter of fact, I'm pretty sure you're probably holding yourself from me just like my father, just the way my father used to."

Looking back on his outburst, Peck said, "I, who used to think I was much too smart ever to fall into the trap of 'transference,' realized I'd done it." Peck described "transference" as childhood ways of dealing with the world that are inappropriately carried into one's adult life. "Dr. Aikers and I worked it out. The basis of my neurosis—and I needed help from him to see it—was that my father was such an attractive man, in looks, in his brilliance, in his sense of humor when he was in a good mood, so loving, that I deeply wanted to be dependent on him as a young child. But I also knew that to be dependent on him would be to be emotionally steamrollered by him. He would have just obliterated my psyche and made me who he wanted me to be. And the only way I could deal with that was to say, on a very deep level, 'Who needs him?' And to say that I had to say, 'Who needs anybody?'

"So I'd become this hyper-independent individual. But at the same time I was going around unconsciously, totally unaware of this, looking for a 'good father' figure. And whenever somebody who was a potential father figure for me turned out not to be the good father I wanted I'd get furious at him." Peck continued, "As soon as I became aware that I was, in some ways, a dependent person—I'd figured where some of this rage was coming from, and that I did want a father figure—I was able to do things in the military and in executive life that I just never would have been able to before." Peck liked to insist that this therapeutic year "cured" him of his "father" and childhood neuroses.

The Army was freeing Peck from some major constraints. In the closing months of his military career, it would enable him to cry again. What couldn't have been anticipated was that the Army, inadvertently, also helped Peck further along a road he had not yet embarked on: toward Christianity, and in such ways his nine-and-a-half years in uniform contributed markedly to the Scott Peck of future fame, through its accidental role in his faith formation, and its deliberate molding of him as a psychotherapist.

In 1966—as he prepared to depart San Francisco for service in Okinawa to honor the required "pay-back" period for his medical training—he had been a constant student for twenty-five years. Now emotionally less constricted than at any period in his early life, he was about to step into a freedom he had neither experienced nor anticipated. He'd be psychologically and physically distant from his father, and financially independent of him. He was thirty years old.

CHAPTER FOUR
Captain Scotty of Okinawa

The Japanese province of Okinawa is a sub-tropical cluster of 161 islands, half way between the Japanese mainland and Taiwan. The United States, since the end of World War II, has maintained a large military presence on the main island, and ruled it until governance of Okinawa was returned to Japan. When Scott Peck arrived in 1967, Kadina Air Force Base, Okinawa was home to 115,000 troops and their dependents, plus U.S. military psychiatric patient evacuees from Vietnam.

If his island home and this posting represented some potentially formidable problems to the newly promoted Major Peck, the climate wasn't one of them. Work aside, he and Lily and the two girls had an idyllic family life in a place where the summer temperature rarely exceeds 73 Fahrenheit (22.4 Celsius) or drops below 60F (16C) in winter. A fulltime local nanny was available for $65 a month. The nanny also loved to baby sit, at the rate of one dollar a night, and for the entire night, if required. An evening at the movies was 25 cents each.

At work, Peck's first challenge was he had to immediately become a top-flight administrator. His department had forty personnel who handled thousands of cases. His senior staff was one veteran non-commissioned officer—a sergeant considerably older than Peck—three psychiatrists about his own age, and two junior officers in their late twenties. The remaining thirty-five personnel were enlisted men and women in their late teens or early twenties. For the number of military personnel at the base, the department was seriously understaffed for psychiatrists. Peck started training enlisted personnel as "psychiatric technicians" to shoulder some of the load.

The sergeant was African American.

Peck said he had an easygoing if ambivalent personal relationship with black people, a fact he credited not only to Aunt Sally, the Pecks' housekeeper of his childhood, but to an affair he had with a black woman who, he said, enabled him to cross cultural lines. He also said that until that affair, he'd had a deplorable habit of not seeing black women except to undress them with his eyes. Later, he said, he found African-American church groups open and capable of offering "instant community," which he enjoyed. But there was a place in that community which a white man could not reach or enter, he said.

He explained his relationship with African Americans this way: "At fifteen I looked like a WASP because certain things get tattooed into your skin, but under that skin I'm half black and half Mediterranean." He said he was a reverse Oreo, white on the outside and black on the inside. Peck seemed to stereotypically envision Latins and African Americans as enjoying some form of easygoing emotional release of their passions, a release that eluded him. It had eluded him in San Francisco, too, when he was exposed to the burgeoning "free love" movement when, he said, he marched in anti-Vietnam War protests, but out of uniform.

In Okinawa, Major Peck was determined "to be 'Mr. Nice Guy,' as different as possible from every authoritarian boss who had ever been in charge of me," he said. Rank was ignored; he was soon "Scotty" to one and all. His daily operating model was that no decisions would be made until everyone involved had been consulted. Wherever possible, his subordinates were encouraged to make the decisions that affected their own work lives. The mood was euphoric, morale was superb, and the mood held for about six months. Then things began to sour.

Peck could see that working conditions were cramped, but those would shortly be addressed when the new outpatient complex opened. He anticipated morale would improve as the moving date approached. It didn't. "The staff grew worse," he said. "Files fell behind schedule. Finally, it was my responsibility to do something about it." He told the entire staff there'd be meetings each morning in the new building's conference room "until we got to the bottom of the problem." What he got, in two four-hour morning sessions, "were the stormiest meetings I ever attended. Everyone took pot-shots at me and everyone else. Yet all the complaints were picky, superficial and seemingly unreasonable." An innocuous remark from an enlisted man on the second morning set Major Peck off on a fresh tack. The soldier said, "I feel I don't know where I stand." Asked to elaborate he couldn't and became inarticulate. "It's like we're all at sea," was all he could offer.

That lunchtime, Peck sat in his office in the old building and stared at the ceiling, lunch uneaten. Was it possible the department needed more structure than he'd provided, he wondered. He called in the senior sergeant and asked for the plans for the new building. Then he assigned everyone on his staff to an office in the new psychiatric department. Job done, he handed it to the sergeant and said, "Now go inform." The result was "you could practically hear the howls of dismay across the island," he said, but everyone now knew where he or she stood, and "by evening morale had began to improve. By the end of the week, it was back to where it had been." They still called him Scotty—his overall leadership was still relatively non-authoritarian—but everyone knew who was in charge. Morale stayed high for his remaining tour of duty, he said.

Having dealt with the staff, Peck felt it was time to deal with the Pentagon regarding his now acute shortage of psychiatrists. He'd pleaded long distance by military mail to no avail. When a crisis erupted in Vietnam that affected Okinawa Peck was quick to read its signs and make his move.

Long Binh Jail, Vietnam—the "LBJ"—was a major brig that held U.S. servicemen, a majority of them black troops, found guilty of extremely serious crimes. The brig was holding at least twice the number of prisoners it was built to accommodate. When there was a race riot in the "LBJ," the Army tried to hush up the affair, but the news got out. The Pentagon had to make a move to show it had the situation in hand. The president ordered a large contingent of black militants shipped to Okinawa, sixty of them as prisoners. The Secretary of the Army ordered a psychiatric evaluation of a dozen or so of the key militants.

That was when Peck made his move or, rather, his slow-down. "My only other psychiatrist had just gone on leave. I was the sole psychiatrist on the island." A colonel telephoned Peck and said he immediately wanted psychiatric evaluations of twelve particularly militant prisoners. The Secretary of the Army had requested the evaluations. Peck said, "'Well, fine, let's see. It's the fourth of September now. I'll see the first one or two on the seventh of October. And then I can see one on the eighth and then maybe two on the ninth.' He said, 'No. These are urgent evaluations.'" Said Peck, "I hear that they're urgent. I'm giving you the first times I can possibly give you." When told again it was the Secretary of Army who wanted the evaluations, Peck repeated, "'I hear that very well, great priority.' The guy hung up on me in a fury. I called my Colonel at the hospital, and I said, 'Colonel I just wanted to warn you that shit is going to hit the fan.'" The next day there was a psychiatrist en route from Hawaii TDY, temporary duty. Within six months there were nine new psychiatrists.

That was only the first wave of trouble emanating from the Okinawa stockade, however. The Kadina military police proved no more adept at understanding the problem on their hands than had the LBJ's guards. Consequently, the Okinawa stockade soon had a rebellion on its hands. In a six-man cell occupied by five blacks and one white, an African-American held a razor-blade "shank" to the white prisoner's throat and said he would keep it there, ready to slit the throat, if the black troops' grievances weren't addressed. Peck was called in, by which time the stockade was surrounded by a SWAT team, a fire crew, and armed soldiers. Peck's commanding officer, Major General Michael Finn, told Peck no one knew what the riot was about, and the issue was how to end it.

"Mickey Finn was a two-star general when he should have been four-star. He was a man of considerable courage," said Peck, "but somewhere along the line he alienated somebody." Then Finn asked Peck if he'd be willing to go into the jail to discover why the prisoners were rioting. Peck said he went into the jail, "scared as hell. The reason for the riot was eminently clear, and eminently cruel. The stockade had run out of segregated disciplinary cells, those used for solitary confinement to isolate particularly unruly prisoners. Short of cell space, the military police had taken to using conex shipping containers"—those huge metal boxes hauled along U.S. highways by eighteen-wheelers. The military police had punched holes in the containers for air, thrown a mattress in the bottom and started putting prisoners in them out in the broiling sun.

"Not only was this illegal," said Peck, "for there are specifications for disciplinary segregation cells, but the black troops believed that this was the last step before their extermination. Not true, but it was what they believed."

The military commanders gathered to discuss the situation. There were sixty people present, "almost all of whom outranked me and the African American sergeant," said Peck. "We told them, 'We think you ought to get rid of the conex containers.' The other fifty-eight people said, 'We can't get rid of the conex containers. That's giving in to their demands. You'll lose the authority of the guards.'" Peck went to Finn and assured him the prisoners were "going to cut this white guy's throat unless they got rid of the disciplinary conex containers—they're illegal. If you do get rid of them you are going to have a riot on your hands on the part of the guards. But nonetheless I think you ought to get rid of them."

Finn ordered an end to the containers. The guard population was in an uproar, said Peck. Finn addressed the uproar with "one of the most eloquent speeches I have ever heard about rightness and law and America. Everything. It was an extraordinary moment."

With the conex crisis resolved, and plenty of psychiatrists to shoulder the work, Peck took up golf. "Had a lovely time. Okinawa, I still dream of it. It was such a heaven. Beautiful facilities, a comfortable life, all at next to nothing in cost. We figured, heck, if we're ever going to have another child, this was the place to have it. So Christopher was our Okinawa child, born seven years after the girls." It was probably the happiest period of their family life. Peck, the two girls, and a Lily pregnant with Christopher, traveled to Singapore, where Lily grew up, and Thailand, and then spent eleven days in India. Life was pleasant, not difficult.

Though it was the early 1970s, Peck remained mired in a 1950's and earlier attitude toward women. Terry Paiste was a military dependent in Okinawa, her husband, Gary, was one of Peck's "psychiatric techs." She worked for the military base education office and hosted a Friday afternoon television show, *The Teahouse*, on the Armed Forces Radio and Television Service. "People could watch my program on the only station that broadcast in English, or they could watch Japanese television," said Paiste. "I scoured the islands for guests who would expand the minds of the military personnel and their families. Women's Lib was a hot topic. I'd had a woman teacher speak, but I wanted to find a male guest who would promote the same cause."

Paiste, who made these comments in a talk she gave decades later at a Toastmasters Club gathering, said she had a problem—that apart from her husband she didn't know one man on Okinawa who was a feminist. She was about to give up when her husband suggested Dr. Peck. "He'd make a great guest," said Gary Paiste. "He's intelligent and articulate, and he'd make a terrific spokesman for Women's Lib."

"Are you sure he's in favor of women's lib?" she asked her husband.

"Well, we've never actually discussed it," Gary admitted. "But he's very open-minded. I'll ask him if he wants to be on the show."

The arrangements were made. On the air, when asked about the Women's Liberation Movement, Peck said he didn't think much of it because it was the invention of a few malcontented females. Most women, he said, had no interest in equal rights. Paiste said, "I couldn't have found a less sympathetic guest if I had placed an ad in the *Okinawan Times* for a 'Male Chauvinistic Pig.'"

She never saw Peck again, but in the 1980s noticed his name on the best-seller list for *The Road Less Traveled*. She ignored the book. A decade later, his name came up in conversation with a coworker who liked his books. She recommended Paiste read them "because he talks about what a sexist he had been, and how he'd changed." Paiste said that more than a little skeptical, she thumbed through a couple of chapters "wearing gloves so I wouldn't be contaminated. There wasn't a sexist line or thought in them," she said, "and I learned a lot. The most important thing I learned was that people *can* change."

Peck, too, was still learning. "My big education in my prejudice came when a black soldier was transferred to Okinawa from Vietnam for exposing himself. I learned he'd also exposed himself in the United States, and that was why he'd gone to Vietnam—it was either Vietnam or the jail." Peck decided the soldier was not simply a man who exposed himself, but a chronic, low-grade schizophrenic who did not belong in the Army and would expose himself again. "I told him I was going to put him in the hospital and prepare him for evacuation to the United States where he would get a medical discharge and it would be fine." The soldier was bitterly upset, but Peck told him neither of them had any options. Peck said he didn't put the soldier under observation or restrictions, but confined him as a regular, unlocked door, patient.

"That was at 2 p.m. on the Tuesday. At 10 a.m. on the Wednesday," said Peck, "the hospital's adjutant general, who usually called me Scott, called and asked, 'Peck, what the hell are you doing? What the hell have you done?' I said, 'What? What?' And he said, 'I've got 40 Okinawan women in my office all shouting at me at the same time. Apparently one of your patients was hiding himself in the mop closet, and whenever one of the cleaning ladies would come and open the closet door, there he was, all exposed. You get your ass over here and do something about it.'"

Peck went, and through an interpreter gave a lengthy apology for his stupidity, carelessness and the trouble he had caused. And he assured the women there would be no more trouble, the man would be kept under very strict surveillance. He concluded, "I am sorry this happened and I thank you for being so gracious about it." Thirty years later, he added, "But I realized it was the first time I had ever looked at these Okinawan cleaning ladies. I really had not seen them. They had been invisible for two years." Peck the non-racist who believed he now saw every black as a person "had never noticed an Okinawan. They had just faded into the wall. For my last year, I'd always say, 'Good morning,' or 'Hi!' as I passed the women in the corridors."

The end of Peck's three-year "pay-back" time for his medical training would coincide with the end of his Okinawa tour. The thirty-four-year-old psychiatrist now had some decisions to make. He knew that if he remained in uniform the place to be was Washington, D.C. He'd learned about working the system to his own advantage, he said, so now knew to add bargaining chips to his demands for a Washington posting. He successfully applied for a Fellowship at Harvard. It was a paid academic position that would allow Peck study time while requiring a minimum teaching load from him.

"It was a magnificent fellowship," he said. "They would pay me $8,000 a year. I could take whatever four courses I chose, and provided I got a B or better I'd have a Master's in Public Administration." Peck wasn't shy about letting it be known in military circles he'd already received an offer from Harvard. He was asked what it would take to have him stay in uniform, and he told them.

"One of my dreams in wanting Washington," he said, "was to try to stop the Nixon push for an all-volunteer Army. I regarded it as a very dangerous idea. I felt the draft kept the U.S. Army sane. When we were marching in protest in San Francisco, we'd go, 'Boy, look, there's 70,000 of us here, the war will be ended in five months.' And of course nothing happened. There was a draft even in the 1960s, but only those who volunteered for Vietnam were sent there then. Things began to happen only when the government started sending to Vietnam those who did not want to go, those who had not volunteered, those whose mothers and fathers and sisters and brothers didn't want them to go. Only then did opposition to the war become powerful enough to do something. That's the one reason I was very much against the very popular idea of an all-volunteer Army."

In December 1970, his military masters gave Peck the nod and he flew to the United States to be interviewed for available openings. He was a markedly different young man from the one who'd flown to Okinawa. He'd had to time to see his parents in a clearer focus. He was returning to the United States as an adult, as a professional who'd grown on his own. That was soon to be tested.

Peck had decided to stay in Washington with his old friend from Exeter, Tim Childs, and his wife, Hope. Then he traveled to New York on New Year's Eve to see his parents. He combined the journey with a shopping expedition in New York to buy gifts for Lily and to FAO Schwartz there for gifts for the children. Holiday festivities still in the air, he went into the toy store, "and as I did so an incredible wave of depression came over me, so powerful I just had to run from the store. Walking back to my parents' apartment, I said to myself, 'God, what happened there?'" He decided that "searching for presents for the kids just reminded me how much I missed them, and that I was almost exactly on the other end of the world from them." When he went into his parents' Park Avenue apartment he told his mother about the feeling he'd had while looking for presents for his children. He said he was a bit depressed by it all.

"No, you're not," she said.

"Not what?" he asked.

"You're not depressed," she said.

"I said, 'What do you mean, I'm not depressed?' She said, 'Well, you've got no reason to be depressed.'"

Peck said this exchange crystallized for him the nature of the emotional suppression in his boyhood home. He said that fortunately he'd already, "realized some of the stuff I'd grown up with," but he was "jolted" by his mother's "capacity for denial. Mother's attitude, that I could not experience depression, was just a mind-blower to me." It was as if showing emotion, even for missing one's wife and children half-a-world away, revealed personal weakness, he said.

Evidence of personal weakness was not an acceptable WASP trait.

CHAPTER FIVE
In the Pentagon Basement

If Peck was interested in climbing up the military ladder, the nation's capital was a fast-track career move. He'd still have a long way to go in a Washington setting where two-and-three star generals are as commonplace as archbishops in the Vatican. Peck was a lowly major. In Washington, Peck was named Assistant Psychiatry and Neurology Consultant to the Surgeon General of the Army. Under the Army Surgeon General's command is the Army Medical Department system. It provides healthcare for the entire military and their families.

Freshly assigned, he had to find somewhere for the family to live. He bought a small house in Southeast Washington in the District of Columbia, not far from the U.S. Capitol, and reported for duty. The house's location suited him, "I could walk to work, and I wanted to be close to the black population rather than be totally isolated from it." Unless one lived in northwest Washington or Georgetown, it was almost impossible to be isolated from the African American population in a city then 70 per cent black.

On Peck's second night in town, tense from the trauma of moving and facing a new job, "I got really nice and mellow drunk." The next morning he arrived at his office with a hangover and found he was due at the Pentagon for a 10 a.m. meeting of the Army's morale and discipline committee. So I said, "Okay. How do I get to the Pentagon?" Peck arrived at the Pentagon early enough to learn how to find the meeting place. The enormous table in the cavernous meeting room had place plaques, including one for the Army Surgeon General.

High-ranking military types arrived and took their seats. Peck suddenly was aware that practically everyone else was two to four ranks above him. In Washington it was a condition he'd have to learn to live with.

A three-star general bustled in, took his seat, called the meeting to order, went around the heads at the table asking if anyone had any business. No one did. He came to Peck. Recalling the meeting thirty years later, Peck said that given the committee was "morale and discipline," he thought he'd better speak up. "Through the cobwebs of my hangover," he introduced himself as representing the Surgeon General, newly arrived in Washington to work on precisely these kinds of problems. The general continued on around the table. No one had anything to report. The meeting ended with the general closing it, adding, "'Major Peck, I'd like to see you in my office right after this meeting.' And I thought, 'Oh my God, he knows I'm hung-over.' I went into his office, a huge waiting room with a secretary in it.

"He kept me waiting for about ten minutes wondering what the hell was happening. Finally I was ushered in and he was sitting behind his desk and he said, 'Close the door, close the door.' So I closed the door. He said, 'Sit down,' looked piercingly at me and said, 'What do you know about transcendental meditation?'

"Out of the cobwebs of my mind I recalled some article I recently read on TM, and said, 'It may help people get off drugs.' His eyes lit up and he said, 'Oh, God, finally somebody I can talk to about this. There's nobody in the whole Pentagon I can talk to about this Maharishi Yoga program that's going to be the salvation of the Army.'" At which point, said Peck, he decided he'd better quickly become an authority on transcendental meditation. He did, "and that way became a favorite of the general's." In such ways, said Peck, "I was very successful politically."

Peck had studied social relations at Harvard and consequently, he said, found himself alternately amazed and entertained by the institutions around him. "I was interested in the psychology of politics, and the psychology of power," he said. He turned a critical eye on the military with its doggedness for detail, and Congressional politics with their momentary passions.

Peck also regarded as "good and graceful" the advent in his life of his newly arrived boss, Colonel Stewart Baker, the chief psychiatry and neurology consultant. "He turned out to be just the right kind of person—we were co-conspirators." As "sort of consultants" to the military, he and Baker, Peck said, were "in a hot spot because we were the center of dissent against the Vietnam War, the center for examining drug abuse problems, and the center for racial problems." He said there wasn't much attention being paid to racial antagonisms in the military, though whatever surfaced spilled over into Baker's and his domain.

The Pentagon's anxiety about drug abuse among the military in Vietnam, however, was reaching fever pitch. The Army was petrified by what Peck called the Vietnam War "drug thing. I guess they got scared because of *The Man With the Golden Arm* syndrome [a 1955 movie starring Frank Sinatra that dealt with heroin addiction and the difficulties of overcoming it]." The current Army General Staff reasoning, Peck said, was that because some 50 per cent of all U.S. military serving in Vietnam had tried heroin, ergo, 50 per cent of the military would return home addicted. "My boss and I kind of knew the actual figure would be around 1.5 per cent, but we couldn't get that through anybody's head."

Peck said he wasn't above leaking useful tidbits to the press—through Jack Anderson, a leading and respected Washington syndicated columnist. Colonel Baker and Major Peck developed an anti-drug proposal to deal with the problem as they envisioned it, and forwarded it up the chain of command with a request for $8 million, to run at a cost of $1 million a year. It was not funded.

Next it was Congress, alerted to and alarmed by the heroin in the military topic, began investigating. Peck contended that the military is just about the only population Congress can study with impunity. "If you're [a Congressman] investigating drug abuse in somebody else's state you're going to step on your colleague's toes. If you're going to investigate it in your own state, you're going to step on some important toes in your own state. But you're home free if you investigate it in the military, the federal population." Part of the heroin scare being blown out of all proportion, he contended, "was because everybody under the sun wanted to investigate it. There were like six [Congressional] committees all investigating it at the same time.

"It just escalated and escalated until [President] Nixon had to take action." Jerome H. Jaffe, MD, was brought in to form a new office, SAODAP, or Special Action Office of Drug Abuse Prevention. It reported directly to the President. Jaffe, in Chicago, had pioneered a mix of methadone, detoxification and therapeutic programs. In Peck's assessment, "Jaffe was a sort of hard liner, a 'By God we'll get these guys to pull out their peckers and pee in the bottle no matter how humiliating it might be.'"

An evening meeting was called in one of the Pentagon situation rooms, said Peck. "It had one of the longest tables I'd ever seen, 50 feet long. The room was just jammed. Anybody who was anybody of importance sat at the table—the less important on seats away from the table; me in particular in the darkest, furthest corner, and my boss about three seats from me. SAODAP officials told how the urine testing would work—soldiers were to be tested just before they got on the boat or the plane to leave Vietnam. If they tested positive they would be held over and put in a drug rehab program of some kind, in Vietnam or someplace else. Questions came up about managing these guys: 'Supposing they didn't want to be in a drug rehab program?' 'Supposing they ran off, what do you do? Detain them?' It got more and more ridiculous."

A Peck friend, an assistant secretary of the Army, was at the table. Peck passed him a note: "'John, this is getting crazier and crazier. It's really got to be stopped.' So, John spoke up and said, 'Well, on some of these issues maybe Colonel Baker would have something to say.' Much as I loved him," said Peck, "Stu was kind of over-awed by the high rank of the assemblage and just had nothing to say. Finally, I stood up in my little dark corner, the lowest ranker in the room. I think I just said, 'Stop. This is getting out of hand, getting totally insane.' They said, 'Who are you?'" Peck explained he was from the Army Surgeon General's office and that he and his boss knew "a fair amount about drug abuse, and I'm glad Dr. Jaffe is here. But one of the things not mentioned thus far is that most of these people you're going to urine test are draftees leaving Vietnam because their tour of duty in the Army is up. It is highly unclear—at least it's not clear to me yet, perhaps you would tell me—by what legal authority you would have to hold these people past their tour of duty?'"

That made them pugnacious, said Peck. He retaliated that there was no way that the media would not get word of the decision and have a field day with the violation of civil liberties. Peck said the meeting turned into a shouting match, not least between Jaffe and himself. Three-plus decades later, Jaffe said he remembered the meeting, recalled that it was an extremely high level gathering, but had no recollection of Peck or the scene Peck described.

Ironically it wasn't only the low-ranking military in Vietnam doing drugs. Peck, for example, was using marijuana. "I was turned on to pot by a colonel in San Francisco in the 1960s. Tried it a couple of times, and I didn't smoke any again until my last year in Okinawa," he said. There he'd worked on drug abuse lectures in conjunction with the Army Criminal Investigation Division officer. "One day, in a joking sort of way, I said to the CID officer, 'Do I really know what I'm talking about? I ought to smoke some of this stuff. Can you sneak me a bit to smoke?' He snuck me quite a bit, and I smoked with some regularity, I'd say two to three evenings a week, for the next, oh, dozen years." Later, as a famous author, one of his stock answers in interviews regarding drugs was, "I think marijuana should remain illegal for everyone under 30 and made mandatory for everyone over 30. Fortunately I didn't start smoking until I was 33. If I'd smoked during adolescence I think I would have blown my brain out."

Peck did make one attempt, he said, to scuttle the idea of an all-volunteer army. He usurped a military psychiatrists' annual conference by getting the topic on the agenda, with a panel that included "the Israeli ambassador, the chief military sociologist from academia, a U.S. senator, and a couple of other big people." Once the invitees had accepted, Peck said, it was difficult for the Surgeon General, "who looked at it very dubiously," to cancel it. As a meeting it worked well, said Peck, "but it had absolutely no influence on the president. The psychiatrists, justifiably I think, resented me for what I done because what was normally their private conference had half of the General Staff over."

The Pentagon's tricks never ceased to amaze Peck. He'd helped organize a program in Texas to develop military drug counselors. He learned they were being yanked out of their programs and re-assigned with other troops to Germany. At a cocktail party he discovered what was happening. U.S. Senator William Fulbright wanted a two-thirds reduction in troop strength in Germany so the Army was sending over three to four hundred thousand extra men over to Germany so they could just send them back again when Fulbright got his cuts. "God, a horrible story," said Peck. "Think of the costs, plus screwing up 400,000 people's lives, just to play a paper game with Congress."

Whatever his personal grandstanding in recalling some of his battles, Peck, was quite modest about how he and his boss almost changed U.S. military policy in dealing with Army personnel brutality during wartime. Had Peck and Baker been successful in getting the Army to deal with the psychology of an atrocity in Vietnam, later brutalities at Abu Ghraib, Guantanamo and elsewhere might have been prevented. The atrocity was the massacre at My Lai.

On 26 November 1969, while Peck was still serving in Okinawa, General William C. Westmoreland, chief of staff of the U.S. Army, directed Lieut. General William R. Peers to investigate "the nature and scope of the original U.S. Army investigations of the alleged My Lai incident. It occurred 16 March 1968 in Quang Noi

Province, Republic of Vietnam." The massacre and cover-up had been made public by the American journalist, Seymour Hersh. The Peers Inquiry concluded that U.S. troops had massacred a "large number of Vietnamese ... that efforts were made at every level of command from company to division to withhold and suppress information." Despite numerous officers and enlisted men being charged with a wide range of offences, the Army authorities dealt with My Lai by dismissing the charges as they surfaced. Out of an initial three dozen charges, only one made it as far as a court martial, and the soldier was found not guilty.

In 1972, Westmoreland decided to retire. The General had remained deeply disturbed by My Lai, and prior to leaving military service, he picked up on a sentence in the Peers Report that stated, "We have made no effort to investigate the psychological and sociological implications of My Lai, which is something that ought to be done." Westmoreland echoed that sentiment, ordered a psychological and sociological investigation, and that left the Department of the Army trying to figure out what to do with Westmoreland's request. "So," said Peck, "we, or rather I, went over to the Pentagon and essentially grabbed this floating paper and said, 'We'll take care of it.'"

The result was that a three-medical officer panel, Baker, Peck and a colonel who was head of research at Walter Reed U.S. Army Hospital, produced *Recommendations for research and training changes in response to General Westmoreland's request relating to My Lai and the report of the Peers Inquiry,* with eight recommendations listed. The Walter Reed colonel filed a minority report dissenting from the Peck-Baker recommendations. Peck was insisting that the first step was to authorize a study of atrocities and brutal behavior by U.S. troops both elsewhere in Vietnam, and in other wars. The study was quite feasible. The Army General War College was willing to undertake it, Peck said. In recommendation after recommendation, with the relentlessness of a man who understood the significance of what had occurred, Peck said he outlined how to research the atrocities issue and how to arrive at some conclusions that could lead to change. The Department of the Army immediately shelved the Baker-Peck recommendations and they were never heard of again. That ended a bid to makes changes.

Peck had decided that he, too, needed to make a change, and that he was nearing the end of his military career. Not only was he tired of the game, there were reports circulating that the Office of the Surgeon General of the Army was to be relocated from Washington, D.C., to Texas. Peck had little interest in staying in Washington, and less in going to Texas. If Peck was foiled in his attempt to give the Army a lasting gift, the Army in its turn munificently—and inadvertently—dropped two gifts into Peck's lap. The military set him firmly on the road to becoming a Christian. It also taught him how to cry again.

On the belief front, Peck said that by the early 1970s he was becoming dissatisfied with Zen Buddhism and wanted something more earthy, "something more carnal and flesh and blood-real than Buddhism." He hadn't settled on anything, but he was reading a little and cogitating a lot. In November-December of 1971 Peck was assigned to a high-level inspection tour. With a U.S. Senator's aide, they toured the military anti-drug programs Peck had helped establish. Because of Senatorial and Surgeon General Office rankings, the expedition meant a high degree of eager-to-please attention from their military base hosts. At Fort Jackson, near Columbia, South Carolina, said Peck, "the people taking care of us were terribly embarrassed, all they'd been able to get for our evening entertainment was tickets for something called *Jesus Christ, Superstar.* I knew nothing about it except it had been talked about a lot. I didn't know whether it was heretical or not." They decided to attend.

Peck noted two things. First, that there were no black people in the huge audience, and next, that once he got over the music's noise level and concentrated on the words, "for the first time Jesus became real to me." In the second assignment, so did crying. In 1971, the heyday of "encounter sessions"—a frequently demeaning and sometimes psychologically brutal "total immersion" program—the military was weighing the possibility of a contract with the National Training Laboratories in Bethel, Maine. NTL had developed a twelve-day "sensitivity groups" program. In June that year, it was what brought tears to newly promoted Lt. Col. Peck's eyes.

In *The Different Drum: Community Making and Peace,* Peck glosses over the worst aspects of encounter sessions, but describes how he became so wracked by the emotional release the group activities provided one woman became concerned that he couldn't stop sobbing. He assured her, he said, it was because he hadn't cried in thirty years. It was the Army's final assignment for him, for within a month of the encounter session, said Peck, "Lily and I were house-hunting." They were looking for "an area where I could establish a private practice. By Labor Day we had found our house, and I submitted my resignation. We left Washington on November 4, four-and-a-half months after that night I had first sobbed."

Few people have been so happy to leave Washington that they've written poems to commemorate it. Peck's *Leaving Washington* reads, in part:

> *The rugs were taken up,*
> *The cleansers like wooden soldiers in formation stand waiting*
> *for action on a cardboard battlefield*
> *Plymouth Van Lines will rescue us tomorrow*
> *from this soul-sucking sterile marble town.*
> *The sapless trees bear National Trust Blossoms*
> *And the mean, ugly real blacks mock us all.*
> *Do I escape to the wild hills to lick wounds and return?*
> *Or retire to sit early old in the sun*
> *Recounting brief honors and showing shallow scars.*
> *Or are we being maneuvered there by some distant general*
> *To fight a war more elemental yet than little skirmishes for position?*
> *I do not know.*
> *I know that if the fight must again be here*
> *I will need a better army or greater love.*

CHAPTER SIX

Master of All He Surveys

The Road Less Traveled *was my own journey and I was even working out my journey as I wrote it.*

—M. Scott Peck

Though his plan was to become "an ordinary country psychiatrist," Peck said, "I was terrified—terrified I wasn't going to find enough work to support myself. Practically everybody I know who has left the practice of medicine under the aegis of an organization, trying to break free and go into private practice, has been terrified. There's something about having to deal with the paperwork, the insurance, your own health insurance that's terrifying." The Army had tried to keep Peck, either as Chief of the Outlawed Drug Abuse Programs for the Veterans Administration, or as Medical Military Attaché at the U.S. Embassy in London. But Peck was done with military life: "I'd learned everything the Army and Washington had to teach me. It was time to move on." He was 36.

He and Lily agreed he should go into private practice, but where? They considered Santa Fe, New Mexico, thought about Maine, but concentrated on Western Connecticut. They'd saved $10,000; "We couldn't even handle the down payment on the houses we liked, they were well over $100,000." Manhattan wealth has always kept its Western Connecticut summer home locations' prices high. Lily and Scott kept looking. Finally, in the village of New Preston, the Pecks "stumbled across a house" at a price they could consider. It was a few steps across Bliss Road from Lake Waramaug. The price was low because it was unoccupied and hadn't been painted in twenty years, said Peck. "The grounds were overgrown, the inside neglected. It was one of the many acts of grace in our lives. We bought it for $79,500. It was a wreck, but it was gorgeous."

The house is typical of old houses throughout the rural areas of the Northeastern United States. Its 18th-century self was probably a two-or-four-roomed cottage. Then came 19th-century additions, then 20th century. The Pecks would add more, until it became today's five-bedroom house with a guest house to the rear. At the time, in the downstairs configuration, they wedged in a sizeable home office for Peck. Later Peck would say setting up his office in his home was a huge error. "The children would see daddy at home but not available. It would have been much easier for them had I had an office and then, when I came home, be available."

New Preston village is about a ninety-minute drive from the Hartford-Springfield airport and a two-hour drive from New York City. It was located a mere thirty miles from his father's summer home. The village's popularity comes from its lake, the second largest natural lake in the state. The Peck house, rimmed to the rear by hills, sits in the sheltered Bliss Hollow up from the lake edge. Peck insists the previous owners had named the house "Hollow Bliss"—"would you believe it?" "Hollow Bliss" may have been prescient.

Peck chose New Preston in part, he said, because there was a dearth of psychiatrists in the region. The town of Torrington is about 20 miles north and Danbury some 30 miles south. There was no psychiatrist in practice within perhaps 45-50 miles. "Before I even got here I had employment arranged at a clinic in the Torrington hospital, and two days at a clinic in Milford, and a two-hour set-up to be psychiatrist at the jail in Litchfield," he said. For first the time in his adult life, Peck had to answer to no one other than himself: he was a solo practitioner, and paterfamilias. He decided to call the house, "Imladris," the place in Tolkien's Middle Earth magically protected against the forces of evil. "Imladris" was not protection for the occupants against some of Peck's developing whims and demands.

He contended that an early childhood phobia about being lost mutated into always wanting to know where Lily was. Thirty years later he said he realized that to Lily it must have looked as if he was trying to control her when he'd ask her what time she'd be back from shopping. It wasn't control, he said. "If she wasn't back I'd begin to worry like crazy that something had happened to her."

On the seasonal calendar, as Lily and Scott moved in, Lake Waramaug had begun to freeze. They had a dollar bet on a date by which time the lake would be completely frozen. It was an annual contest they kept up for thirty years. They settled in. The lake thawed, the work for both of them continued. There was the steadying routine of normal middleclass professional life: school for the children, work for the parents, much effort put into family vacations, and maintaining the home.

Terrified though Peck might be about losing Lily, or not making enough money, he was nonetheless fortunate. The era, as his friend psychologist James Guy later remarked, was indeed "the Golden Age of psychotherapy." Within six months of arriving in New Preston, Peck could report more patients than he could handle with more money coming in than he'd ever made. "I came with no ambition higher than that of simply being a country psychiatrist who played golf, hopefully, on Wednesday afternoons. It was one of the times in my life that I've been truly without ambition." With more patients than his schedule permitted, he asked Lily if she would like to take on a patient. The small summer house to the rear of "Imladris" became the practice's waiting room, and Lily's office. Peck said, "From the word 'go' I knew that Lily was a born therapist. She had a practice, fifteen to twenty hours a week, for the next ten years, maybe fifteen." Lily was also the manager who ensured the practice operated efficiently, and that the patients were welcomed and comfortable. Said the Peck family friend, Hope Childs, widow of his Exeter friend Tim Childs, "Lily made everything work." The Child and Peck families were close during these years, their children of a similar age.

Another close couple was the Allens, and while Peck could talk of being a simple country doctor, his intellectual dynamism hadn't slowed. Elizabeth Allen (nee Elizabeth Peale, daughter of Norman Vincent Peale), who had also attended Friends Seminary, said she and husband John, would spend "snowy afternoons in our home when Scotty would expound on his latest train of thought. My husband and I would marvel at the range of his dynamic thinking. We would always come away aware we had been in the presence of a great mind."

Immediately on setting up his practice, Peck said he'd become "extremely focused on his work whereas Lily had the great capacity just to flow with the kids—and she loves to shop, which I hate. She'd play dumb games with them. It's rather hard to flow with children when there's a paper you want to write on religious ecstasy. I left 95 per cent of the burden of raising the children to Lily. I put in my five to ten per cent.

"Parenthood is a lot of work, but I enjoyed that work. Lily wasn't so keen on feces and I was used to them. So I didn't mind changing diapers, washing them [these were pre-disposable diaper days], and taking the girls for walks. As soon as they began to talk, and started telling those endless sorts of stories that children can talk about that never go anywhere, I found taking care of them very difficult. I would do some of it, but I thought it very boring. I really had to work at it until they became old enough to have dialogues." He said he and son Christopher were always close. "We used to dance incessantly and had great fun. I spanked less than I was spanked. The oldest, maybe five times when she was a kid. The next one, three times. Christopher not at all. I would be hesitant to say never spank a child."

Decades later he regretted that he competed too much with his children, and wrestled with them too hard in horseplay. He even gave them the same type of Christmas joke presents his father had visited on him and David. "I didn't pay them enough attention," said Peck. "If you asked them they would say, 'Well, Dad was really good in a crisis, but you had to have a crisis to get his attention.' I regret not having paid them, particularly the girls; more attention than I did. By the time they were adolescents they were exciting. I gave them lots of attention. Of course, they had lots of crises then, too."

He and Lily were keen to develop the land around the house into a fine garden. Just as Judge Peck had been able to boast of the finest lawn in Connecticut, so, in the decades ahead, Scott Peck, with a wave of his arm, would be able to introduce visitors to "one of the finest gardens in New England"—due in major measure to gardeners who created and maintained what Peck and Lily envisioned. Peck had his own patch, for growing pot, which he would offer to friends and guests. "He was the only man who ever offered me pot," said Hope Childs. She declined his invitation.

Peck continued his heavy smoking, his drinking had not lessened, and he'd developed his taste for marijuana into a three nights a week habit. He said, his relationship with the children improved with pot. "It made me more playful and more able to flow. Simon and Garfunkle music would have left me cold, but suddenly, under pot, I began to hear it." Peck tuned out what he didn't want to contemplate, such as the effect on his children when he asked them to roll his joints for him.

Peck answered questions about his drinking, his pot-smoking and his ability to see everything in terms of his own needs first with a few stock phrases—the quick retorts of the cornered performer or politician. He'd say the children were better than he was at rolling joints; that he was nicer to have around when he was on pot or drinking. "I get mellow," he'd say. Then he'd try to deflect the question by adding, "whereas [brother] David was a nasty drunk." That would develop into a riff about David in order to avoid the further answers for more probing questions. Sometimes Peck would use another stock phrase to conclude that topic of conversation: "I wished I could drink and smoke more," he'd say, hoping the topic then had nowhere to go.

In the 1990s, psychologist Guy asked Peck "in looking back, do you find yourself being kind of sadistic towards your kids the way your folks had been?" (Guy, at the time, was considering writing a book on Peck, but dropped the idea.) Peck replied, "Yeah. Not to the same degree. But that's some of the stuff I would take back." His instance was the same: "they loved to roll my joints for me because Daddy was so much more fun when he was on pot. And again, that's something I wish I could do over again, it gave them the added burden of the secret they had to keep." Many around Peck have chosen to keep their secrets secret.

Marijuana allowed him to become more passive, he said, and "get more in touch with my feminine side. C.S. Lewis said, 'In relation to God we are all feminine.' I also think it had a great deal to do with my spirituality. I became more able to more or less 'hear' God, and for the first time, while stoned, I began to carry on serious conversations with Him—or Her. No great revelations, just an ever-increasing closeness. I was still smoking marijuana when I first listened to the music of Marilyn Von Walder, and was turned on to the Christian core of her music and lyrics in a way I don't think I would have been otherwise." Sister Marilyn von Walder was a Discalced Carmelite nun known for her sacred compositions and joyful songs of praise. (In 1987 Peck and von Walder produced *What Return Can I Make?* a multi-media liturgical celebration kit subtitled "Dimensions of the Christian Experience.") Then he'd add, "Once again, I don't want to recommend marijuana to everyone. I am damn glad I did not start smoking it until I was in my 30s, and with a very well developed lifestyle and clearly focused. Under those circumstances it did have the effect of loosening me up so that I could become like a little child, and emotionally a child a God."

Vacations were another break for Peck from the routine—if not from the pot. His son Christopher was rankled by the contrast between vacations paid for by his father, and the annual getaways to Bermuda or elsewhere funded by the easy munificence of his grandfather. "The odd thing with Scotty," Christopher said, "was there was generally enough money for luxuries but not enough for comforts. He had this strange way with money. He was a Depression era baby. His father was doing well financially, but the Depression had an effect on everyone's psychology. So, when we went to Europe, we often stayed in very grand hotels, but the three of us would pile into one room. I guess our last family trip was we went to Paris one Christmas. Julia and Belinda both brought their fiancés, or they became fiancés during that trip. And they were given separate accommodations. I was the fifteen-year-old having to share my parents' bedroom. It was kind of odd in a very nice hotel. Obviously, if I'd had my druthers, we'd stay in a cheaper hotel and I'd have my own room. This was typical of him."

"He was very tight with Mom," continued Christopher, "but on the other hand she'd buy a lot of cheap things. That was her rebellion. They were always fighting over all this stuff she was buying. I think they only installed air-conditioning in the mid-'90s. It's an old house, so air-conditioning was kind of spotty in places. Mom bought a couple of window units, which actually worked really great. Dad on principle didn't like the idea, even though he was sweaty and miserable. He could be very Spartan." Christopher retained "warm memories of my grandfather. He was a grand old gentleman by that time. Both Scotty and David were still burdened with memories of the way grandfather had done things, the way he'd been before. Each year we had Thanksgiving at grandfather's apartment and watched the Thanksgiving parade from one of his office windows."

"We were often together as two families," said the Rev. Peck, "but almost always with my grandparents as hosts, whether Easter holidays in Bermuda or in the country." In addition to grandparents it was David Jr. and his wife, Greg, and their three children, Heather, Lisa and David III (the Rev. Peck). There was Scott and Lily, and their three children, Belinda, Julia and Christopher. Said the Rev. Peck, "Some of my happiest memories are of us playing, singing or dining as cousins in Greece or Bermuda. They were also shadowed on all sides by family dynamics of which one is only vaguely or subconsciously aware. But there were shadows only because the light was so bright." Said Christopher, "The Greece trip—we cousins had a great time. It may not be relevant but it's amusing, all the sailors on the yacht were gay and they were always perpetually fondling each other." Even on vacation Scott Peck didn't fully relax; he preferred turning a vacation into an experience. When the Pecks, *tout ensemble,* were in Greece, Scott "laughed at the notion" that that the Greek Isles, the Cyclades, might be the site of the lost city of Atlantis. But after hearing the tales, he sought out the Akrotiri, sunken city exhibit in the Athens museum. And after viewing it he decided he was a believer.

Peck said he regarded vacations and travel as a time for family bonding, whether taking Belinda, his eldest daughter with him to a Salt Lake City conference ("a time together to enrich our relationship"), or he and Lily taking Christopher a few years later to Puerto Rico for deep sea fishing. On a more modest scale, for parental relaxation and refreshment, Scott and Lily would go into New York, to catch up on art and music, or to hear speakers such as the Afghani writer Idries Shah, a Sufi mystic, teacher and storyteller (1924-96). "He was a brilliant man," said Peck. "He turned me on to the wonderful explosion of 13th-century Persian mystics. He talked about false Sufis and true Sufis—very important because there were a lot of New Age people floating around calling themselves Sufis who weren't."

Peck, the professed anti-WASP, discovered in Sufism more ammunition for his blasts against The Establishment's idea of the proper social ordering of things. "Muslims tend to believe there are seven levels to everything," said Peck. "One Sufi teacher said that esthetics is the lowest appreciation of the Real, with a capital R. And I suddenly said, 'Aha!' The number one ultimate value of WASP culture is good taste, and in worshiping good taste WASPs have caught on to a little piece of the Real. What WASPs don't realize—and generally don't care—is there are six further levels higher than that."

Americans didn't care much about WASPs anymore, either. America was changing. The Beatles went East, many young Westerners to India, too, souls on a spiritual search, with, for many, cheap drugs as a bonus. Back in the United States, "religion" was changing, too. World religions scholar Melissa Jones, PhD, explained that academically, "religion" was no longer simply confined to divinity schools, theological colleges and seminaries. For more than a decade, major U.S. universities had been creating Departments of Religious Studies. Said Jones, "To be authentic in the academic community you have to be scientific. Academics were trying to turn religious studies and theology and that whole area of inquiry into a social science. Dr. Peck [with *The Road Less Traveled*] would make that connection. He did have the scientific credentials, he was an MD, and a psychiatrist." (Peck had his own addendum to this. When he was on the lecture circuit he'd frequently be asked why he didn't go to divinity school himself. His view was that while he'd have loved to take time off to attend, "it would be the bloody stupidest thing I could possibly do for my career. It would almost de-credential me." In other words, people paid attention to the spiritual side of psychotherapist Peck's writing and lectures precisely because he was not ordained, or a credentialed theologian, but a scientist.)

If Americans were headed to the East, the East was also making its presence felt on Western shores. Idries Shah was an example of those who brought the Eastern experience to the Western armchair traveler. He appeared on the scene as Peck was emerging from his industrious psychiatrist shell driven to do more. Peck liked the challenge of new ideas, and liked Idries Shah. To *Psychology Today* Shah was "a major cultural event of our time." One of Shah's aphorisms possibly lodged in Peck's subconscious. Shah's response to a person complaining about life's problems was, "It is my view that your real problem is that you are a member of the human race. Face that one first." Peck opened *The Road Less Traveled* with "Life is difficult," same thought, tighter construction. *The Road Less Traveled* was an instruction to "face that one first." It was probably not lost on one-time Zen-Buddhist Peck that Shah blended Eastern teachings with Western needs. A newly stimulated Peck, the man who'd abandoned thoughts of a writing career for medicine, suddenly found he couldn't keep thoughts off writing a book. Further, he'd begun his first long-term affair.

How one assesses the fact that Peck could conduct this sexual relationship and subsequent affairs and flings, while working on and believing in what went into *The Road Less Traveled* on love and marital love, is a personal call. And there is a quite personal answer. Years later, Peck's friend the Rev. Stephen Bauman, said a good preacher preaches out of his own needs. Seen in that light, *The Road Less Traveled* is Peck's emotional, spiritual and psychological autobiography. He is preaching to himself, not least about sex. Psychiatrist Guy probed Peck's sexual development with him.

"I had wet dreams starting at about thirteen," Peck said, "and so I instinctively knew what sex was about. I wouldn't masturbate, but

I had wet dreams. And I said I would never have sex or enter a woman. I can remember my first couple of dreams clearly. I was with my father and we had picked up a couple of Hawaiian girls, beautiful Hawaiian girls, and we were in my parents' bedroom, which had twin beds. And he was in the bed with one of these girls, and I was in bed with the other, and penetrated her, and had the sense that I was going to urinate in her. I can't do that. I can't do that. I tried to withhold myself and I exploded. I woke up and there was all this semen around. So that was my first. I don't know exactly what to make of the fact that my father was there and the girls were Hawaiian."

Guy—referring back to fifteen-year-old Peck's five weeks in Silver Hill psychiatric clinic, and the Silver Hill psychiatrist detecting a certain fear of sex—said to Peck, "The issue of the fear of sex came up again in your 30s. A mentor mentioned it to you after seeing one of your poems (*Death Wish*)." Peck replied, "I just don't think the poem shows it. The poem on death I called "Life Wish," and the poem on sex, "Death Wish," and the last couple of lines have to do with sinking into that dark furry hole where I will expire. Of course, orgasm is referred to by the French as 'le petit mort,' the little death. But there's no question that in my earlier years I was plagued unconsciously with a fear of sex, which I don't know to this day where it came from. It never surfaced in the course of my analysis. My marriage was not an intimacy issue, it was a boundary issue. Lily proposed we have separate bedrooms; three years later I was ready for it and proposed we stop having sex [in the mid-1980s]. I think our marriage began to get better as a result.

"My infidelities were never about searching for a new wife or a better wife. They were some relief time from marriage, but not a substitute for marriage in my mind. They were primarily about sex, not intimacy. The majority of them were very brief, if not one-night stands, two- or three-night stands. One woman I had a two-year relationship with, really quite constant, say twice a week anyway. The other was much more occasional, limited to when I was on speaking engagements—eight or ten times a year, but lasted close to ten years between the time I was 45 and 55. If I could have lived without being unfaithful to Lily, I wish I could have, I would rather it had been that way." Nonetheless, Peck could say of the two longer-term liaisons in particular, "We're still in some communication, not much." They were "rich relationships. They gave me a great deal and I think that if they were talking to you they would say I gave them a great deal."

Winter. Lake Waramaug froze again, thawed again. It was 1975. Like rain filling a lake behind a dam after a drought, Peck's ambition as a writer began to build. Months into 1975, when he was supervising a pastoral counselor, Peck remarked to him, "Gee, it would be good if somebody wrote a good book for patients to tell them what psychotherapy is about. What to look out for, and what to go with." The conversation led nowhere, the thought died (except that in 1984, Peck did write an introduction to the *Clinical Handbook of Pastoral Counseling, Vol. One*).

Peck at twenty-two was "the great American writer" with nothing to write about. At thirty-nine competing inner forces and raw edges from how he was living—ambition and restraint, searches and lapses—created an internal friction. The spark from that friction ignited the mature writer. He would try to write honestly. He would write from what he knew about life being difficult, about love being difficult, about what he understood of sexuality and sex, and its demands; and infidelity. He would bring in what he was experiencing in family life as husband, father and son. Peck—the wounded healer (without acknowledging many of the wounds were self-inflicted). At this time his clandestine sexual life was a muted, unseen, unspoken backdrop to the marriage—in the long term a more corrosive backdrop than Peck was prepared to admit.

In the Introduction to his Harvard thesis, Peck had described his writer's *modus operandi*. It was a method of operating he would carry into *The Road* and all his other nonfiction. His explanation would certainly not defuse his critics. "My efforts have been severely criticized on two counts," he wrote in 1958. "First, that existentialism is a philosophical topic and it is not the function of a social relations thesis to deal with philosophy; second, the subject is much too general and theoretical ever to be dealt with adequately by an undergraduate." This was the future psychologist who, without any deep background in religion, and no underpinnings as a theologian, wove through his manuscript a cord of faith strong enough to tug a troubled life forward.

His Harvard thesis hammered home his non-fiction writer's creed: "I am of the belief it is unrealistic to divorce one area of study from all other areas, to divorce psychology from philosophy or the 'natural' sciences." He believed for his thesis, as he believed for *The Road*, "that the eclecticism practiced in this paper is necessary to my approach."

Inspiration hit. Whatever the level of discontent in the family circle, for Peck, this was a winter of creative excitement. As he tells it, and has done repeatedly, he was stoned on home-grown pot, listening to Simon and Garfunkel. Whatever he was wrestling with spiritually came encapsulated in three words: discipline, love and grace. "The words were in my mind and wouldn't leave. I said, 'Well, Scotty, you've had this idea for a book many times before and it's never turned out. Let's see how it floats in the morning when you're sober.' And in the morning it looked good, and I said, 'Well, let's look at it again in three weeks.' I would keep saying, 'Yes, and let's wait another few days.' At the end of those three weeks I felt as compelled to write it as I had the first morning after."

Decision made, Peck spent the next five or six weeks reorganizing his schedule so that, starting in mid-January, 1976, he'd cut his practice back to four days a week to allow three days a week for writing. "I'd learned from Marquand that the way to write was you did it as an eight-to-five job. For me it was eight-to-six. Back then I could write for ten-twelve hours with ease, for the most part in longhand on yellow pads, which were transcribed." Seven days a week was a decision that meant a grueling work life. The main burden, however, was really to be borne by Lily Peck. All writer's spouses can attest to that.

Peck's decision to write semi-full time had been aided, psychologically at least, by an unexpected turn in his fortunes. His father paid off Scott's mortgage, though the father later felt he'd made a mistake. As Peck single-mindedly settled into his book writing, Judge Peck would regularly chide, "What are you doing writing a book? You know that books don't sell. You've got a good career going now and a shoemaker should stick to his last." Peck said that at the time of his father's generosity, they were actually making more than they were spending. He could have used the money better a little later, he said, when, before *The Road*'s financial bonanza hit, with children in private schools and college, plus inflation, finances were tighter. Other sons might have been simply grateful to father for paying off the mortgage.

Peck stuck to his therapist's last *and* made a career shift. He had the dream, the theme, the determination, and a title: *Psychology of Human Spiritual Growth*. While he didn't have a deadline, he did have a stark reminder that the years were pressing—in May 1976 he'd turn 40. Peck kept up the brutal pace for a year, and in January 1977, twelve months after he began, the first draft was done. This graduate of Harvard's social relations department, who referred to himself as "an unusually socially conscious person," had packed his experiences together, "and on some unconscious level all this stuff fed into, by the grace of God, my writing the book."

Peck at Harvard had finessed his thesis, cleverly, a masterly stroke. His thesis wasn't academic research but a lengthy, speculative essay based on little more than his personal observations and reactions to the thoughts of others. Fascinating his thesis might be, but as his main critic said, scholarship it wasn't. As in his thesis, so with his book, finally titled *The Road Less Traveled*. Academics pointedly ignored *The Road* with its general lack of footnotes and academic rigor.

His books always generated a split decision, unevenly split—the majority: reviewers, religious authorities and readers, generally on his side. The professional and academic community: usually thumbs down. Peck would always be quick to admit he didn't invent anything new; he simply pulled together what already was in a different way. That's not what the academic community wanted to hear. They want obeisance to the goddess.

Writing a book is one thing, getting it published is another. Peck's is a cautionary tale for anyone thinking of a future in the writing business. He gave the book to Carl Brandt Jr., son of his mentor, Carol. Peck said Brandt called it "sellable" and said, "It will be sold." He took it to the top editor at Random House who said, "You know, I've been going around telling everybody about this marvelous manuscript I've got and then I got to your third part, which is called 'Grace,' and you just totally blew it. It was too 'Christ-y.'" Peck said, "I only quoted Christ a couple of times. We argued for a while and finally the editor said, 'Well, I think you really ought to go looking for another publisher because I don't think we can resolve this.' Carl Brandt then took it to Simon & Schuster, to Jonathan Dolger. Dolger said it was a wonderful book, here's the contract."

Dolger suggested to Peck that as Freud had intimated that faith in God was a neurosis, he thought Peck ought to address the issue. It was incorporated into part three, Grace, and Peck set about cutting part four which, by his own admission, was too long. Dolger also did not like the original title. Said Peck, "I kept doing titles and they weren't pleasing to Simon & Schuster. Title number 47 was *The Road Less Traveled,* which Jonathan liked. I recognized it had a Frostian ring, so I didn't know whether I'd have to pay royalties or not." He repaired to his Frost, he said, and saw that the words were not precisely as Frost had used them in his poem. Peck's original title was reworked into *The Road's* subtitle: *A New Psychology of Love, Traditional Values and Spiritual Growth.* Shortly after the title change, Dolger left the publishing house. Several years later he became Peck's agent. In publishing parlance, Peck's manuscript was now "orphaned to the trade"—a book without an editor, a literary sheep without a literate shepherd. It floated around and was taken up by editor Alice Mayhew. Simon & Schuster decided on a press run of 5,000 copies.

Peck had achieved one thing; he now had a book that was about to be published. Next, his private life in upheaval, Peck, undoubtedly on edge, waited for reviews. Fueled by the energy and ambition of completing one book, Peck had immediately started on a second book. It would become *People of the Lie.*

For writers, waiting for reviews is a soul-destroying time. Sometimes it brings redemption—a decent review. Sometimes damnation—a panning. For many writers, it brings the worst of all possible worlds, no reviews at all. Even a bad review is worse than none, for at least someone noticed. Shortly after publication, a review of *The Road Less* Traveled surfaced for Peck in the *Washington Post.* Peck loves serendipity. Nothing and no one in his writing life would ever be as serendipitous as Phyllis Theroux' decision to pop in on an editor at Simon & Schuster to discuss a book she was working on.

Theroux tells her Peck story with ease, a sense of fun *and* in the full knowledge she launched the Peck phenomenon. "All I did," she said, "was nudge the boulder and it began to roll." In 1978, at a time when her essays in the *New York Times* were attracting some attention, she called on Simon & Schuster editor Alice Mayhew. She was just starting a writing career that would later include such books as *California and Other States of Grace: a Memoir* (1980), *Peripheral Visions* (1982), *Night Lights: Bedtime Stories for Parents in the Dark* (1987), *Giovanni's Light* (2009) and *The Journal Keeper: a memoir* (2010).

Though there was no meeting of the minds between the two women regarding Theroux' book proposal, they did chat about their similarities, their Catholicism, their studies in philosophy at different Catholic universities. "So," said Theroux, "I said goodbye, and that was that" until a couple of months later when Mayhew sent Theroux galleys of Peck's book with just her card. Said Theroux, "There was no letter, you know with, 'we just love this book, blah, blah, blah.' Just her card." Theroux said that at the time, "I was just divorced, it was early days, everyone was still bleeding, and I was figuring out how to support myself with my writing. I opened up the Simon & Schuster galleys. It said *The Road Less Traveled,* a guide to spiritual whatever, and I just thought, 'Oh, really boring,' put it down and didn't do anything. But a couple of weeks later I had a moment and came back to it, picked it and read the first sentence, 'Life is difficult. This is a great truth because once you acknowledge that life is difficult, life is no longer difficult,' or words to that effect.

"I was hooked pretty early on," Theroux continued. "I got about halfway through and I thought, 'Well, if the rest of the book is horrible, it doesn't matter. The first half is worth it.' So I called Brigitte Weeks, editor of Book World at the *Washington Post* at that time, and said, 'Brigitte, I have a book I want to review.'"

Weeks said she probably had the review copy in her book pile and she'd see if she could find it. "She called me back later that day or the next and said, 'Well, there must be something going on between you and this book." Theroux told her, "'I just think it's an amazing book.' She said to go ahead and review it."

For the next two weeks Theroux spent all her time "trying to write the most compelling review on the face of the earth so that people would be forced to read the book," she said. It appeared on Sept. 29, 1978. Even as the review was headed toward the presses "I couldn't keep my hands off it," said Theroux. "I called up Scotty. He was actually in the middle of a session, counseling somebody. I said to him, 'You know, I'm breaking all the rules by calling you and telling you that I have reviewed it. This is an amazing book,' I said, 'and I just want you to be prepared, it's going to be a big hit.' It didn't happen my way. It became a best seller, but only in Washington."

The problem, she said, and Peck quickly noticed his dilemma, was his publishers would neither publicize *The Road* nor commit themselves to another press run beyond the original 5,000. Theroux was also perturbed, she said, because "in New York I would keep running into people like the number two at Simon and Schuster at the time. I remember specifically running into him at a book party and he gave me a ride home. I said, 'You know, I want to talk to you about one of your books.' And he said, 'Which one?' And I said, "*The Road Less Traveled*." He said, 'Oh yes, it's kind of like an in-house discovery.' I mean they never took it seriously. They never did anything for it even after it became a best seller in Washington. Ho-hum."

Simultaneously, Peck, knowing the book was selling out, was becoming increasingly anxious. At which point, Peck and Theroux, in a manner of speaking, joined forces. Said Theroux, "My nature is such that I love promoting other people's books." She called Peck and asked, "Can you and Lily come down here? I'll give you a book party. All the people that already love the book can come and meet you." It was at that point Theroux discovered Peck as micro-manager, "no detail too small. By the time he got here I had gotten 18 different letters from him [about plans for the party], and three different revisions of several," she said. She kept telling him things such as, "'Scotty, this is going to have to wait, I haven't even thought about what I'm going to give people for hors d'oeuvres. You know, I don't do that until a couple of hours before the party.' Anyway Scott and Lily came, and a lot of people came." M. Scott Peck, author, was launched.

Theroux said that when Peck was leaving he told her, "'You know, I have to confess you weren't what I expected.' I took it, rightly or wrongly, as a compliment, you know, he thought I was pretty?" The attractive-looking Theroux said, "I don't know what he thought. I guess as a writer he'd probably created sort of a grim image of somebody. So I said, 'Well, you were exactly what I expected.' And he took that as a compliment."

Peck couldn't help taking Theroux's remarks as a compliment, especially since she'd written in the review: "Books by psychiatrists on spiritual growth dot the ocean in great number these days. But *The Road Less Traveled* is a clipper ship among Chris Craft, a magnificent boat of a book, and it is obviously written by a human being who, both in style and substance, leans toward the reader for the purposes of sharing something larger than himself, that one reads with the feeling that this is not just a book but a spontaneous act of generosity."

By then, there was a second review, in the pages of the *National Catholic Reporter,* an independent newsweekly. Dr. Gerald May, a psychiatrist with a fine reputation in the field, said bluntly, "A book for our times. [Peck's] discussion of love is the freshest since Eric

Fromm's, and his approach to spirituality is simultaneously honest and understandable. It meets our culture directly, encourages us to move forward, and points a trustworthy finger in the direction of wholeness."

The next seven million copies of *The Road Less Traveled* had a brief excerpt from Theroux in the *Washington Post* on the front cover, and a slightly lengthier one from May in the *National Catholic Reporter* at the top of the rear cover. But what Peck had already realized, given Simon & Schuster's ho-hum attitude, was that *The Road Less Traveled* would not bring success to M. Scott Peck unless Peck first brought success to *The Road Less Traveled*.

CHAPTER SEVEN
Author! Author!

Two favorable reviews do not a best-seller make; newly minted author Peck was up against hard reality. "My fantasy was it was going to be reviewed across country," said Peck. "It was on the *Washington Post* best-seller list in a week. In two weeks it was sold out in DC. I called up my imperious editor and got her assistant. 'When are you going to do another printing?' She said, 'We haven't thought about that yet.'" The problem was that excellent reviews and strong local sales in Washington, D.C. made no impression up in magisterial Manhattan where Simon & Schuster remained unsure as to what they had on their hands.

Theroux' *Washington Post* rave was confined geographically to the Washington, D.C. area audience. The *National Catholic Reporter* review had a national audience, and a sophisticated, literate and highly educated Catholic readership, but circulation was limited to about 45,000 readers. As 1978 turned into 1979, Peck's anticipations for the book soared exponentially. He needed more copies. He said he sought legal advice to see if his contract could force Simon & Schuster into a second printing. Nonetheless, armed with the promise of another press run, self-publicist Peck had the Theroux and May reviews photocopied in the hundreds. Throughout 1979 his packet was mailed out to anyone likely to have reviewing credentials in print, on the radio or in television. The package offer was simple—"Here's what others are saying, we can send you a review copy, too." It was a blitz. Peck was relentless in making himself available.

If editors glanced at the *Washington Post* and *National Catholic Reporter* reviews they were likely to be impressed. Theroux was one of the few reviewers to mention what a fluid, engaging and persuasive writer Peck was. (Fred Hills, Peck's future Simon & Schuster editor, said, "All of his manuscripts are well written. He's a pretty clean writer. Occasionally his syntax could be strengthened, but whatever editing was done he always went over it again and often would rewrite in order to keep it absolutely in his own voice.") Theroux wrote, "Peck begins with what we all know, 'Life is difficult.' Yet Peck the psychiatrist sees people every day who have not come to terms with this knowledge, or rather have come to terms with it, by developing neuroses and character disorders which are efforts of the conscious mind to avoid legitimate suffering. If there were not problems, we would never evolve from weakness into strength. If we do not grow into our full strength, we might as well not live at all …. 'Real love,' Peck defines as 'an act of the will to extend oneself for the purpose of nurturing one's own or another's spiritual growth.'" Without knowing of Peck's ongoing personal spiritual journey, Theroux identified him as moving along a God track on a journey that had a spiritual destination.

Psychiatrist Gerald May's *National Catholic Reporter* review followed the Theroux review like the baton passed in a relay race: "This book insists that the path requires hard discipline, willful attentiveness, constant questioning, and responsible loving. Even then it is only through grace that true wholeness comes to us. This is a refreshingly serious business, the more so because the author refuses to fall into pessimism or pietism about the heaviness of the struggle. In fact, the pages of this book express a bright and buoyant vision of hope. His discussion of love is the freshest since Erich Fromm's, and his approach to spirituality is simultaneously honest and understandable. His spirituality mixes traditionally non-threatening images of humanity with just enough gentle mysticism to keep one enticed and encouraged. He deals honestly and clearly with issues of evil and sinfulness, again from a metaphysical base which will be acceptable and understandable to most western minds."

Theroux lighted on one statement Peck wished he'd never written: "Psychotherapy should be (must be, if successful) a process of genuine love, a somewhat heretical notion in traditional psychiatric circles." Theroux, writing rhetorically, asked, "Are there pitfalls to this commitment? Peck admits there are. 'Were I ever to have a case in which I concluded after careful and judicious consideration that my patient's spiritual growth would be substantially furthered by our having sexual relations, I would proceed to have them. In 15 years of practice, however, I have not yet had such a case … It is out of love for their patients that therapists do not allow themselves the indulgence of falling in love with them.'" Even before publication, said Peck, "ninety per cent of me felt the book wouldn't go anywhere, but ten per cent of me had intimations not of immortality, but that it was going to be quite an extraordinary book. I thought, 'If that should happen to be the case, and it should become famous, how am I going to deal with that fame?' The notion came to go into a monastery for a two-week retreat."

In three batches the publisher printed a further 4,500 hardback before releasing it as a Touchstone paperback. They sent Peck on a publicity tour, just to sign books. "A publicity tour which isn't a speaking tour. That's a laugh," said Peck. Through word of mouth, not least through Alcoholics Anonymous meetings and church reading groups, Peck was creating a drumbeat, or "buzz."

Peck, ambitious but ambivalent about what lay ahead, understood how the game might play out. The book was his entrée to the public stage. He had his themes, those would be his topics. He also had his hang-ups. He was painfully shy. He had absolutely no capacity for small talk, and he had even less interest in extended conversations he could not control and direct. Because Peck was comfortable in control and uncomfortable when others were, he was in inner turmoil. He needed help. He was already deeply into writing his second book, *People of the Lie: the Hope for Healing Human Evil*, and was coming face to face with the fact that he'd committed himself at some level he could yet not yet fathom to become a Christian. To give himself some space in a different environment, he decided to find a monastery somewhere in the Hudson River Valley and go on a silent retreat. There, he imagined, away from family, his psychiatric practice, and writing, he could gather his thoughts about possible fame in the offing.

"The Episcopalian Convent of Saint Helena, in Vails Gate, seemed just right the moment I walked in," he said. "It has the most beautiful chapels, the nuns made me feel very welcome. I had a number of items on my agenda—one was to stop smoking, which I managed to do for two days. But the major issue was how would I deal with fame. Should I go public? Or, like J.D. Salinger [author of *The Catcher in the Rye*], should I immediately get an unlisted number and retire deeper into the woods. I didn't know which way I wanted to go. And I didn't know which way God wanted me to go." While it is reasonably safe to comment that fame was not the initial spur for Peck, by this time it was certainly a lure. Indeed, fame holds an allure few authors want to resist, for the financial rewards are generally inseparable from the author's name.

He told the nuns he wanted to make a silent retreat. Sister Ellen Stephen—she liked to be known as "ES"—the person in charge of novices at the time, said the nuns were agreeable. Peck liked what he heard, liked what he saw, and soon returned to the convent in its 50 acres of fields and woods with a backdrop of the river valley mountains. His yellow Beetle was packed with books for a ten-day silent retreat. The nuns were surprised as the monastery had an excellent library. They were possibly even more surprised that Peck began talking to the sisters and more or less interviewing them. At the end of it, said the nun, Peck "seemed to have gotten what he wanted and became interested in us." She did not feel he had talked away his silent retreat.

Lily's role in Peck's Christian search is not known, but she was baptized and a believer. As the daughter of a fundamentalist preacher and pastor she'd have a considerable background in conservative Christianity's teaching tenets. If Peck had a relevant question about Christianity, Lily had more knowledge than he did. Their son, Christopher, said that for a period prior to Scott's adult baptism, Scott and Lily were Anabaptists. Anabaptists do not hold with infant baptism, and believe in the re-baptism of baptized believing adults. The Mennonites and Amish are among those groups that can trace their roots to Anabaptism. Sister Ellen Stephen, who later became her order's provincial, said she did not talk to Peck about his Christianity or his exploratory reading.

"Scotty was a mystic in his approach," she said. "It was always the personal with God he was interested in, not philosophical proof. I think his reading was maybe C.S. Lewis." The nuns later invited Peck to receive the sacrament of the Eucharist with them.

In 1980, two-and-a-half years after he'd for entertained the possibility of baptism, Peck returned again to the Episcopalian Convent of St. Helens and was baptized in its chapel by a Methodist minister. "God kept tugging, pushing, kicking, prodding, and pulling," said Peck. It was a joyful family affair; Lily and the children were present. An Episcopalian priest celebrated the communion, "and afterwards," Sister Ellen Stephen recalled, "we had a jolly reception with some wine, and Scotty led us in *Amazing Grace*."

Members of his nationwide audiences had their varied assessments of this new Christian. At one gathering Peck addressed, he said, the poet Maya Angelou was seated next to Lily. "She nudged Lily and whispered to her, 'He ain't no white boy. He's a black Southern preacher.'" Meanwhile, "*The Road Less Traveled* was being hailed as the great self-help book," he said. "I may not have known why I wrote it, but it was fairly clear to me at the time I was not writing it to be a self-help book." The readers—not surprisingly—were making their own assumptions about that. One former Nixon aide (Peck declined to name him), a man "who got saved by religion, said to me, 'Scotty, it was just so clever of you the way you disguised your Christianity in *The Road Less Traveled* so as to get the message across to people.' I said, 'No, it wasn't clever of me at all. I wasn't a Christian.'"

Not everyone who loved *The Road* loved all of it. Magazine writer Gary Dorsey was one reader who liked some of the book, but not all of it, and provided a reason. Dorsey, writing in the *Hartford Courant*'s magazine, North East, said, "Surprisingly, the first two thirds appeal to me as a journalist because of its tough-minded insistence that people question everything, never shrink from doubt—from dedication to the truth. Values such as discipline, delayed gratification, personal responsibility and truth are carried like banners through these pages. At the same time, just as he describes them as tools to holiness, Peck reminds that if used properly they will unlatch pain and emotional suffering. What bothered me was the section entitled, 'Grace.' Here his theory makes gargantuan leaps ... 'be ready to accept ethereal gifts that are unsought and inexplicable.' The very guy who had pledged an allegiance to skepticism and the scientific method was now asking me to have faith that he was right."

Overall, the 316-page *The Road* was a book like his Harvard thesis—no index, no bibliography and barely a handful of footnotes. Peck, cleanly, cleverly, possibly unwittingly, had put himself forward—in the words of a later writer—as "the nation's shrink." It was a tag he detested, but that doesn't mean he didn't take advantage of it—any self-publicist has to have a handy sound-bite or two ready.

"The mail you get can tell you a lot about the book," Peck said, "and I knew within two-three months of publication that I had a good selling book on my hands. My first fan letter, from Washington, D.C., began: 'Dear Dr. Peck, you must be an alcoholic.' The writer couldn't believe I could have written this book without being humbled by alcoholism and having spent years in the program. AA was terribly influential in *The Road*'s success because AA is an ideal grapevine. It's all very quiet, and you don't know anything about it, but it was picked up by AA people and kind of zoomed through every AA meeting."

A fellow psychotherapist wrote, "I especially enjoyed the flow of your text, traversing the delicate connections of psychotherapy, love, evolution, and spiritual growth. It often seems to me courageous to speak of soul and spirituality, without apology, in the field of psychology." The writer continued, "Missing for me in your synthesis was a differentiation of the masculine and feminine elements in oneself, one's growth, and in our culture …. Choosing to use non-sexist language is difficult and cumbersome, and I think it a very loving act. I challenge you to engage in a loving dialogue with a committed feminist regarding this issue."

Sex quickly reared its controversial head. "I found myself disagreeing with your characterization of what you term 'romantic love,'" one woman wrote. "I couldn't tell whether you thought this kind of love identical with sexual infatuation. I don't, incidentally. The characterization struck me as too easily dismissive of something that has acted historically as a substantial force in human affairs; as internally somewhat inconsistent with other views you expressed; and, finally, as at odds with my own experience. I do think you might want to be a little more cautious about the equating of 'falling in love' with 'a genetically determined instinctual component of mating behavior.' You describe a very real phenomenon—people imposing their needs on other people in the name of romantic love—but ignore another very real phenomenon—people experiencing joy in each other precisely because of the suspension of need."

A soul sister to that writer's opinion wrote: "I thank you for writing it. I also, however, found myself demurring at some points … your observations … on romantic love seem inconsistent with your other observations that you see grace abounding (as I do) in so many spheres of human activity and yet deny its operation in the sexual/romantic sphere."

A group of seven women in Oregon, who formed a study group around *The Road*, wrote, "We have really built up a trust level and felt your guidance in our lives. But we are stumbling on our interpretation of your ideas on open marriage. In our varied experience we find that fidelity is a necessary part of all marriages. Even though an open, trusting relationship may survive an outside sexual experience, it does not contribute to the spiritual growth of your partner. It does reduce the amount of trust and openness within your relationship."

These were the readers who kept up with Peck with each

succeeding book. They are the ones who were horrified when he began publicly rationalizing his infidelities. Peck could tell a psychologist that his affairs were "never about searching for a new wife or a better wife, but relief time from marriage" but he was not allowed much leeway by the class of women who wrote in response to *The Road Less Traveled*. Decades after these events, the American essayist Michael Dirda (not with reference to Peck) addressed the topic of marital love in France. It was in the St. Valentine's Day Eve, 2003, *Washington Post* Book World. Dirda spoke of "settled men and women who realize that a well conducted liaison can enrich and refine the spirit like a work of art. At the very least, wit, attentiveness and delicate flattery—all the social graces—enhance every encounter, whether over dinner or in bed …. At its best (or its most cynical), the relationship could be less a betrayal of marriage than its safeguard. Such measured delicacy is probably not for Americans, burdened by a Puritan past …."

To most Americans, this was a concept that spoke more to unacceptable French sexual orderliness or Italian marital practicality than to their own lives—even though some 50 per cent of U.S. marriages end in divorce.

While some letter writers poured out their own sexual experience woes, others asked for advice, for a chance to talk on the telephone. Many were highly literate—an indication of the type of readers he attracted. Some readers he confused on sex, others he confused about God, or even psychotherapy. A California woman wrote, "The confusion I had dealt mainly with your theory about the relationship between a therapist and the patient. In fact, at times I think you forgot entirely about the 'patient' in this process of psychotherapy. Take for instance, the ego boundaries and love. The professional was told to let go of the ego boundaries. But what about the patient? The patient wouldn't be there if a problem didn't already exist. Is the patient supposed to read between the lines at this point? Don't you think you leave the poor patient hanging in mid-air? To my way of thinking, now would have been the time for the patient to be told that the therapist is to be looked at like a loving parent figure. My psychologist recommended *The Road Less Traveled*, and I did receive a lot of insight as to what 'love,' 'grace,' and 'lazy' meant."

One man wrote, "Would you be so kind as to indulge my confusion by offering an explanation of the last sentence in the section of Love and Psychotherapy, by offering an explanation of what is meant by 'they are content to be ordinary men and women and do not strive to be God?'"

Theologian Dr. H. Wayne House, later president of Oregon Theological University, said, "Peck wrote *The Road Less Traveled* at a propitious time. Whereas psychotherapy stood at a distance from the average person—wrapped in scientific jargon and devoid of spiritual dimension—Peck offered solutions in a non-scientific and easy-reading style. He addressed the spiritual cravings of Americans who apparently were not being satisfied through the church or their culture." House added, "Peck denies practically every major doctrine of Christianity while advocating an unbiblical morality." (*The Psycho Heresy Awareness Newsletter* would later lambaste Peck for a lack of clear standards concerning the nature of truth, for viewing Scripture more or less as mythology, for denying God as sovereign. Peck's reliance on evolution and the evolving nature of man came in for a drubbing, as did his views on salvation, resurrection, heaven and hell.)

Peck's book was liable to do more harm than good wrote Roy H. Smith of Phillips Graduate Seminary in Enid, Oklahoma. Smith said Peck had taken the wrong road in claiming mental illness as a "manifestation of grace" and his other errors would further afflict the afflicted.

"I do want to air one bad feeling I had," wrote a New Yorker who was "glad" he'd read the book, "and that was to a remark about 'passive homosexuals' who might benefit from the risk of asking a woman out. I am a homosexual and I don't feel that this is a disease or a lack of development psychologically—that 'old' Freudian stuff is something I, and most healthy people in your field, don't believe in any more. I am in a life style that was chosen for me by a High Power, and one that takes as many risks and disciplines etc. to grow in as in a heterosexual life style."

Despite the criticism, the letters were overwhelmingly grateful, quick to point to personal growth that had resulted from reading the book. They were particularly appreciative of Peck's tentative, but quite apparent, belief. "It took my breath away," one woman wrote, "to read about 'recognizing,' to be confirmed that what I feel and have felt about God being me—my unconscious—that amorphous, ephemeral 'something' within me that I can feel, but which hasn't, up until now, seemed to fit in the world in which I live." A Charlotte, N.C. woman commented, "There are many case histories where 'the church' has laid a real number on the young

92

mind—taking [them] some time to get out from under." Then she asked: "What 'formal religious training,' if any, did you allow your own children to be exposed to?"

Others wrote of their problems and addressed them to Dr. Peck the psychiatrist. One man wrote, "I finished reading your chapter on dependency and I can't do anything until I find help for my problem in that area. I want to live so badly and yet I am not living now. I am numb and empty and helpless to change." Wrote a woman, "I am in the middle of reading your book … I like it because you so honestly say what is wrong, as in facing problems. I have never heard anyone speak so honestly. I want to thank you for that. I also want to solve my problems. I want to try to escape suffering. I want to feel the pain inside. I want to help myself grow emotionally. I want some mental health. I need these things." A doctoral student wrote, "I can't tell you how wonderful it feels that I am not alone. So many times your words echoed my own thoughts—my years of feeling alone, outside the group of others who seem so certain about God and what life is all about. Now I feel that I'm not just a misfit who couldn't accept the religion I grew up with …. I feel that I am becoming myself. It took me eight years to leave a marriage that, in is many respects was 'ideal,' looked upon by friends and family as perfect, and which I could easily have remained in for the rest of my life, but which felt empty to me. As I read your book I knew certainly and instantly why I had to leave."

A dean of students applauded Peck: "You are to be congratulated on this very difficult although important synthesis of psychology and religion. Your writings have done much to help crystallize some of my thoughts and to raise other far-reaching questions." While the file drawers in Peck archives at Fuller Theological Seminary are packed with such letters to Peck, the latter letter touched on a thorny topic for scholars—that of the blended frontier where psychotherapy, psychiatry and religion meet, and Peck's contribution, if any. Peck admitted he wrote first and researched later, consequently he'd probably little knowledge of the depth and width of the academic arena he'd entered. He'd soon begin to hear.

Peck had dared to be different in order to care for the individual reader as warmly, though as disinterestedly, as if the reader were in his consulting room. He was telling them that if they were in therapy, their assessments of their condition or situation were probably correct, as long as their assessments were honestly, candidly arrived at. Readers could detect the difference in what this man was saying from what they'd previously heard or thought. They could not always describe what they detected, but they accepted it because it was so reassuringly familiar. As for his "erroneous theology," Peck was genuinely unconcerned about what the religious or psychiatric professionals might say. He would have liked their endorsement, but he didn't crave it.

To some, Peck smacked of New Age. One article on New Age "leading voices," placed Peck in a group that included the Jesuit philosopher Teilhard de Chardin, movie star Shirley MacLaine and former United Nations assistant general secretary Robert Muller. Peck was described by Drs. John Ankerberg and John Weldon as an "important New Age voice, despite his lack of religious consistency."

His spiritual statements often had a pick-and-choose quality. Whatever that says about Peck the personality, none of it undermines what Peck the writer created. Peck's personal weaknesses were his strength as a writer. Surely his emotional pain was a major element of the tension that sparked his creativity? In his narcissism, however, he seemed to believe that admission of a wrong was itself exculpation, hence his absence of genuine remorse, not least for his treatment of Lily and the children. He would paint his behavior, his rarely restrained drug and alcohol consumption, and philandering in shades of genteel naughtiness, but no more than that. Toward the very end of his life, he admitted his burgeoning success had a role in his behavior getting out of hand. "It was happening so fast that when it came I was in over my head, I couldn't control it," He admitted. "I was profoundly affected by the Sixties in that first glorious year in San Francisco. It was one gigantic sort of love-in and it was spectacular." He'd missed out on it then, but a decade later, successful and becoming wealthy, the worst part of him wanted it. And who was to say no? So he pleased himself.

From his reviews (and later travels), Peck learned, he said, there were three groups of Christians that did not like him, "and they are very distinct. There's the real, hardcore fundamentalists. They don't like me because I am not a literalist—I do not believe the bible is the directly transcribed word of God; there are places where it should be interpreted. The second group have been the New Agers. I have to acknowledge that they've been big attendees at my lectures, and that many have been supporters despite my criticism—and my biggest criticism is that they are total imminentists. They believe God dwells within them, not outside them. Therefore, any thought or feeling they have can assume the status of revelation, which is a very dangerous heresy. The others who haven't liked me have usually fallen into the Catholic camp, although they are a minority of Catholics. They're such transcendentalists they're into the authority and majesty of God to such a degree they can't deal with the fact that God can talk to the likes of Scott Peck, except through a priest, maybe."

Don Avirom wrote in *Aurora Magazine*, that *The Road* "seems to have struck a reawakened nerve of interest in looking at life from a spiritual point of view. Peck 'attacks tunnel vision'—the pitfall of most religious revivals—while he simultaneously tills the all too neglected ground which separates psychology from religion." *Campus Voice's* Cynthia Lollar said *The Road* "is a bold synthesis of psychological and spiritual insights into mental health that speaks to the modern American's alienation from a sense of higher good." Peck would repeat in interviews that "mental health is a process of dedication to reality at all costs. There are any number of fears" people must face to reach that reality. The *New Age Journal's* Jeff Wagenheim consequently spoke of Peck as the "spiritual therapist and psychological guru to the millions of lost souls he had led along *The Road Less Traveled.*"

One mid-1980s reader of *The Road Less Traveled* was Omar Khan, son of a Pakistani diplomat and today founder and senior partner in Sensei-International, a global management and business consultancy "that blends Eastern approaches to people development with Western process improvement experience." Khan had gone to high school in the United States and the Netherlands, where he was when he read *The Road*. "I was intimate with it as I headed off to Oxford, and it has continued to be a seminal book for me at many levels." Two decades later, Khan recalled that "what came through was the honesty of it, and the fact that this man had the ability and willingness to say things that I knew I had inescapably grappled with—even though parts of me didn't want to. Parts of me wanted an easier, simpler, fortune cookie remedy, and the book wouldn't let me have it."

Where did Peck find it all? At a cocktail party a younger woman remarked to Mrs. Peck she "must be very proud" of Scott and his book. His mother replied, "No, not particularly. I had nothing to do with it, really. It's his mind, you see. It's a gift." The ability to write *The Road Less Traveled* was a gift. It was also his reaction to what he perceived as a lack of love from his parents.

CHAPTER EIGHT
A Bourbon with the Devil

There cannot be many exorcists who, having just made contact with Satan during an exorcism, leave the room to place a telephone call to ask what to do next. Not a bad idea when in doubt; the problem lay in the man Peck telephoned, the Irish-born former Jesuit priest, the Rev. Malachi Martin.

Equally, probably few exorcists grab a shot of bourbon on the way back to the room to help with the coming encounter. But Peck was convinced that the woman on the bed with the crucifix on her chest was possessed, and that the latest manifestations of her muttering and declamations meant he was facing either the anti-Christ, or Satan, or a combination of both. These details were not in Peck's second book, *People of the Lie*. Indeed, Peck did not reveal he was the exorcist mentioned. He merely said he'd witnessed exorcisms. Peck waited more than twenty years to unveil his role. That came in his 2005 book, *Glimpses of the Devil: a Psychiatrist's Personal Account of Possession, Exorcism and Redemption*.

People of the Lie opens with evil, and some excellent cameos of people whose behavior he labels "evil." To the *Charlotte Observer* the book was "so compelling in its exploration of the human psyche, it's as hard to put down as a thriller ... such a force of energy, intensity and straightforwardness." His *People of the Lie* passages on the Devil and exorcism, in fact prepare the way for *Glimpses of the Devil*, just as his four pages on evil in *The Road Less Traveled* paved the way for *People of the Lie*. This "hope for curing human evil" was half completed in first draft even before *The Road Less Traveled* received its first review. Peck lauded *The Road's* "four extremely well done pages on evil—for when I was writing it I hit on evil and I just took off. I wrote about 50 pages, and was still writing away when I said, 'This is ridiculous, you've got a totally unbalanced book, condense everything you know, Peck, into four pages. You can write about evil in your next book.' And so, before I was even done with the final rewriting of *The Road Less Traveled*, I knew that my next book would be *People of the Lie*. The other thing is, almost all heresy arises with somebody running with one side of the paradox. And so [having presented God and Love at length in *The Road*] I just owed it to present the other side."

Peck said that the first agent to whom he gave an initial chapter of *People of the Lie* turned it down. "She said, 'It's probably a very good book but I can't represent it because it scares me too much.' She did me a great favor though. She said, 'Where you are [in terms of *The Road Less Traveled* selling well] I don't think you need an agent—agents are needed by people who are not yet published or don't have a reputation, or are too busy. You're sort of in-between.' So that saved me a great deal of money, actually."

Peck might be developing a reputation, but that didn't mean anyone wanted his next book. Simon & Schuster didn't, he said. They passed on it twice. Finally, Peck surmised, *The Road*'s rising sales convinced them otherwise.

People of the Lie, a 270-page book that would also become a bestseller, was received with accolades. Readers coming to *People of the Lie* from *The Road Less Traveled*, if not scared out of their wits at having to face up to evil in their lives, would settle quickly into Peck's engaging style. He began with stories from his casebook designed—rightly so, given their content—to startle the reader into setting aside some reservations about even delving into the topic of evil. Storyteller Peck provides précised-biographies of evil characters and evil couples, and surrounds them with Peckian analysis and commentary. These evil people in the everyday world are "people of the lie," they lie to themselves about the evil they do. Peck's account of the couple who give their son for Christmas the rifle with which his brother committed suicide is an example of how Peck can startle, unsettle, and keep the reader fascinated.

When his pen is at its best, in those bursts of writing that hint at a novelist's skill, Peck attracts the reader deeper and deeper into the topic's abyss, luring her or him further along with tales that have mini-saga overtones as they detail acts conducted with a frightening ordinariness—acts with horrific consequences. But devilishly evil? The reader has to decide. The goal appears to be to get the reader to the bedside of an exorcism. Some critics might say of *People of the Lie* what magazine writer Gary Dorsey said of *The Road Less Traveled*—that it switched at the two-thirds mark as it went from cogent argument and declaration to asking the reader to suspend disbelief (or, rather, to accept Peck's version of belief). In *People of the Lie* there are factual cases clearly discussed, then the switch from the everyday to the paranormal, to accepting that Satan exists, and that people can be physically possessed by the devil. At the end of the book, perhaps in an attempt to return to the ordinary world, Peck ends with an account of "group evil." The U.S. Army massacre at My Lai, Vietnam is his example.

Even readers with an open mind regarding possession might well take issue with Peck's blanket use of the term "evil" to cover a variety of aberrant behaviors and cruelties. The Dominican theologian, Richard Woods, said, "In fairness, Peck was not a theologian. Technically he's right—that moral evil is still evil whether we call it sin or badness. My problem is when the language becomes used as a weapon—not that Peck did, but others might." What the book did do in its first two thirds was attract an interested readership into the discussion of evil in ways to set them wondering. For that it was widely admired. Equally, whatever the percentage among Peck's readers, a significant percentage of U.S. Christians does accept that Satan exists as a corollary to accepting the existence of God. They were favorably impressed with Peck's dual grasp of evil and Satan's presence in the world.

Simon & Schuster editor Fred Hills joined the firm as *People of the Lie* was in final proofs. He summed up Peck's first two books this way: "I don't think *The Road Less Traveled* was written as a self-help book. It evolved to the extent that people—many readers—found it was a life-changing experience for them. *People of the Lie* was not written as a self-help book. I mean it doesn't have sections on how to apply it to your own life, but ironically, that book has sold just about a million copies." Money wasn't the root of all evil in *People of the Lie*, but as a book it did rather well generating it. Some twenty years later, it had a renaissance, in Japan where, said Peck, it became a best-seller and brought Peck a further several hundred thousand dollars. One point to make about Peck's first two books—and perhaps *Denial of the Soul*—is that they are "original" to a high degree. That isn't the case with the others.

Peck owed his mounting interest in evil and possession to the Rev. Malachi Martin (1921-1999), a headline-grabbing, "bald-faced" lying, book-writing Irish-born Catholic priest. Martin had a reputation with many inside the Catholic Church as a troublemaker, a liar and a cuckold. In the eyes of the exorcism crowd, Catholic and otherwise, Martin's reputation switches from infamy to fame. Peck was in the latter group. He dedicated his *Glimpses of the Devil* to Martin.

The two met through Simon & Schuster. Martin was one of the

publishing company's authors, and when Simon & Schuster circulated copies of the Peck book to its authors seeking publicity comments, Martin, was the only one to reply. He wrote "a nice long comment," said Peck, "and I said, 'Well, who's he?' I figured he must be a psychiatrist. I looked in my big tome of American psychiatrists. No Malachi Martin. So he might be an author, and in Books in Print, lo and behold, he had plenty, including his most recent, *Hostage to the Devil,* on a subject I was already interested in. I called him up, got through his formidable phone defenses. He was eager to meet me and have me down for lunch in New York, the first of four or five lunches we had." *Hostage* convinced Peck that Martin was the authority on exorcisms.

Dominican theologian Woods had interviewed Malachi Martin on television. "It fell to my lot to conduct a pre-publication review of Martin's *Hostage.* I was allied in this with an internationally celebrated clinical psychologist. Working independently, our conclusion was the same: Martin's 'five cases' were the fabrications of an inventive but disturbed mind, lacking all psychological, historical, theological and pastoral credibility." When Woods interviewed Martin, he found him "a clever, charming engaging Irish rogue who evaded every effort to document the instances of possession he so graphically described." When Peck's *People of the Lie* appeared, Woods said he was "appalled" that, Peck, a newly committed Christian "of a vaguely evangelical stripe, had accepted and endorsed the Martin's fictional ravings [about exorcism] as accurate and instructive."

Peck's regular lunches with Martin had sealed their pact. The psychiatrist's adulation of the priest-exorcist fairly drips off the *Glimpses of the Devil* pages. Peck was not blind to Martin's failings. "He was a bald-faced liar, and I believe that what Robert Kaiser wrote [*Clerical Error: a True Story* by Robert Blair Kaiser] was probably correct, and that Kaiser got him kicked out of the Jesuits for sexual activity." Peck said that when he first met Martin, "Malachi had this cover he was a plain clothes man for the Vatican, for the pope, to hold back the progress of Vatican II. It was all a bunch of bullshit. Malachi also had a good side and it, too, was of heroic proportions. As I say in the book *[Glimpses of the Devil],* that other than his identity, he never lied about anything important. I asked him at our first luncheon, 'What is the effect upon an exorcist of doing an exorcism?' and he just looked at me and said, 'It will give you greater authority and make you more lonely.' And, of course, it was exactly correct. After I was baptized, Malachi Martin started sending me cases to evaluate for 'possession,' and I got involved in the first exorcism, which was a profound spiritual experience and a profound teaching experience."

In spite of Peck's claim to have been "cured" in therapy of his attraction to and subsequent willing dependency on likeable father figures, it may not have been so. Peck idolized and idealized the strong men on the Letterman faculty in San Francisco. His gushing comments on at least two military commanders he served under went far beyond admiration. He was in awe of his friend Tim Childs—to a degree that Mrs. Child's found, if not unsettling, at least misplaced and somewhat naive. Then he met Martin and came under his baleful influence. Martin was a fabulist. In person, he was an entertaining cross between a chameleon and a faun, a priest who flaunted a "charming variety ... of blarney and piety" (to paraphrase A.P. Graves). During the sessions of the Second Vatican Council (1962-65) in Rome, the Jesuit not only cuckolded *Time* magazine correspondent Robert Blair Kaiser by leaping into Blair's half of the marital bed during the writer's absence, but slept in than man's nightshirt and wrote a fallacious account of Vatican II on Kaiser's Olivetti typewriter. Martin also ruined the reputation of at least one fellow Jesuit by planting false stories about him, and wrecked the marriage of at least one Irish couple with his cuckolding ways.

Peck wasn't long on gratitude. When Martin was old, Peck ignored his devilish mentor. (He was much the same with his own father, an attitude that caused a serious rift between Peck and brother David. The Rev. Peck said his father, David, "loathed Scotty for many things. How unwilling Scotty was to shoulder equal responsibility as their father was sick and dying. He just left my father to face the death and estate on his own, which certainly left my father saying Scotty's view was not much more than, 'all I want is my half when it's over and you've worked it out.'" The Rev. Peck said it was "a really shitty and spoiled thing to leave someone with. It hurt my father deeply and fueled the resentments and wildly complex issues that existed between the two brothers." (Judge Peck's estate was just under $1.5 million.)

Now it was Malachi Martin whom Peck neglected. "A good decade after our work together," said Peck, "Malachi asked me to dinner. Malachi somehow embittered and slightly over the hill. This was during a lengthy period in which I had allowed myself to become inhumanely busy, and I made no effort whatsoever to reach out to him. I suppose one reason I dedicate this book to Malachi is as an act of contrition." A publicly guilt-stricken Peck was a rare sighting.

At one level Peck believed in the possibility of possession by Satan. At another, what he really believed in was his right to explore whether indeed there was such a thing. Despite his psychiatrist's declarations of what an exorcism is or ought to be at the close of *Glimpses of the Devil,* an air of ambivalence creeps in toward the end of the book. Indeed, not every participant in the Peck exorcism was a convinced believer, even Peck's Anglican nun friend, Sister Ellen Stephen, one of the team for the first exorcism, though she didn't stay until the end, said she had "an open mind" on the topic.

Peck nearly became an on-call exorcist. When a man in Buffalo telephoned Peck one day, it was to describe his wife, as a "very sane and sober church-going, church-involved Presbyterian," who had left that for a New Age church, and a year beyond that "suddenly went crazy and had been hospitalized for three years. And nothing was working for her." Peck told him "one of the things that might have to be considered is the possibility that your wife is possessed." The man said, "Why do you think I'm calling you?" Peck, who had just finished the second exorcism, was exhausted and told the man he'd get back to him. Peck said he was in tears when he called Sister Ellen Stephen and complained, "You know, God could have waited at least a week, couldn't He have? Just a week." Peck said the nun replied, "I have no doubt this timing is not accidental, but it does not mean God is calling you to do another exorcism. It is quite possible that what God is calling you to do is say no to another exorcism." Eventually, Peck did see the woman in the hospital.

"The insurance was running out," Peck said. "Consequently the issue about who was going to do any exorcism was taken out of my hands." During that time Ellen Stephen told him, "You know, God never calls anyone to do something that doesn't feel right in his heart." Peck continued, "I think that's true even for Jesus. I am not into philosopher [Joseph] Campbell's 'follow your bliss.' I don't think Jesus went to the cross following his bliss. He went sweating blood."

The most exciting thing about his participation in these two exorcisms, Peck told *The Wittenberg Door,* "was not meeting the devil, instead it was sensing the palpable presence of God. That presence of God was not an accident because in both cases there were teams of people [seven in one and nine in another] that came to work with the patient. When you get seven people in a room at considerable personal sacrifice and risk who have come in love for the purpose of healing, it's not an accident that God is in the room."

The Wittenberg Door, later known as *The Door,* was published by liberal evangelicals with a keen sense of humor and a discriminating use of the tongue-in-cheek. It was known also for excellent in-depth interviews that could run for considerable length. *The Door* interviewed Peck three times. In the "devil" interview, *The Door* reversed the type, white lettering on a black page, with Peck's photograph altered to include horns and a pointed beard. *The Door* interviewer, W. "Bill" McNabb, said it was on the strength of Peck's persuasiveness that he, previously open-minded on the topic, came to believe possession was possible.

In a comment that perhaps explains the ambivalence at the close of *Glimpses of the Devil,* Peck told *Door* interviewer McNabb that "demon possession should really be called partial or imperfect possession because clearly in these two patients there was a struggle going on between the demonic and the soul. One of my theories is that good people are more prone to possession than bad people precisely because Satan, in accord with traditional Christian theology, is on the run and its trying to put out fires, so he goes where the action is. Possession is not an accident. You don't go walking down the street one day and all of a sudden a demon jumps out at you from behind a bush and penetrates you. Both patients I saw had very, very difficult childhoods. They were terribly lonely, both of them repeatedly sold out to unreality. Their possession was a gradual phenomenon for which the individual has a considerable amount of responsibility." Other psychiatrists might suggest the patients were not possessed, but stricken with multiple personality disorders (MPDs).

As for a definition of evil, Peck told McNabb the best he'd heard "came from my son when he was eight years old. I asked him what evil was and he said, 'That's easy, Daddy, evil is "live" spelled backwards.'"

Once *People of the Lie* was circulating Peck was soon hearing from his readers. As with *The Road Less Traveled,* his admirers were not hesitant to simultaneously admire and play critic regarding his opinions. One reader, in a typed, three-page, single-spaced letter, wrote: "*People of the Lie* is interesting but also disturbing. It recognizes evil because of your examples of bad parents and others. It is easier to see your evils in others than in yourself. But I thought you could have been a lot more effective if you had not labeled the parents as evil. If one of your readers has done or said some of the bad things your examples gave, the reader, instead of seeing evil, will be tempted to get angry and close the book. But on the other hand, if you gave the parents the benefit of the doubt about whether their ruling loves were good or evil, but called [their] actions destructive and harmful, you would be less likely to lose your reader. In fact, this is what the Lord meant when He told us not to judge. We are not to judge the person but the words and acts. We can and should say, 'This act is evil and it will hurt you and hurt others.' But once we say, 'You are evil,' we totally antagonize that person. Men like Stalin and Hitler were pretty obviously evil and we can say, 'If this man is what he appears to be, he is evil.' Most people are not that easy to judge, although you would be in a better position than most."

The woman continued, "We are not evil until we have looked at our evils and said, 'I come first and I don't care who I hurt' …. A lot more people are mixed up because of ignorance … because of upbringing that is immoral, prejudiced, faulty and/or destructive of self-esteem."

A Presbyterian pastor weighed in. He saw communism as evil and mildly chastised Peck for opposing capital punishment. A troubled student wrote to say, at great length in tiny handwriting, that he thanked Peck for the book but was "deeply troubled for it exacerbated my belief that something evil was influencing the course of my life." From Texas, a female reader wrote, "I join with others in thanking you for naming 'evil' a 'religious' concept in the midst of a scientific profession. Almost a heresy, perhaps, for you! But as a person who is both a Christian and a believer in psychotherapy, I believe that this naming is crucial to a correct diagnosis and treatment."

A man with an apparent background in the scriptures chided Peck. "In a book that deals insightfully and compassionately with the quality of evil and the nature of the lies that precipitate evil," he wrote, "is a repetition of the *lie* that has caused more malevolence and suffering than any other … the allegation that 'fat cat' Pharisees murdered Jesus." In a defense of the Pharisees, the writer argues a historical context defense and asks Peck, "Was your intent evil? I more than doubt it … it suggests a lack of knowledge."

There was another element running through some of the letters. Writers spoke of their experience of "corporate evil," working in corporations "where," a Londoner wrote, "I saw what happened to individuals in a group under pressure, and how easy it is to make that one first step of disowning responsibility for one's actions. It is so easy to talk oneself into doing something to save one's skin. So easy to convince yourself there is nothing wrong in this. So easy to betray everything you thought you believed in until your position is threatened. I can say from experience that the only thing that prevented me from going against everything I was taught, the only thing that gave me the strength and support not to put myself first, was my Christian faith." The Londoner told Peck, "You give many reasons for group evil, but I do believe you missed out the most important of them all: self-knowledge. If we even have an idea of what we are capable, we are then on our guard when faced with certain situations. But if we truly believe, or talk ourselves into believing, that we are 'good' people who aren't capable of those terrible deeds we read about—and most people feel this way—then when we are in a similar situation we will act similarly. We still may, but at least we will know we are wrong while we are doing it, we will at least have a conscience, and hopefully will be stronger the next time."

A computer analyst told Peck, "You are right, *People of the Lie* is not a nice book. It is a disturbing book … I constantly draw on portions of the book in meeting various situations which arise. Thank you for that." She then questioned Peck, "As well as the consistency of the destructive behavior, surely the magnitude of the offense should be considered in determining evil behavior? I also associate a purposeful-ness, a directedness, and an awareness of the evil deed being committed. The intent of the do-er, whether conscious or unconscious, is a factor. It is the unconscious element which concerns me. Can an individual be considered evil or held morally responsible for acts which inadvertently injure others? You say in the subtitle, 'Toward a Psychology of Evil'; you are brave to begin. May you be protected from any ill effects in your study."

Through *People of the Lie*, the reviews, and the related interviews he gave, Peck created a different sort of stir than he had with *The Road*. In *The Road*, folks read the book and looked into themselves; with *People* they looked out at others. Peck's friend, the psychologist Dr. James Guy, said *People of the Lie* has "something in there to bother everybody, to bother therapists, theologians, and churchmen. It's a little too scary. When I read it, I said, 'Ah, this one's not going to help him, but he's telling the truth about how he feels about this.'" Peck's Harvard roommate Jake Severance called the book, "Quite a different piece of work, but that was to be expected. I was fascinated with the discussion of evil. I'm not at all sure that I agreed with all of it but there were some fascinating takes on just what evil is and [that] the friendly postman on your block might also be an evil person, that sort of thing. But I didn't go as far as some of my relatives who said [of *People of the Lie*], 'My God, it's Halloween.' They thought he'd gone around the bend. I didn't think so."

One person wrote that as a victim of oppressive relationships she was unable to finish *People of the Lie* because she found it "so overpowering." A New Yorker told of his own jarring insights into evil after "being trained by my mother only to see good in people." But the most compelling of the many letters was from a retired U.S. Marine Corps pilot. He had napalmed My Lai on orders at the time of the massacre. In a harrowingly emotional letter he convincingly traced My Lai's evil effects into the broader reaches of the military and society. "My wingman and I refused to be decorated for attacking the village for what then appeared to be no reason. My observation [is] there is more evil in this affair than has ever been imagined." The writer believed that with the air attack "I think we covered up a massacre by killing the few survivors, but I cannot be certain. When I found out I had attacked and destroyed My Lai under dubious circumstances, I did report it a number of times and was told to stay out of it. I'm the last person alive to see My Lai, and may have killed hundreds of people & nobody cares."

Peck had cared about My Lai, valiantly so, when he served in Washington. He cared, almost violently so, about the presence of "group evil" in the world, and the lack of interest in seeing it explored and analyzed scientifically. At the end of his life, in a desperate effort to have his say on the topic, he wrote a proposed coda to *Glimpses of the Devil* that dealt mainly with group evil. It was too late in his writing life, too rambling, and fortunately never published.

Including anthologies, Peck would write fourteen books in all. His writing was "eclectic"—in the Greek sense that he selected from the many schools of thought and teachings that appealed to him personally. Some of his books were extensions of earlier ones.

People of the Lie, and his final book, *Glimpses of the Devil,* came decades apart but they are coupled wagons on Peck's "evil" track. *The Road Less Traveled* and *Denial of the Soul: Spiritual and Medical Perspectives on Euthanasia and Mortality* (1997) are coupled on the "life" track.

Peck's other works would include *What Return Can I Make: Dimensions of the Christian Experience* (1985), with Carmelite Sister Marilyn von Waldner's music and Patricia Kay's artwork. *What Return* is a sort of antidote to people perspiring after *People of the Lie.* It is a Christian prayer service with a series of sermons by Peck on cassette tape along with his text in the volume itself. Next would come *The Different Drum: Community-Making and Peace* (1987); *A Bed by the Window: A Novel of Mystery and Redemption* (1990); *The Friendly Snowflake: a Fable of Love, Faith and Family* (1992); *A World Waiting to Be Born: Rediscovering Civility* (1993); *In Search of Stones* (1995); *In Heaven as on Earth,* a novel about Purgatory (1996); *Denial of the Soul* (1997); *The Road Less Traveled and Beyond: Spiritual Growth in an Age of Anxiety* (1997); *Further Along the Road Less Traveled* (1997), *Golf and the Spirit: Lessons for the Journey* (1999), and finally, *Glimpses* in 2005. *The Friendly Snowflake, In Search of Stones* and *Golf and the Spirit* were illustrated by Peck's son, Christopher. In addition there was *Meditations from The* Road (1993), daily readings excerpted from *The Road Less Traveled* and *The Different Drum.*

In *People of the Lie,* Peck declares his Christianity on the second page of the Introduction and reinforces it on the third page. Doing so, he places any skeptic among his readers, reviewers or listeners, at an interesting juncture. If the reader, interestedly or pruriently, accepts Peck's candid account that he cruised Manhattan as a teenager to pick up gay men for sex, accepts his claim that he was not always the world's best parent or most attentive husband, accepts his account of two-and-three night stands and long-term affairs, accepts his claim that he is narcissistic and somewhat lazy, then the reader is more-or-less obliged to accept Peck's sincerity regarding his Christianity and its role as a prime motivation in his life after his baptism at the age of forty-three.

In Christianity, said Peck, he'd found his ultimate paradox. "What I suddenly discovered after being a mystic for years was the richness of Christ-ness. The central doctrine is that Jesus paradoxically is both human and divine, not fifty percent one or the other, but fully human and fully divine. There's probably no more indigestible paradox than that," just as there's no escaping *People of the Lie*'s evangelizing edge. Through the encouragement of Sister Ellen Stephen, Peck took to daily meditation, not a large leap for someone who'd begun a belief life with Zen Buddhism. His prayer life, he said, "is 99.9 per cent spontaneous, my own dialogue with God about what I'm feeling. Sometimes when I'm worried in particular about the state of the world, or a bunch of people, I will often pray over and over again, the *Agnus Dei*, 'Lord God, Lamb of God, you take away the sins of the world ....'" As for organized religion, Peck said, "In a gun-in-the-back situation, asked to join a denomination or die, I would become a Catholic." When he was dying, he blurted out, "I want to be a Catholic," but discouraged his wife, Kathy, from summoning a priest.

The Wall Street Journal might herald Peck's works as "groundbreaking, the long overdue discussion between psychology and religion has begun," but in academic circles, Peck was pummeled for being proclaimed the synthesizer of psychology and religion. Dr. Hendrika Vande Kemp was one who excoriated "Peck's highly narcissistic views of his contribution to psychiatry and religion—he often erroneously implied he was the first Christian psychiatrist." Vande Kemp, a psychotherapist in private practice in Virginia, was a former member of the Fuller Theological Seminary faculty, and also a past-president and Fellow of the Psychology of Religion and History of Psychology divisions of The American Psychological Association.

Religion and psychology were once in harness, said Vande Kemp, in her chapter, "Historical Perspectives: Religion and Clinical Psychology in America," in *Religion and the Clinical Practice of Psychology* (1995). Further, she writes, "Psychologists trained in the dominant historical tradition of the twentieth century may be startled to learn that psychology and religion have historically been intertwined." She wrote that when the Latin term *psychologia* was first used, around 1524, it referred to one of the subdivisions of *pneumatology,* the science of spiritual beings and substances. The term *anthropologia* was coined later in the sixteenth century for the science of persons, which was divided into *psychologia,* the doctrine of the human mind, and *somatologia,* the doctrine of the human body. Vande Kempe argues her case down to recent times, not least mentioning the impact and importance of how the psychology of religion was treated in college textbooks, and the work of the various interested academic and professional organizations.

Leaning back in his wicker chair in the sunroom of his New

Preston home, Peck listened to these criticisms unconcerned and unimpressed. Despite his periodic flights of hyperbole, Peck at heart was the consummate realist regarding his limited range of knowledge. He made no claims to an extensive understanding of the existing and wide-ranging scholarship around psychology and religion that Vande Kempe ably marshaled. He preferred to let others, like *The Wall Street Journal*, lay claim to his popularizing the interface between the two fields—psychiatry and religion—for the nonscholar. In effect, Peck leapfrogged over the back of the academic discussion to land on his feet in front of the popular audience. But then, had he done any less with his thesis at Harvard for an audience of three—his invigilators?

CHAPTER NINE
The Foundation for Community
Encouragement

In November 1981, borne along on the currents of *The Road Less Traveled's* success, Peck arrived at the George Washington University in Washington, D.C. He was an all-day visitor to someone else's group. His task was to facilitate a spiritual growth workshop. Peck declared it "the day I had a miracle happen to me. I was leading my first workshop, at the end of which sixty people were hugging and yelling and screaming and saying it was the best $120 they ever spent, the best thing they'd ever done in their lives. I knew I'd be invited to do further workshops; yet I knew I could never do a workshop that would approach the success of this one."

Consequently, whether future Peck workshop attendees wanted it or not, Peck now deliberately developed every future *Road* workshop into a how-does-it-happen community building laboratory for an audience of one. He wanted to learn how to do run a workshop well. "I gave the workshops the title '*The Road Less Traveled* and The Way of the Cross.'" ("The Way of the Cross" refers to the crucifixion of Jesus Christ.) He provided a brochure that warned "in this highly experiential, and at times, painful workshop people might have personal experience of the Way of the Cross." Call it what he liked, it was a reworked version of the encounter session he'd experienced while a Lieutenant Colonel, with an overlay of everything he'd learned since. Where the encounter sessions were geared to freeing up individuals, Peck wanted to free them up enough they could come back together as a cohesive group in the same period of time.

In running his "*Road* and Cross" workshops he quickly acquired the nuts-and-bolts skills for handling the community-building workshop he sought. He reduced what he learned to set prescriptions, and decided his community building workshops "laws" were teachable—so he could create other workshop leaders in the Peckian mold. He used an old medical school surgery dictum: "Watch one, do one, teach one—watch an appendectomy, do an appendectomy, then teach the next one how to do it." Peck's dilemma was where to go with these new skills. The answer appeared in 1983, during a workshop at an Episcopal retreat center in North Carolina.

Said Peck, "A well-to-do businessman said to me, 'Look, I believe in what you're doing. I would like to help out in some way.'" Peck explained that he was himself uncertain which way to go, and needed help in making his decision. "I think it ought ultimately to be my decision," he told the man, "but I need community advice, and I would like it to be international, totally ecumenical, inter-racial and so forth." He asked the businessman, "Would you organize, pay for, such a group to meet and advise me on what I would do in my life?" The man agreed.

Fifteen months prior to this, during the period Peck was still exploring how to produce community, the Rev. Stephen Baumann (later, senior minister at New York's Christ Church on Park Avenue, where Peck's parents attended services), was in his first church appointment, in Connecticut. He read *The Road Less Traveled* and "on a lark," he said, "I picked up the Yellow Pages and in those days 'M. Scott Peck, MD' was still listed. I thought, what the heck, I'll give a ring, thinking I'd get his secretary. He didn't have one, and he answered the phone. I tumbled out something like, 'I sure liked your book ....'"

A week later, at Peck's invitation, Baumann went to see him. For the next 18 months, Baumann said, they developed "a short, therapeutic relationship. Scotty was clearly in a state of transitioning. By the end of [our therapeutic] period, his life was radically changing course." Baumann realized that the phenomenal success of Peck's book was catapulting him into very prominent places. Peck's also mentioned that a friend had volunteered to pay for assembling folks for a several day retreat to consider issues of community. "He asked if I was interested. The Danbury conference," said Baumann, "was the beginning of the rest of our friendship."

In late winter, 1983, twenty-eight people gathered in Danbury, Connecticut. "It succeeded in building community," said Peck, but, he added, sounding a mite sorry for himself, "by that time there was really no energy left to guide me, no time left to focus on me or anything that I fashioned. So it did not succeed in that sense. I did ask certain key people for advice." The Danbury "community building" was so successful in tear-inducing terms, its attendees became known as "the People of the Kleenex." Peck's encounter session crying jag a decade earlier had convinced him of the therapeutic value of tearful release. Danbury also confirmed his conviction he had hold of something powerful in terms of organizing, yet he was still at a loss as to where he should concentrate his efforts.

His personal behavior, meanwhile, was bordering on late Hippie-movement abandonment—alcohol and drugs and sex— though not to the extent it diminished his ambition. The Danbury sponsor also suggested to Peck he consider a run for the U.S. presidency. Given that the United States at that moment had a former Grade B movie star as president, the idea of the popular author-psychologist campaigning for the office was not extreme. Peck added it to his ponderings.

There were several more gatherings of theologians, businessmen, doctors, therapists and others from around the country in various locales, some more successful than others. The important ones had pet names. In 1984, those attending a session at an Episcopal retreat house, Valle Crucis, North Carolina, became known as "the People of the Balloons." By that time, an organizational outline was taking shape in Peck's mind. But he still had caveats about getting too close to the potential throng. His *Road Less Traveled* journeys and workshops had produced in him a strong personal reaction against those he described as craving a guru and "wanting to touch the robe"—groupies. Or *Roadies?* Journalist Cindy Lollar, who attended a North Carolina workshop in order to interview Peck, immediately spotted his groupie difficulties. "There were a lot of 'disciples,' a lot of that weirdness of [people] kind of falling all over themselves" to get close to him, she said, "a lot of young women about who hung around him." (When interviewed for this book, Lollar added, "I hope you haven't found out he was sleeping with all his young acolytes. I hope he wasn't one of those who was a really good man who couldn't keep his pants zipped up.")

Janice Barfield, first met Peck when he facilitating a workshop at St. Joseph's Hospital, Atlanta. She witnessed over the three days that many people placed Peck on a pedestal, their guru. "I mean it was unbelievable. One of the things I liked about him was, he'd say, 'I'm not your savior.' I appreciated his honesty and candor in saying that 'I'm not going to be your salvation here.' I liked that because it was important to me not to follow a man. I did not want a savior. I already had a Savior. I didn't want a guru. I wanted somebody that would facilitate and lead."

Barfield, an Atlanta-based, Delta Airlines flight attendant, said she "was completely blown away" by the session. He was a wonderful facilitator because he listened so well, she said. She was struck by the fact he appeared to be a little nervous. "He would say some outlandish things that I had trouble believing, you know, then he would just kind of zap me with something so profound." She believed him to be "a very, very deep and a very spiritual person. And because I myself am a spiritual person, I was very drawn to that part of him. It was easier for me to understand the spiritual part than a lot of the intellectual stuff he would say. I was even more drawn to the work because I realized that the work he was talking about was a lot bigger than him."

In Atlanta, Peck told the group that because of all the letters he'd been receiving, he and his staff were talking about forming some kind of foundation. "If you're into prayer or meditation," he said, "I would appreciate your prayers or meditation." Said Barfield, "That's all he said, but I was hooked. I felt a great sense of I don't know what. So I wrote him a letter after this and he was kind enough to write back personally. That was in the spring of '83." Early that year Peck was seriously ill with pneumonia. One outcome was he rid himself of the idea of a presidential run. Barfield said when Peck was ill she telephoned to say she would keep Peck in her prayers. Peck recovered. In 1984, he returned to St. Joseph's for another workshop. There was still no formal organization for the intended organization he and his wife Lily want to create, but Peck invited Barfield to an inaugural meeting Memphis. "On my part," she said, "I was more convinced than ever this was a calling for me, but I didn't know to what." She went to Memphis.

That assembly, in the Peabody Hotel in 1984, created the Foundation for Community Encouragement (FCE) with offices in Knoxville, Tennessee, where its first president, Patricia White, lived. As hotels go, the Peabody is unique in one respect. Daily, at 11 a.m., four ducks and a drake, accompanied by the hotel's Official Duck Master, are escorted from the birds' rooftop Duck Palace to an elevator, which descends to the hotel lobby. The ducks walk across a red carpet to frolic and feed in a hotel fountain pond until 5 p.m., at which time they are escorted back to their rooftop pad. No one suggested the meeting was for the birds. The eleven people at the Peabody Hotel gathering were an interracial cross section of society, from churchwomen, to a Dallas lawyer, to a Catholic priest. Texas lawyer Vestor Hughes suggested the foundation's name.

For Peck, the gatherings that produced FCE opened him to a new world of personal involvement and acceptance. "Until I started FCE," he said, "I generally enjoyed communicating with black Americans more than I did with whites." While he had to "penetrate" the African American façade, he said, "once that was broken they were remarkably honest." The meetings from Danbury on had enabled him, he said, to penetrate white facades. Peck and Lily were sufficiently delighted with FCE; they boosted its start with several million dollars of their own money. Lily wryly remarked that if the Pecks were ever to create a second foundation, it ought to be for the preservation of WASP culture because Scotty was so anti-WASP.

"We spent probably close to $3 million," said Peck. "We were its largest donors, but there were several other large donors, too. I think it the best money we ever spent. We also donated an enormous amount of our time. It closed not quite knowing whether it had been a tremendous success or a failure."

Omar Khan, the Pakistani ambassador's son who read Peck's books prior to attending Oxford, now entered Peck's orbit. Khan and his wife, Leslie, had established Sensei-International, a consultancy business in Pakistan and Sri Lanka. Khan said that when he read *The Different Drum*, "It occurred to me the community building described by Scotty could be of great value in [Asian] communities." He wrote "an honest letter" to Peck about his life, and what in Peck's work had been valuable to him, in community building terms. The Peck form letter—"Dr. Peck doesn't correspond with members of the public"—was followed by a personal one in which Peck enclosed a copy of one of his speeches and said FCE would be happy to cooperate with Khan's venture. "So," said Khan, "I brought FCE out to Pakistan and Sri Lanka and got to know ES, Sister Ellen Stephen, very well."

Khan explained the intent and method of an FCE community-building workshop. It was to create people who could conduct workshops themselves. It was accomplished through "an experiential interaction." In two or three days, a group of people, previously strangers to one another, passed through four stages in order to learn how to take on leadership themselves. The first was

"Pseudo-community—when everybody pretends to love each other already." Next came "Chaos—when people start expressing what they actually think and feel rather than what's politically correct to say." The third stage was "Emptiness—where people stop posturing, stop trying to heal and convert and fix everybody other than themselves." Finally, "Community—if the group was fortunate, the context and conditions right, and if there was enough honor and heroism and guts. Whether 'community' actually arrives is really the choice of all the people there, and how far they're willing to take it. It is a hard tension," said Khan.

Peck described a successful community building result as "an experience of community so complete it's like watching a ballet. Everyone knows what the task is, and, fluid yet coordinated, everyone knows what needs to be done at any given moment and does it." Frequent facilitator Sister Ellen Stephen said the "emptying" process was "a letting go of one's biases and fears, prejudices and defenses, intellectualization and all that kind of junk. The strength of it is it brings people into reality; it makes it safe. Without doing much talking at all, facilitators have to know how to guide these people into being who they really are instead of who they think they ought to be."

To Janice Barfield, who facilitated some thirty to forty FCE workshops, FCE's strength "was this incredible commitment to spread 'community.'" With groups ranging from ten to forty people, it worked when "the facilitators were committed to authenticity, to following the guidelines. People would rise through chaos above their differences. With the FCE process we found a way to build community without the crises. It was very, very powerful and, I might even say, very holy," she said. One essential component of success in Barfield's view was that the facilitators could more or less take it for granted that the attendees had read *The Road Less Traveled, People of the Lie* and *The Different Drum*. Consequently, one distraction at the workshops, said Barfield, was Peck himself. "People would fixate on him," she said. "People would get past that if we stuck with it, but it could be a really sticky point sometimes. Even if he wasn't in the group, he was present."

Most Americans, by nature, are a garrulous lot. The FCE stipulation that people attending the workshop not unnecessarily break the workshop's "silence." It was an element of FCE that came from Peck's Quaker experience. It led to misunderstandings. "There was a Jewish-Christian-Muslim workshop in which the people could just not tolerate silence," said Peck. "We told them, 'Listen, if you want to talk, raise your hand. But count to ten first.' And some guy raises his hand and starts, 'One, two, three, four ....' Worse than that," said Peck, and despite the advance notice, people would come to workshops "and get from 'pseudo-community' to 'chaos' to the beginnings of 'emptiness' and then begin to complain, 'This isn't what I expected from this workshop at all. This is really painful. This is not, you know, the way a workshop should be.'" Peck would ask if they'd read the brochure before attending, and they'd say yes. So he'd ask if anyone had a copy, show it to the complainer, who'd usually remark, "Well, I guess I didn't read it very carefully." Encounter sessions were painful.

To create FCE, said Peck, all he did was synthesize what already existed. Some community building rules came from the Quakers, others from Alcoholics Anonymous, and Christian monasticism. "AA's twelve steps are absolutely extraordinary," said Peck, "but people have to be in a crisis to get to them. As we integrated these rules they worked for people of all cultures—not that everybody wants to buy into them. But we've never seen anybody who couldn't participate and benefit because of their race or their sex or their religion or what not. We've also seen some very sophisticated people who just don't follow the rules."

North East Magazine writer Gary Dorsey went to a 1986 FCE workshop to scoff and stayed to cry. His account confirmed that tears were an integral part of the community building. He described a veritable weep-a-thon at which he finally burst into tears himself. On his first full day, a Thursday, he announced he was a journalist writing a profile on Peck, and that the profile might not be favorable. "I heard one of the staff members gasp." Dorsey said that by the time he'd finished speaking, "several people were in tears. Peck cried too," as people recounted "horrible incidents in their lives each personal revelation triggered an unexpected sob and another sad tale. Some people choked on their own tears; others wept quietly .... As people cried, others rushed to hold then, hugging them around the shoulders or at their knees, or simply clasping their hands." By the Friday morning, said Dorsey, he was having his own problems. He felt the group had closed him out. "I needed to be accepted," he wrote. Late on Friday afternoon, as Peck "started to close the workshop," Dorsey "spilled out a rambling monologue" until he reached point at which the journalist said the word "'healing.' I broke down," stated Dorsey. "The man beside me put his head on my shoulder and sobbed with me. The man next to me was crying …. When I lifted my head, people all around the room were crying. When I stood up, there was a line of people waiting to hug to me. Scott Peck was one of them. That night we all went out for a big meal and celebrated. 'We are a soft and wounded organization,' Peck said."

There is little doubt FCE was a shining period for Mrs. Lily Peck. Kazimierz Gozdz, who first attended an FCE workshop in 1987 and later became an FCE facilitator trained with Lily. "I went out on my first community building experience with her as my co-facilitator—a lovely woman." In Lily Peck, said Gozdz, he found "a kind of introversion that was appealing. She had a good sense of humor and a capacity to move beyond herself. Scotty is a kind of egomaniac. He has a personal power to him, spiritual, social. She was the opposite. She was a person you could feel you fit in with comfortably." She was a peer to people, he said, whereas Peck, "by the power of his ideas and experience—was kind of at the commander level of professional respect. Lily was a human being you could relate with and wonder how she could tolerate all of this sense in him. There wasn't the same kind of power and politics to it with Lily. She showed that the ordinary person could gain mastery in a domain. For a person like me it built confidence that she cared, [and I was] able to approach her comfortably."

Janice Barfield saw Lily as "very sensitive to people." They'd met in Memphis. Where Peck was "strident," Mrs. Peck was "softer, authentic, a good searcher, and judge of character. Quite shy and wonderful. She was very kind to me. Lily and I did become very good friends." There was a playful side to her and she was "incredibly patient and very, very kind." When Omar and Leslie Khan met her for the first time in New Preston, said Khan, he found her to be "clearly, a very private person, never touchy. I could also see that she sometimes would try to be helpful, to make sure Scotty had heard something we said, or that we had gotten enough air time for some of the things we wanted to talk about—other than what he had in mind. I could see that she perhaps played that role at other times in her life."

FCE closed its office doors in the late 1990s with "the wake at Wake Forest," an honoring ceremony at Wake Forest University. Scott and Lily, who by that time had been its "elders" for several years, did not attend. Janice Barfield was present. "I don't think FCE died because something went wrong," she said. "I think it was time for it to die. It was a process, just like anything else. I remember Scotty from the very beginning saying this is not going to last forever." But, Barfield said, it lasts a lifetime for people who went through it, and there are thousands of them. "It was phenomenal for me personally, very significant in my spiritual and intellectual life," she said. "I learned to build community with myself. I think I listen better. I learned to reflect more, learned to love silence more." The "wake at Wake Forest" recalled the names of those who'd been FCE. "It was very sad, very precious," she said, "and I think reconciliations were made there."

What remained, apart from the network of facilitators—and CBiB (Community Building in Britain)—was what Peck described as a "viral gene" in the field of creating community, one he'd hoped would create a "planetary culture" of community building. At its starkest, FCE was about being open, about tearing down personal facades. Peck was still trying to peel away the vestigial veneers of WASP culture.

In retrospect, said the Rev. Steve Bauman, Peck had identified "a very powerful process, not completely original, a collection of learning he gleaned along the way." Bauman understood Peck's skill, perhaps genius, for packaging the process "so it worked. It doesn't work universally and there are certain constraints on it. Another strength: there were some really interesting, creative people attracted to it. It was a genuine learning community." If FCE had a weakness, said Bauman, it stemmed from being based on a charismatic founder. Peck himself was a something of a cipher, said Baumann, with a capacity to see some distance from him "with a searing laser. He had a difficult time seeing anything close up. Both these qualities, this ability to see far and not seeing near, were pronounced. They were exaggerated so that his strength was really, really strong, and his weakness was really quite weak. Scott could be soaring the heights, and on the other hand be just dumbfounded or dumbstruck at something that's right there in front of everybody's eyes to see."

Peck, as a loner seeking community, was a built-in paradox, he said, and "it was particularly paradoxical for the organization because the organization was a product of that person's personality." He described Peck as a phenomenal synthesizer of information into palpable and otherwise unseen truths. These truths were "his strongest gift, along with a boyishness and an innocence, and a petulance and a self-centeredness that goes along

118

with the boyish innocence—sort of the dark side of the same thing." Bauman said he had a great affection for Peck, and that he'd been an important mentor in many ways. "But I don't have rose-colored glasses about that."

Nor does Kazimierz Gozdz, though in 2005 Peck paid Gozdz the ultimate compliment. "He is somebody I really worked at mentoring," said Peck, "and now he is becoming my mentor. Kaz is absolutely brilliant. He's been a researcher on the cutting edge of community, and has deep insights on the best and worst of FCE." Gozdz, who first heard Peck in 1987, said he knew "more than most" about him. "He has played various roles in my life and I know him differently from each of these perspectives, a complex man of significant depth and breadth."

Gozdz' critique centered on Peck's model of community. One focused on psycho-social-spiritual development. "It did not focus on professional, cognitive, economic and other lines of development classically associated with building community in society," he said. "Peck's theory and methodology was: teach anyone to experience community repeatedly, and over time they make a developmental leap to a new stage of integration. His theory works, but not the way it was implemented at FCE, and not the way Peck envisioned it."

Gozdz mused on potential modern applications of FCE's "old programs." One is large-scale social recovery from disasters, natural or man-made, sending in FCE trained facilitators "to a group experiencing disaster trauma, like survivors of the 9/11 attack. I have toyed with the idea of pulling a cohort group together and focusing on re-integrating veterans returning from the Iraq War. By using large-scale group process methodologies, such as those developed within FCE, Post-Traumatic Stress Disorder could be treated on a much larger scale than the VA hospitals are equipped to handle. Further, non-technical professionals [say, veterans with little economic opportunity], could be trained to facilitate experiences of community with returning soldiers. I'm pretty sure what Peck and FCE taught me would work on this type of problem—I am just not as naïve about the costs and commitment to make something like this work as I was in the old FCE days."

Khan, who took FCE out to Pakistan and Sri Lanka, said that the FCE organizationally went into a tailspin when Peck retired from it, for it was kept alive "by his stewardship and to some extent by his charisma. If we were able to marry ability with need,

FCE could very quickly come out of hibernation because the people are still out there, the abilities are still out there. The organization was secondary. It's not like a brand, or as if it had some particular supply chain, it was more like a network."

As for Peck himself, Khan said those who knew him would agree Peck's universal appeal was he was able to "take his own failings and extract the universal value out of them so that they could guide not only himself, but the rest of us." He praised Peck's "remarkable honesty in terms of taking a look at issues we probably all thought about. He put them before us in an accessible way that we can all recognize and resonate with. Rather than fleeing from the demons he discovered inside himself—and I don't mean demons in the literal sense he's written about in his ultimate book, I mean the shadows he discovered," Peck was able "to face the shadows, look beyond them and illuminate what was dark with direct reference to what he lived through." It was not glib, not frothy; it felt real "and that's very captivating," said Khan.

Peck came across to Khan as an extremely thoughtful person who took his time processing things. He never leaped in with an answer, was not the quickest with a riposte. The listener had to slow down and wait a little, but slowing down was worth it, Khan said, because what came out of Peck's processing was "well worth waiting for."

CHAPTER TEN
In the Money

By the early 1980 Peck was living the author's dream: sales doubling each year. In 1980, *The Road Less Traveled* sold 30,000 copies. The next year, 60,000. In 1983, when it gained a foothold on *The New York Times* non-fiction bestseller list, it was 120,000. The only book ahead of it was *The Joy of Sex*. Peck soon pushed that aside, and in 1984, with *The Road's* sales at 240,000, his second book, *People of the Lie: the Hope for Healing Human Evil* (Simon & Schuster, 1983), also made it to the best-seller list. The audiences were overwhelmingly female, but men were reading the book. Anthony J. Centore of the American Association of Christian Counselors, later wrote, "His self-help writings were absorbed into the mental and spiritual lives of thousands, if not millions, of men. His views on life, evil and personal growth deeply impacted our culture."

The reviews and letters for *The Road* continued to pour in. Readers' letters jammed the mailbox at the house on Bliss Road, for Peck had included his address in both books. He later dropped the practice. Nonetheless, he claimed the final tally of letters over two decades exceeded 22,000 pieces of correspondence from all over the world. If that's the case, only a fraction of that number made it into the Peck archive at the Fuller Theological Seminary in Pasadena, California.

The scores of letters that survived were arriving even after his death. Thirty years after the book's first appearance, a new reader of *The Road*, who did not know Peck was deceased, wrote from Australia: "I want you to know it has given me courage and hope and has helped, in part, to clear the mists of confusion and doubt more than anything else anyone has written or said to me. You have been a Prophet to me by speaking my own language, by being a translator, a conduit, a transmitter, a conductor—I am now allowing myself to accept the Grace that is offered to me. It is hard to take, but I cannot throw it back any more."

On the road, and toward the end of a *Road Less Traveled* speaking engagement, Peck would ask the audience, "'Would you like to know about yourselves? Would you like to know who you are?' And they'd say yes. And I would say, all right, you are not an ordinary cross-section of Americana, but there are some things you do have in common that distinguish you. An extraordinarily high percentage of you either have had or are currently receiving psychotherapy, either through traditional routes or 12-step programs." He'd ask those to whom this applied to raise their hands, "and 95 per cent would raise their hand." They loved it, he said. So did Peck, he was becoming addicted to it. He was attracting something like adoration.

Scott's son, Christopher Peck, said, "I think his angelic compassion, as others describe it, and his scathing cruelty, were different tricks from the same bag. Scotty's narcissism left him a very lonely person, and his saintliness, which I found creepier than his cruelty, was a plea for love. I don't think he loved because he enjoyed loving others; he loved in order to be loved back." Despite personal shortcomings, however, Scott Peck was a committed healer and Christopher praised his father's openness. "On principal and in fact, his door was open to everyone who was not delivering a court summons. It was his most noble stance, and perhaps the least discussed of his noble stances. Although he erected baffles to secure his safety and some privacy, and regardless of whether he was a quack who could do you more harm than good, anyone in the world could, with little effort, gain an audience with Dad at no charge. That was exceedingly brave and defies any question of motive."

Most of Peck's audience members were, like his readers, actual or potential *Road* converts. On the page or from the stage he spoke to his readers conversationally, clearly, and with genuine conviction. He wrote as he counseled. When he spoke, he addressed their needs. He was compassionate. Convinced and converted, they were particularly hurt when his later books addressed his own failings. Yet still the people came. His directness, his reluctance to nuance, gives his writings and talks—at their best—their pleasing conviction, their acceptable, magisterial yet spiritual quality. Equally, the inability to nuance left him naked to his observers, critics and enemies if they got close enough. Sister Ellen Stephen said, "I think Scotty has been more vulnerable than [many spiritual writers or gurus] because he is dedicated to truth and humanity. Others [who transgress] make these great manifestations [regarding their fall from grace]. He doesn't. He doesn't beat his breast or anything. He says, 'I am a human being just like everybody else.' I don't know of anything that Scotty has done to hurt anybody. I don't think he has done anything that most human beings haven't done."

Peck in person was frequently less engaging than his stage presence. He had no capacity for, and no interest in small talk. He had it built into his contracts he'd do no cocktail parties, and there'd be no social meetings with boards of directors, or similar. He avoided cocktail parties, he explained, because he never knew what to say.

With his polished performance in New Jersey, Peck was now master of the public platform craft. It was a far cry from his first amateur sortie into the post-*The Road* spotlight. That was in Buffalo, New York in the fall of 1979. A woman in Washington, D.C. had sent her college roommate a copy of *The Road*. The result was Buffalo book sales of 600 copies in a remarkably short time. Two local churches, one Episcopal the other Presbyterian, combined to bring Peck in for a two-day session. "I read my speeches," he said. "It was absolutely awful. They paid me the vast sum of $900." (A decade later he was charging $15,000 a workshop.)

He offered his Buffalo audience his own angst and experiences, and the angst and experiences of his patients. It was the lecture circuit version of the book. In his book he wrote in declarative sentences. On stage he was the calm, mellow-voiced, reassuring and appealing psychiatrist declaring these things even when his delivery was dull, or soporific. "There was such a kind attitude dumped on me, such good feeling going around," he said, and on the Sunday "I delivered a good sermon."

The adulation Peck received on the road was not feigned. Fred Hills, Peck's editor at Simon & Schuster, said that within a few years of the publication of *The Road Less Traveled*, Peck "had become idolized by many, certainly of people in attendance at churches where he spoke." Yet Peck was a prophet without honor in his hometown, Manhattan. He never got much of a reception in New York City. Hills said, "I think that's true." Hills explained, "New York is a very tough town, a difficult town, for any speaker. Speakers seem to be a dime a dozen. It's a major metropolis with a vast array of entertainment, intellectual or otherwise. Very few speakers find they get a great reception in New York. Often, speakers who come to the New York area do not speak in

Manhattan or New York City. They speak in New Jersey or Long Island, where it's a much bigger event." Hills did hear Peck speak in Manhattan, in an auditorium in Paramount Pictures local headquarters. At that time, Paramount owned Simon & Schuster.

Peck found regional variations in how audiences responded to him. "I used to routinely get standing ovations when I spoke," he said, "except in the Midwest. Finally, after the longest time, I got one in Chicago. Once they started they couldn't stop. But I was aware how unresponsive Midwestern audiences are, how little feedback you get from them. I'm told there are some musical conductors that will not conduct in the Midwest. Finally, I was in Sioux City or Sioux Falls, one of them, and hit the absolutely deadest audience yet. Back in my hotel room I said, 'What is it with these people?' It occurred to me that a hundred years earlier, these cities didn't exist. They hadn't time yet to form a culture. No one wanted to be out of step. And the reason you get no standing ovations, of course, is that to start one somebody has to stand. They don't know how to behave except to see what the next guy is doing."

As an extemporaneous speaker, pontificating on a subject he enjoyed, Peck gave inspiring and clever talks. Early on, when he was still reading his talks, his tapes reveal he was a tad preachy. That changed radically after an engagement in the American South. His host praised his presentation but said he would have greater impact if he did not read it. Peck worked hard to alter his presentation method so he could operate from a few notes of key words and phrases. Reworked as a speaker he projected a convincing authority—something he'd apparently always had when delivering earnest pronouncements on topics of his choosing.

One example of that was in his senior year at Harvard. The students were each responsible for a patient in the state hospital. Said Peck, "We ended the course with a kind of group therapy session among us students. There was one student—an old man for people at Harvard, more like 30 when we were 21 or 22. He said, 'Scotty, this is not meant as either praise or criticism. But whenever you open your mouth, it's like the voice of God.' I did not know what to make of it at the time. I think part of it comes from my father who, at times, albeit rather rare times, spoke with the same kind of authority."

Recounting the incident thirty years later Peck suggested, "Sometimes I think it comes from God." Peck's friend, psychologist James Guy, mulling the question of Peck's authority as a speaker and writer, said, "Peck was a *kind* of guru; but for his authority he doesn't fall back on others writers and thinkers, not even the Bible. What I've seen, what I've heard, what I can measure, what I've detected, is that he comes with a mighty message but the vehicle is that he's a human being. People want to be able to say the messenger is as mighty as the message—otherwise where's the message really coming from? You look at Peck, he's not so mighty. He's got all sorts of vices and quirks and he's as human as my neighbor. Yet he's the bearer of a message that helps people along the way."

In the early years on the road he was addressing a gathering in Jackson, Mississippi. The venue was an Episcopal cathedral. In the group discussion, people did ask, among themselves, "Where does he get his authority?" One woman present was Louise Mohr. She was sufficiently impressed with Peck, she told him, that she was conferring on him the mantle of Gert Behanna. Peck smiled, but barely knew the reference.

It's hard to imagine a Gert Behanna—or a Peck—surfacing in any country other than the United States. Behanna was born to extreme wealth and raised in the old Waldorf Hotel in Manhattan by a series of governesses of doubtful ability and quality. Her father, a canny immigrant Scot who made an early fortune, had one aim for Gertrude: education. Like Peck, Behanna was a cosseted child of comfort who nonetheless felt smothered by her circumstances. She grew up extremely lonely. After her parents' divorce she was sent at age nine to school in Europe and was there until the onset of World War I. She felt inadequate, a plain girl with a brilliant father and a beautiful mother. At Smith College she broke loose, and became involved with a man who, she wrote, "was silly enough to marry me the first night we met." Behanna's "the bull and the virgin" autobiographical description of her wedding night in *The Late Liz: the Autobiography of an Ex-Pagan*, comes close to an account of conjugal rape.

She had a child, and after four years of "the nightmare, the contest macabre," she quit the marriage. It was back, with her young son, to the Waldorf and her father's "I told you so." From then on for Behanna it was booze, men—"I learned about men from men"—and the downward slide. There was a trail of three broken marriages, alcohol and drug addiction until, during a bedside moment confronting the loss of someone she truly loved, she heard "the Voice" that led her, "one climb up, one slip back," to Christianity. She was 53. She became a preacher, with a cigarette dangling from her lip. She was a sassy, appealing Episcopalian evangelist. Her life was depicted in a 1971 movie, starring Anne Baxter. She wrote one of the most catchy of all 20th-century prayers:

> *Dear God*
> *I ain't what I wanna be,*
> *And I ain't what I'm gonna be,*
> *And I sure ain't what I ought to be.*
> *But thank God I ain't what I used to be!*

Gert's was the mantle Mrs. Mohr conferred on M. Scott Peck.

Back in the Edison, New Jersey motel, magazine writer Yagoda penned a snapshot of Peck's operation. It was a three-day program that cost $95 a person, and brought Peck an $8,000 speaker's fee. The attendees got their money's worth. Frequently, toward the end of an appearance, he would read poetry, usually T. S. Eliot, infrequently it was one of his own poems. More rarely yet, Peck would sing "Amazing Grace" in a light tenor.

Life on the road is tough. Anyone who has traveled for a living, even business class and four and five star hotels, knows how quickly, despite any momentary limelight, it turns into grueling work. Peck would arrive, do his shtick and be out of there and off home—or on to the next appearance—as quickly as possible. The lecture organizers who expected nothing but light, calm, and order when Peck hit town sometimes found themselves considerably disconcerted by Peck's manner. A control freak, he utilized his skills to make people keep their distance. Constant travel, uncooperative hotel reception desks, late planes and disinterested airline counter agents can make monsters even of mild-mannered men.

"It was an exhausting schedule," Peck said in 2004. "I think that, as well as my cigarettes, is a reason I'm early old. I got to do all my writing on planes, a precious time for me. I'm a very shy person and don't like to talk to the person next to me, who's often intoxicated." There was a rare exception, he said. "I was riding on a plane to a speaking engagement in Minneapolis. The man sitting next to me was a man about my own age at the time. I gave this man my usual non-verbal messages that I was not interested in talking and he had absolutely no interest in talking to me, either. We sat there, me writing, and him reading a book, on an hour-long flight from Hartford to Buffalo. We sat together in total silence in the lounge at Buffalo airport, then silently got back on the plane together. It wasn't until 45 minutes west of Buffalo that out of the clear blue sky, the first words that passed between us. He looked up from the book he was reading and said, 'Excuse me, I hate to bother you, but you don't happen do you to know the meaning of the word *serendipity*, do you?'"

Peck, puffing himself up, said it was probably serendipity for his seat-mate that he was "seated next to the nation's authority on the subject. I was the only person I knew who had written a substantial portion of a book about serendipity. Serendipity is sort of my scientific code word for grace." While Peck might have regarded himself as an authority on experiential serendipity, it was typical of his approach that he hadn't bothered to research the word. (Peck neither knew nor cared that Horace Walpole coined the word "serendipity" from the title of an ancient Sri Lankan fable about *The Three Princes of Serendip:* princes—not unlike Peck, perhaps— "always making discoveries by accident or sagacity, of things they were not in quest of.")

Peck's seat-mate asked about Peck's book, and Peck described it as a sort of "integration of religion and psychiatry. The man said, 'Well, I don't know about religion any more.' He was a Methodist boy from Iowa with significant questions and doubts. I told him that unlike what most Christians believe, in almost all instances, doubt is not a sin, but a virtue. The path to holiness," Peck told him, mentioning him this was also in the book, "lies in questioning everything, and that I thought what he was doing was very holy. As we got off at the Minneapolis airport, he said, 'Well, I have no idea what the hell this means, but maybe I don't have to leave church after all.'"

Peck's comment on the encounter: "Moments of serendipity, moments of pure grace."

Peck, who didn't know the difference between bad temper and anger when describing his father's eruptions, could erupt himself. Once, at the end of a speaking engagement in Virginia Beach, Virginia, he was driven to the airport by the sponsor who remarked what a gentle person Peck. He particularly admired in the gentle way Peck handled questions. The men arrived at check-in about 45 minutes before flight time, but stood in line for a further fifteen minutes to reach the counter. Once there Peck produced his ticket for his seat, only to be told the flight was overbooked. He was informed he would be booked on the next flight and arrive four hours later than the current flight.

Peck remonstrated, "I was here. I've got a ticket. I've got a reservation. And I'm going to get on that plane." The counter agent told him, "No, I'm sorry, sir, you can't get on the plane. It's overbooked." Peck said, "Let me talk to the manager." The man replied, "He's not available and he would just tell you the same thing." The exchange escalated until Peck said, "Then you'll just have to call the police, because I'm getting on that god-damn plane." Then Peck turned to his sponsor and said, "You see, I'm not always so mild." With that, he boarded the plane.

Distance lent charm to Peck. At close quarters, meeting him for the first time, Peck did not always impress. These contrasting views make the case. To Cindy Lollar, one among a large crowd of several hundred people at an outdoor event, described him as "a compelling speaker. They were rapt as he articulated so well the confluence of science and religion. I came away thinking he was an ethereal kind of guy: calm, gentle, clear and, I thought, creative." By contrast, Barbara Rich was the appointed official greeter at the Thomas Jefferson Memorial Unitarian Universalist Church in Baltimore, Maryland at an early 1980s Peck appearance.

"The minister at the time," said Rich, "was a man wedded to the art and non-science of New Ageism, a keen admirer of Peck; therefore, the invite, and the healthy cash paid out to the self-help guru of his time." She said she already loathed Peck: "I adhere to the principles of skepticism whenever faced with somewhat hysterical fervor about some new messiah." She entered the small sitting room adjacent to the sanctuary to where Peck had been directed. "He was looking extremely bored," said Rich, "and when I approached him and held out my hand in welcome, he remained firmly seated, outwardly bored. Not having his divine insights I had no idea—to this very day—what was going on within his exquisitely sensitive self. I asked whether he'd like some water, and he refused. 'Anything else?' I asked. He shook his head. So then, being me, I thanked him for his courtesy and walked away." She continued, "Peck barely reacted to (I say this with pardonable pride) a small attractive woman not used to this kind of boorish behavior." Rich called his talk "solipsistic" and Peck "a fraud. Some of the stuff that's come out about the way his personal life has been conducted tends to bear that out." Rich, later a theater critic for a newspaper in Virginia, takes herself seriously when she criticizes: she was once quoted in the *Washington Post*, saying, "I think irreverence is the greatest quality anyone can have."

Paula Matuskey, later dean of Montgomery College in Takoma Park, Maryland, also heard Peck speak in Baltimore. "I was reading Peck's book and was inspired to think more deeply about my life, beyond the day-to-day challenges and trials." Presbyterian-raised Matuskey had been away from church attendance for fifteen years, she said, and was thinking about returning when she read *The Road*, "which really affected me. I subsequently purchased all of his later books, although I think the first was best. In a restaurant in California one time, reading one of his later books while waiting for my husband to meet me at the table, the waiter saw what I was reading and said, 'His first book changed my life.'" She gave the waiter the one she was reading. In Baltimore, up close, she said, "I found Dr. Peck to be less engaging than I expected. He did not seem really approachable one-on-one, if you know what I mean. Yet I still got a great deal from his presentation. His lecture on death and meaning was particularly helpful to me when I had lost four close family members and my best friend all in the course of three-and-a-half years."

Business executive Ron Sharpe heard Peck speak "three or four times, and I met him once." At their meeting Sharpe offered Peck a paper he'd written. "I can remember him snatching it like it was full of serendipity, like he would find something magical in it. I wonder sometimes if he ever did. He I always actually trusted—for lack of a better word—to be unflinchingly honest. I tried to take apart his books to find any flaw. I could never understand how anyone could know so much [and] actually communicate it so simply and efficiently. The answer is obvious: God. Though he smoked, drank and had an affair, he let others know he that was not their hero—although a mentor—and that he was flawed. My background was a lot of business battles. The paradox is, that it is in fighting the battles one learns the most about oneself and the ability to extend oneself. I often tell people that *The Road*, and *People of the Lie* are the best 'business' books ever written."

Peck at his peak had a phobia in his suitcase along with the cigarettes and gin. He would never check luggage. Traveling once with his then executive assistant, Mary Kay Schmidt, they got in the car with the sponsor. The sponsor said to him, "Oh my God, you've brought no luggage or extra clothes." Peck replied, "I would rather stink than check luggage." His hosts were amazed by his frankness.

Peck, constantly traveling, was going through a mid-life crisis *and* initiating the longer of his two long-term affairs. That liaison lasted almost a decade.

What ended Peck's eighteen-year career on the road wasn't the sudden drop in his libido in his 50s. It wasn't that he'd lost his popularity or that the crowds were thinning; his fees and his crowds were increasing. It wasn't because a woman who claimed he'd seduced her after a spiritual growth seminar went public with her charges, or that *Life* magazine broadcast the story. He stopped his public appearances because of an article in *Rolling Stone*. It portrayed him having a temper tantrum because his suite wasn't ready in the Boston luxury hotel where he was to appear before a thousand people.

By being captured in print haranguing the help, he'd sullied his public image of himself. What he didn't know yet was why he was so tired. He was in the early stages of Parkinson's Disease. He either wouldn't know, or wouldn't admit the reality for a few more years yet.

CHAPTER ELEVEN
Golf—and Parkinson's

In 1992, in a happier phase, Lily and Scott bought home on a golf course in Bodega, California. They began to spend months at a time on the Pacific Coast. They kept their western Connecticut house, their home for 20 years, and returned regularly for long periods. The 1990s California idyll turned into a working retirement. Peck was commissioned to write a golf book. In 1997, a Booklist reviewer commented, "Peck, very productive of late." Eight books appeared in the 1990s. The reviewer didn't know the half of it—for Peck was now under attack on two fronts: from an aroused media, and from Parkinson's disease.

Despite being "productive of late," life on the edge of a California golf course was not bringing soul-peace, his game was deteriorating, major U.S. magazines appeared to have declared an open season on him, and his misogynistic remarks increasingly drew the ire of women.

For almost two decades, in interviews with dozens of newspapers and magazines over the years, Peck had recycled the familiar, or was diversionary when pressed with new lines of questioning. He told a *Playboy* interviewer that one way to maximize sexual experience—a craving he said was part of God's design—was extramarital liaisons with someone new for "a day or two or a year or two." When asked if he was a graduate of that school of thought, Peck changed the topic to paradox and game playing. The big magazines generally treated him gently. An October 1988 *Omni* magazine Q-and-A was mild, and the 14-page *Playboy* interview, December 1991, was softball treatment. A year later, however, in *Life* Magazine, he was carefully and effectively dissected. *Life* broadcast to a wide audience the claim of a former Peck admirer, Judy Andreas, that Peck was "a drunk and a womanizer" who'd led her into having an affair with him following a spiritual growth workshop.

The phrase "a drunk and a womanizer," gained some circulation, and not a little currency. New York writer Geoffrey N. Smith heard a variation of it at a Manhattan gathering when a psychiatrist referred to Peck as a "boozy womanizer." Smith, an author himself, said the charges of "booze" and "womanizing" were scarcely germane to the issue of Peck's qualities as a writer. (Smith's opinion of Peck's work was that *People of the Lie* was his best book and he should have kept going with that topic—probing individual and group evil, not waxing at length about Satanic possession.)

Peck's own self-defense, quoted in the *Life* magazine article, was, "People are flabbergasted that I should drink or smoke or that there might be some question about my fidelity, because they put me on such a pedestal. They're horrified that their idol has been broken, or they look at him and say, 'Let's pull him down.'" Playing catch-up to *Life*, in 1994, *Time Magazine* worked Peck over and attributed *The Road Less Traveled's* continuing sales not to the fact that people were helped by it, but because they bought the book as a gift for friends whose habits irritated them.

No article irritated Peck more, however, than the October 1995 *Rolling Stone* article that revealed him on the road. Writer John Colapinto caught Peck at his worst, hectoring the reception desk staff of a Boston luxury hotel because his suite wasn't ready. Peck contended he "was generally very gracious to most people even at the very end when I was dead tired. What *Rolling Stone* picked up on still infuriates me. In that instance I'd arrived in Boston, one of two plenary speakers for an audience of over a thousand people. They made a mint off me. Well, I arrived at 3 to 3.30 in the afternoon to check in. At the registration desk I was told my room was not ready and they wouldn't even tell me when I'd have a room. So I went to the woman running the conference and said I would really appreciate it if she would damn well see to it I got a room. I was tired and needed to rest. And that was what it was all about. I made myself very nasty until about 4.30 when they had a room for me."

Peck could argue it how he liked, Colapinto recorded what he witnessed. The writer also visited Peck at home. Peck said Colapinto "criticized my gin and my four cartons of Camels, but he didn't mention that he helped himself to the three packs he smoked while he was here. He ended with me sitting on my private golf course. As a householder I owned 1/780th of it." Not surprisingly, Peck was chagrined, and alarmingly aware how vulnerable he was becoming. He made one trip to Canada then canceled all his scheduled appearances. He made no announcement, he simply ended his speaking career. "I retired from speaking a year before I intended to," he said later, "almost on the heels of that Boston engagement, before the article came out. I just said, 'Christ, I quit.'" Presciently, Colapinto's article was headed "M. Scott Peck at the End of the Road." A decade later Peck was still fuming, damning the *Life* and *Rolling Stone* articles as the two worst ever written about him.

Done with the lecture circuit, Peck concentrated on his golf game. He'd never been a great golfer, only a reasonably good one, but he now started getting worse. He said, wryly, that Lily's game—and she had Lupus—was improving as his deteriorated. For the constantly competitive Peck, "that made it worse." By 1994, he could no longer compensate for the fact his left hand was "cog-wheeling," twisting uncontrollably. "It's pretty diagnostic of Parkinson's," he said, and he told himself, "Oh, well, you've got Parkinson's, and I didn't pay any more attention. Except here I was writing this book about 'you'll learn something about your soul every time you play and your game might just get better.'"

He was in denial. He knew he had Parkinson's but avoided looking more deeply into his physical difficulties even though "I was lucky if I hit a decent shot any more." He preferred to attribute his poor game to his bad back. By 1996, his game—and health—had deteriorated to the point that at the end of three holes he was exhausted and no longer interested. At that point also, he said, he went "into a very, very dark period of about three years duration." Peck said that about one-third of Parkinson's patients go into a dark period before they are formally diagnosed. "They have some sense that something is terribly wrong with them," he said. He already knew. "For me that was one of the worse parts of Parkinson's disease. I used to have what I called death attacks at 8 o'clock in the evening. I would suddenly feel like I was dying and it was all I could do to crawl up the stairs."

He said that during his medical training in neurology "I don't remember seeing a Parkinson's patient. It's been amazing to me, in retrospect, that during my residency it was a disease in the closet. I had no idea what a devastating disease it can be, only ALS, Lou Gehrig's Disease, is worse. I also had no idea what a gentle disease Parkinson's is, meaning it's slow, you have plenty of time to adjust to it, both physically and mentally." In his late-1990s depths of depression, he said, "Lily kept wanting me to go see a psychiatrist—as did a couple of others. But I knew that what I was experiencing was not an ordinary depression." Sister Ellen Stephen, who "cared for me some years earlier when I'd gone through a midlife crisis, a much more substantial depression," thought he was perhaps going through a dark night of the soul. Said Peck, "This wasn't that. While God didn't seem to be hopping around inside me, I didn't feel He'd deserted me. I emerged out of that terrible time say early 2000."

Parkinson's gradually robs the inflicted of every aspect of his or her control over personal life. The individual becomes trapped in a body over which there is less and less control, and all life's functional necessities, driving, balancing the checkbook, supervising medical services, personal care, are one by one stripped away. The sufferer's emotional anguish, from self-pitying to vicious outbursts of anger, is familiar to many spouses and companions of Parkinson's sufferers. The claustrophobia and loss of control is genuinely threatening and frightening, and the nearest caregiver, particularly if a spouse, is the vulnerable recipient who bears the brunt of the outcry from an individual being gradually deprived of personality. In some cases the threats escalate, from accusations of abandonment and lack of caring, to cries of mishandling money or threats of divorce. In some five hours of interviews specifically on the topic of his Parkinson's Disease, Peck would discuss only the signs of physical deterioration he was witnessing. He would not venture into the psychological or emotional costs and challenges. All he finally said was, "The emotional expenditure on accepting those things can be overdone."

To meet the medical and external demands imposed by Parkinson's, though Lily would have preferred to keep the house, the Pecks sold up in California and returned permanently to Connecticut. Said Gail Puterbaugh, his executive secretary, "Peck was worried about Lily's health issues, too; she had Lupus. Bodega [California] is pretty isolated from good medical care and that was starting to get to him."

In Connecticut, he was a member of the local medical community and had watched it grow. "I've a beloved internist friend [Dr. Morris Clark] from the first day we moved here. So it's a superb medical community and one which I can manipulate to my heart's desire," Peck said, adding, "which is very, very nice because usually the medical establishment manipulates you." As a patient, said Peck, there were both advantages and disadvantages to being a doctor. Being on the inside one knows what isn't being done. Being Peck, he had surfaced this disquiet into a chapter of his book, *Denial of the Soul.* He describes the chapter as "a very good diatribe about pain mismanagement." For Parkinson's sufferers, he said in 2003, "It's terrible that people don't get the kind of treatment I can get with my doctor—because he knows me and will spend the kind of time it takes. Mo [Dr. Clark] refuses to make any appointments for less than a half hour. I don't know how he manages to live financially because the insurance companies say no, no. And he's old fashioned enough to just say, screw it."

Continued Peck, "As a neuro-psychiatrist I can't say that Parkinson's people should be treated this way or that, because it is just so individualized. But if I were a physician today facing someone with Parkinson's symptoms, I would schedule an initial two hours appointment—this is me—to get to know that person. Because any advice that I might give him or her regarding Parkinson's, and my monitoring of him or her, should be tailored by my knowledge of the person as an individual." He acknowledged that the chances of that happening today were slim to zero. "In a back-ass way," he said, "that's the medical dilemma that the United States has come to."

For Peck, the one physical resource that helped him combat Parkinson's, he said, was sitting in his garden. All who knew him well understood the spiritual and emotional tie Peck had to the "little spot in the middle of the garden, where there's a tiny patio I call my anti-Calcutta spot. I'm a great admirer of Mother Theresa's work, there's been a beauty to that. But in Calcutta, to me, death was around every corner. And in this spot everything is growing, life-giving. I am content in this spot. Energized."

Peck was still non-forthcoming regarding his emotional and psychological adjustments. He concentrated on the body's problems with "a general message for Parkinson's patients. If the handwriting on the wall is extremely clear, read it. I mean that when my wife or my staff moved to make changes, like getting handles here or handles there, or a special chair to go upstairs, or a trapeze on my bed, they didn't move a moment too soon." In his one allusion to deeper reactions, he played the stoic: "It isn't, 'Oh, I know now I'm going to die.' But, as the neurologist who diagnosed me told me that first day, 'Your first adjustment is to the disease's variability.' That was very good advice. Parkinson's will not only vary from week to week, day to day, but hour to hour, minute to minute."

He continued that he found his Parkinson's Disease "absolutely fascinating." He said he watched his systems gradually shutting down. "Because the brain controls everything through the nervous system," he said, "any muscle in your body can be affected as the brain function falters and different nerves fail. Swallowing, which relates to the voice problem, is a major difficulty." Two prime causes of death from Parkinson's, he said, are pneumonia related to the loss of the swallowing function, or from choking. Peck told of the day his epiglottis "hadn't woken up," and he poured "the whole slug of coffee straight down my windpipe. It was a little frightening." It was more than an hour later when, considerably weary, he'd coughed it all out, he said.

Every Parkinson's patient, he said, battles with constipation and at least partial incontinence because the nerves are just not working right. Unlike ALS, said Peck, "with Parkinson's the brain, the thinking, is also affected—and that of course is a particularly fascinating thing for me. I have some very distinct brain dysfunction—not just outer nerves of the brain—that I can identify. I don't know whether I could if I was not a psychiatrist and very accustomed to looking at myself.

"Memory loss first. It's not different than the memory loss that most people have as they get older except it's much worse than it should be for a 67-year-old. There's a nominal dysphasia, naming names or nouns. Probably at least every once a half hour find myself searching for a word that I know, tip of my tongue kind of things, which is a higher rate than one would ordinarily have at 67. I've gotten very adept at asking people to tell me, you know, what is that word? That's the first and easiest to spot.

"Then there's expressive aphasia. Aphasia is a disorder of communication essentially. Expressive aphasia refers to a disorder in your speaking, communicating verbally, or sometimes emotionally. That's opposed to receptive aphasia, which is a difficulty understanding what is communicated. I seem to have no receptive aphasia, to date anyway. But I've definitely got a degree of expressive aphasia. I will speak the wrong word. It's sort of like a Freudian slip, only you know it isn't a Freudian slip. I was typing a letter to somebody about three or four months ago and I wrote aggravate and had meant anticipate. And it was not a slip. I can't prove it in court, but it feels different. The wrong word comes out. It's relatively mild, but it's definite.

"Not only the voice goes but the muscles—my lips are not working as well. So I can't pronounce words as precisely as I might like," he said. On the telephone Peck's enunciation was clear, his voice resonant. That, he said, was because the telephone masks how damaged the vocal cords are. "I'm starting to have peripheral neuropathy [sensory loss rather than just motor loss]. My neurologist says, 'Well, that's because you used to drink too much.' Whether it's that or whether it is my Parkinson's I don't know. My drinking reached an absolute peak in the dark period before I was diagnosed. The reason for it was that I had the shakes, the tremor, inside me. Among these other things I just felt very shaky inside me and drinking was magical relief for that. My brother and I were always heavy drinkers." But, related to the state he'd entered three years ago, he said, alcohol wasn't doing much for him any more in terms of relaxation, and he had no trouble in stopping. "Much less trouble than I thought I would," he said. "Before, I drank to calm down. What I miss now is just simply the taste. So I'm drinking nothing now except, occasionally, a sip of communion wine— because of the Eucharist, which is very meaningful to me, not for the wine."

One loss of brain function that particularly disturbed him, he said, was that he had lost his sense of time—not only how long ago things might have happened, but how long he has been talking. "The only time my Parkinson's embarrasses me," he said, "is when I'm suddenly aware that I've talked too much. I ask people to tell me, to interrupt me. Friends will do that."

When asked if he was afraid of death, Peck replied, "Less than I used to be, but yes, still afraid." He admitted he was critical of people who won't face the fact that they're dying until the absolute end. "Terrified they are, and still in denial—even intelligent people. The power of denial among people dying is unbelievable. I mean literally—a brilliant person, a previously introspective person, the body now down to a skeleton, but with a bloated belly, obviously dying and still just not dealing with it." He was concerned about the denial, he said, because it tends to make difficulties for those who would otherwise willingly or lovingly support the ailing person. He spoke of one woman who by her denial "in the end had driven away all of her friends. If I'm dying," he said, quoting the words of a friend, "I'm going to want to talk about it, I'm going to grab the milkman, anybody. So that partly I can deal with my fears by talking about it. I also used to lecture people on dying—part of my missionary work. Parkinson's, in part, caused me to quit the lecture circuit."

He has some very good moments, he said. "Moments of delight

when my voice is somewhat functional." And many moments of constant struggle. "Reading is difficult after the first two pages," he said. "I lose track of the line. I'll find myself either reading it over or reading the previous line or going two lines down. The little tiny muscles that control your eye are activated by nerves. Difficulty with reading is another symptom."

Not surprisingly, he added, "I'll be bloody happy when I'm finished with this present book I'm writing. Can't drive, trouble reading, trouble sleeping, trouble everything, but still writing. Typing two fingers, slower than I would like, but faster than a real hunt and peck." He was also tidying up the paperwork around his life, he said. The financial trust was signed and sealed. The advance medical directives completed. Extraordinary means of life support, such as a feeding tube, he can and will accept, provided he can still communicate. But once it is apparent that two-way communication has ceased, everything is to be withdrawn.

When his Parkinson's Disease was formally diagnosed in 1999, it could have been six years after its onset. At first the Parkinson's medicine nauseated him, "but gradually I got into it and I came out of this dark period singing and incessantly humming, whistling or otherwise making a joyful noise under the Lord. And that has been daily, nightly, for three years now." It also turned Peck into a songwriter. In 2003 Peck made what he referred to as an "anti-secularist" CD, "Free Will." He circulated it among friends. In essence it's a stern chastisement, with some light moments, of those who deliberately close their minds and hearts to God's presence. The CD owed its appearance to Peck's friendship with the country music producer Kyle Lehning. Lehning also revealed how fast Peck's enthusiasms could run once he had an idea between his teeth.

Lehning detachedly viewed Peck as an artist first and all else second. Peck's ability, said Lehning, was to take the best of what he was thinking and hearing, use that as fuel to fire up his imagination, and then find phrasings for it, and the rhythm to it, in order to set it down for an audience. "Just as musicians do," said Lehning. He had come to know Peck through his books, and by attending FCE workshops. (Like some other exFCE-ers, Lehning still periodically conducted workshops.) Peck would regularly try to interest Lehning in different snatches of music he conjured up, but Lehning never took the bait. Until 2003. "I was on the cell phone with Scotty one day," he said, "and he sang me a song. You wish you could take things back—I said, 'I think that song's pretty.'"

Lehning sighed and continued, "I want to fast forward. The next thing is we're working on a musical." Moving at hyper-speed, Peck quickly had a graduate student doing research for the project. Through Lehning, Michael Reid came up from Nashville with Kyle to lend a hand. Reid, well-known as a pop songwriter, was a classical pianist who'd played with the Cincinnati Symphony, a 6-foot-4, 255-pound former all-pro football tackle whose country music includes dozens of 1980s and 1990s hits. Reid met Peck. "Soon Scotty is playing Mike his ideas on the piano," said Lehning, "Scotty's so into it." They play, talk, develop ideas, "and at the end of two days, Scotty, in all seriousness, says, 'About a year from now I'm going to be renting an apartment in New York for when this opens on Broadway—because there's going to be a lot for me to turn to there.'" At which point Reid looked at Lehning and said, "God, if I just had a little of that." Peck said later his enthusiasm was rooted in the fact he came out of his 1990s' darkness, "incessantly happy, imperturbably joyous, either because of Parkinsonian brain damage, or a kind of settled state. Take your pick."

Even as his declining fame ebbed into the 21st century, Peck's new books and statements and proposals continued to attract some attention. His one-time position on *The New York Times* best-seller list still stood; smaller magazines and newspapers still occasionally did none-too-critical interviews. The rare one looked for chinks in the prophet's armor, flaws in the preacher's personal life. *The Guardian* of London headline in 2003 was "Can a Guru Heal Himself?" It continued, "When M. Scott Peck wrote *The Road Less Travelled* 25 years ago, he brought his self help book into our lives and taught us all our problems were solvable. The book has been on the bestseller list ever since but how has Peck's own life matched up?" The writer found it hadn't quite matched up, but discovered Peck was a lot of "fun." Andrew Billen of the Times of London was next. He found Peck to be "colossally self-deluded." Christopher Peck said Billen's searing article eased a burden long resting on his own shoulders. "Now I don't have to say anything unpleasant [about his father]; I can refer people to *The Times* of London article. That's a comfort because, for the first half of my life, no one outside the family believed anything negative I said about him."

The author's admirers remained more numerous than his critics.

Hollywood publicist Michael Levine dedicated his book, *Lessons from the Halfway Point*, to Peck. "Michael's a weird guy, absolutely brilliant," said Peck. "Can't even sit through a community building workshop, writes about a book a year about public relations. *Guerrilla PR* is one of his works. He's been a groupie of mine and been helpful to me a couple of times. He had an idea which I heartily endorsed, which got nowhere: building in Los Angeles harbor 'The Statue of Responsibility'—to counter or balance out 'The Statue of Liberty' on the other coast. Wonderful idea."

Peck wasn't exceedingly wealthy by current convoluted standards. In the final decade of the 20th century, "We were at the point of saying, 'We need to make a major gift, or maybe give away a million of this, and then the stock market brought it down from $11.7 million to about $8.7 million. When Lily left me, we split our accounts. I did very well in the market last year (2003), my equities were up 60 per cent for the year." Given that Peck had pointedly focused at times on the idolatry of wealth, had he ever thought of walking away from it? "I've not seen, not felt God requiring, suggesting, in any way, shape or form, that I put my entire monetary security at risk."

When psychologist James Guy had asked Peck if he saw himself "as being narcissistic—what have you denied yourself?" Peck asked for time to think about it. Finally he said, "I'm just not sure I have ever denied myself in any big way. I've denied myself in little ways all over the place." Five years later, in conversation, he expanded on his self-denial, saying, "I tell you, I turned down $1 million at one luncheon. Peter Guber [*Rain Man, Clue, The Color Purple*], co-president with some other guy at Columbia Pictures, responsible for doing movies on Batman, was interested in maybe doing a movie out of *The Road Less Traveled*. Peck said Jonathan [Dolger, his agent] said he couldn't imagine it. I couldn't imagine it. Guber wanted to talk about it personally so he flew Jonathan and I out first class to Tinseltown for a power lunch in a move set trailer. I took an instant dislike to him, which I think I hid. He spun a few tales about how he might translate *The Road Less Traveled* into film. But they were sort of nonsensical." Peck raised the issue of having artistic control; Guber said that was "a total no-no and [they] needn't bother to talk further." An aide spoke up approvingly when Peck said he could write out five principles so Guber could do the film any way he chose as long as the film demonstrated those five principles.

Peck's principles were that there had to be some way in which the film demonstrated that self-discipline paid off. That it demonstrated there was something called grace, and were three others, similar. Guber's assistant tried to encourage Guber, but he was adamant. The director offered to throw in another $100,000 or $200,000 and make Peck an associate producer. "I figured out by the evening that all he was interested in was my name and the title." Once he returned home, Peck wrote to Guber and said that he and Dolger could not understand what Guber's intentions were for "this non-fiction book. If you purchased *The Bed by the Window*, you could do whatever you wanted with it and people would say, 'Well, Hollywood fucked up another good book.' But *The Road Less Traveled* is basically a book of principles, and if you changed it then people would correctly say that Peck sold out to Hollywood."

He didn't sell out.

But in 2003, Lily walked out.

CHAPTER TWELVE
Wife-less, but Looking

Despite Lily's departure, the household on Bliss Road functioned smoothly, a tribute to Peck's staff, headed by Gail Puterbaugh, supported by housekeeper Valerie Duffy. If Puterbaugh was Peck's amanuensis and general factotum; Duffy, despite her "housekeeper" title, was his valet.

Puterbaugh joined the Peck enterprise in the 1980s as an assistant to Mary Kay Schmidt, who early on managed Peck's speaking engagements and travel, his business correspondence as an author with agents and publishers, collected monies, paid the bills, and kept the "corporate" Peck operating smoothly. Peck handled the money management side of his life. When Schmidt left, Gail took over her duties. Peck's one-page tribute to Puterbaugh at the end of *Glimpses of the Devil* is a platonic love letter. (It didn't need his gratuitous comment on her "great legs.")

Puterbaugh, was a fair-haired, well-built woman with a ready smile, a winning greeting that suggested an ability to laugh at some of life's foibles. She first met Peck in a doctor-patient role in the late 1970s. He was her therapist. When she took over the household her duties expanded exponentially. Even before Lily left, Gail did the grocery shopping and arranged household maintenance. She paid herself and the housekeeper, and ordered whatever was needed for the home. She handled the correspondence and itineraries, arranged schedules for weekend visitors, and shielded Peck from those he did not wish to see or talk to.

When she first joined the staff, Puterbaugh said she thought "Lily and Scott worked beautifully together. They were working on FCE; Lily was chairing different things and taking business management courses. They seemed to be very much in synch, going in the same direction. The kids, well, when I came all three were just getting married. So there were weddings out of the house, there were weddings close by. It seemed, on the surface, to be what you would say a family is. I didn't see any stresses."

Valerie Duffy, who served as the Pecks' housekeeper for almost two decades, kept doing the same once Lily left. She simply divided her time. Lily's new home was eight miles away. Duffy worked for Scott several days a week, and for Lily the rest of the time. Fairhaired Duffy is diminutive, peppy and talkative in an entertainingly no-nonsense manner. She cleaned the house, attended to Peck's laundry, fetched and carried, packed his suitcase if he was traveling. She charged Peck a dollar a time for locating his errant car keys or mislaid reading glasses, and made him laugh by telling him the occasional dirty joke. She brought fun and laughter to the house on Bliss Road.

Peck was cheap and kept the house cool in winter. Duffy would complain but Peck ignored her. "He used to like to keep the thermostat down, save on oil. One day it was cold and I was doing his laundry and he 'powered down' for his boxer shorts and I said, 'Okay, I'll be right up.' So I stuck his shorts in the freezer then I brought them upstairs. 'What's this?' he said. I said, 'That's what my ass feels like coming in here in a morning.' That's the way we got along." Duffy knew Peck was deteriorating physically. If she was packing his case, and he was changing his clothes, she noticed his extended and hard stomach, "his buttocks shrinking like an old corset. He had a fetish about his damn slippers, and I noticed they were not lasting, just flattening to one side."

Peck had preached about dying. Valerie said that some years earlier, "Scotty lost a good friend who was on oxygen when Scotty went to see him. When Scotty returned to the house, he took to his bed. That was it, the curtains were drawn, the whole bit. Now he was going to die. Christopher came to see him. I can remember him having Christopher by his bedside saying his last goodbye. And I don't care how old Christopher is, you're still a child and this is your parent saying his last goodbye. And I was just so irritated. 'My God, he's going to be just like my father. He's going to curl up in a little ball and there's nothing really wrong with him.' And I thought, 'Lily, if ever you're going to fire me, now would be the best time to do it.' I opened up his bedroom door, the curtains were drawn and it was like a morgue in there. I whipped open the curtains and I pulled back the covers and I said, 'Scotty, if you're going to die, you can die on some body's else shift. You're not dying on my god-damn time. There's nothing wrong with you.' And I ran. I ran and hid in Lily's bathroom, and I just looked at Lily and I went, 'Oh my God, I can't believe I just did that.' I thought I'd stepped way over the line, I might as well kiss this job goodbye."

Peck never said a word, but in a few days he was up. "When I would get him something, or say something to him," Duffy recounted, "he wouldn't say a word to me. I'd be walking around for days thinking, 'Okay, I'm going to be in that chair in his office, and the lecture is coming.'" It never did.

After Lily left, Peck, home alone most evenings and many a weekend, was disconsolate and brooding. Until the day he died he firmly believed Lily left him because of his Parkinson's. "And that's wrong. Definitely wrong," said Duffy. "She left him for her reasons." Puterbaugh said the marriage was over long before Lily left the house. "Lily told me once that she wanted to be happy. She realized she had fewer years ahead of her and she wanted to enjoy them and didn't feel she could in the marriage. I think it was easy [to leave]. As in most marriages, you're not in love you're in habit. For Lily I don't think she ever put behind her his infidelities and everything. He thought she did. He thought, 'Oh well, it's over and done with. I've cleansed my soul. I'm being honest.' He used honesty as a weapon." Son Christopher said at the time she left, his mother was also dealing with her own health problems.

Puterbaugh added that once Peck couldn't play golf he became paranoid about his health. "I think Lily would probably have kept the [California] house; he lost interest in it. Looking back," Puterbaugh continued, "I think Lily liked having it as a haven. It wasn't a major strain on them—the house was bought and paid for. He came back home here and I've always thought of it as going into the castle and pulling up the drawbridge."

By the time Mrs. Peck left, housekeeper Duffy said, she knew what else Peck was contending with—in addition to Parkinson's Disease, his hypochondria and his limited mobility. "Scotty had no common sense. He just knew how to put money here and money there, and yes, how to write books, and yes, he knew all this stuff. As he got older it had to be hard, so many people had put him on a pedestal, so to speak, because he had saved so many lives. So many people who were down had read *The Road Less Traveled* and were brought back up. As he got older he wasn't that important. He wasn't the young, the spunky, the good-looking man wanted man by every woman that he thought he was. And maybe was—I don't know that. I didn't see that side of him. It had to be a letdown, not to be so important. Not to be special. To have new people coming up and being the new un-Scott Peck. It had to be a letdown."

His health preoccupied him, said his executive secretary. "He didn't have a headache that it could be a brain tumor, kind of thing; his leg would bother him and he'd have bone cancer. I'd say to him, 'You know, you're going to keep looking 'til you find something.'" Bitter about Lily's departure, said Puterbaugh, he appeared less concerned about the break-up of the four-decades-long marriage than the fact that one of his guaranteed "caregivers," as it were, had deserted him. During this period, Puterbaugh told this writer Peck would find someone else to take care of him.

In early May 2003, Peck received a telephone call from his friend Kathleen Kline Yeates in California. When he told her, "Lily's walked out on me." Yeates replied, "I'm happy for you both. Thank goodness." Later, Kathy Yeates commented, "They had such a terrible marriage. I told Scotty, 'There's a real opportunity for both of you to find some happiness.' He said, 'I'm not called to marriage.' I said, 'You don't have to get married, just have a good time.'"

Yeates was a petite blond, fourteen years younger than Scott Peck, divorced, highly energetic, intelligent, smartly dressed and direct-of-manner. She had worked for more than 25 years for the California State Department of Education, was a volunteer at a counseling center and, with friends, owned and operated a bed-and-breakfast inn in Sacramento. Yeates and Peck first met in the mid-1980s when the counseling center's administrator, impressed by Peck's *The Road Less Traveled,* decided to invite Peck as a speaker and use the occasion as a fundraiser. Because she co-owned a B&B, Yeates was asked to donate a room for Peck during his visit to help keep costs down. She agreed. When he arrived, she dropped him off at a restaurant so he could have dinner. "He spent the night at the inn and did the show the next day," she said. She was no Peck acolyte or groupie. At dinner with him the next evening she refused to be impressed by some of his more outlandish statements, she said, but he liked being challenged. As they talked they discovered they had a companionable ease with each other. That developed into a fondness, which in turn later led to a long-term relationship.

"Scotty said he had an open marriage with Lily," she said. "He talked as if the Pecks were a happy family. I got, you know, what a great artist his son was and how proud he was of his him. How smart Julia was and she was going to Harvard, and she was this and that. How wonderful Belinda was—I mean he talked about them in glowing terms. I don't know if it was pseudo-Scotty. I got the good Scotty, I got the romantic Scotty. He was totally romantic—as much as he fought against romantic love, he had to have romantic love in his life. The happy Scotty, the joking Scotty, affectionate, warm, loving, and for six years he was. He would talk about the open marriage, a marriage that sounded screwy to me, and he was having an affair with a woman in town! All of this was so, like, out of my realm of imagination."

Yeates said she'd "loved him for twenty years," but for some fourteen of those, until 2004, it was at some remove. She broke off their relationship after six years. "The magic was broken in our relationship because he slept with woman on a book tour in Canada." She said it wasn't that he was playing the field, but he was miserable being on this book tour. Early in their relationship, she said, they'd had a serious talk and she'd asked him how many women he'd slept with in the previous year. "He seriously looked at how many," she said, "and it was only twenty-five. I know that may sound like a huge number to some people—but he was looking at every woman with potential, and fantasizing about every woman." The Canada incident was different, she said, because she and Peck had been true to each other, "but with this Canadian woman—he didn't have intercourse with her, he couldn't get it up as it turned out—I just felt, you know, he was willing to go that far. He was filled with guilt and remorse. He called me to apologize and I said, 'You know, Scotty, the spell's been broken—whatever it was that was keeping us in a monogamous commitment to each other. I believed you were not sleeping with Lily, and I believed there was some magic in our relationship. But I don't believe we have it any more.'"

Though their relationship as lovers ended, the memory lingered on and the friendship prevailed. They would occasionally meet when Peck traveled, and call each other around their birthdays, his in May, hers in June. When, in 2003, Kathy made her annual "Happy Birthday Scotty" telephone call, his health and pending death were the major part of his conversation. In addition to calling him with birthday greetings, she said, she needed a letter of recommendation for a new venture she was embarking on. She also asked him some medical questions because her father was very ill, and they "chatted about Scotty's divorce, and this, that and the other." A few days later Peck returned the call with his findings on her father's behalf. He promised to look further, and they continued to stay in touch. In July Yeates intended to fly to Ohio to see her father. Peck, who repeatedly told her he was dying of

Parkinson's Disease, suggested she come visit him on the same trip, which she did. "We had a fun time," recalled Kathy. "I think Omar and Leslie Khan were here on that occasion."

Yeates' father died in December 2003, and in the January 2004, still grieving, Yeates made a second trip to Connecticut to see Peck. He was still trying to convince all who would listen that he was dying, she said. Even so, during those two visits, "Scotty was charming, delightful, wonderful—it was the Scotty that I knew and he was terrific. We had fun, we laughed and all that. It [the potential relationship] was still turning, turning. By then we were talking on the phone every night." A short time after her return to California, as she drove home on the highway from work, Peck called her on her cell phone. When she answered, they spoke for a moment and then he proposed to her. "I can't remember precisely the date," she said, "but I remember I drove off the road, pulled over and caught my breath. I had to get home and we were still talking and I went four exits beyond my exit. He proposed. I said yes. And then I said, 'But I've got to apply for a leave of absence. That's going to take awhile.' He said, 'Come for a year and let's see how it goes and then we'll get married.' And I said, 'Okay I'll get a leave of absence in case it doesn't work out, then I'd go back to California.' And you know we talked about stuff and then the intensity upped because I was shocked that he had asked me. And I said, 'Is this the same guy that said, "I'm not called to marriage?"' And he said, 'Well, now I'm called. I need someone to take care of me.' I told him he knew he wasn't dying."

Yeates visited again in March 2004. It was a pleasant time, she said, and he repeated his suggestion she move to New Preston for a year to see if things worked out. "While we were talking," she said, "Scotty said, 'Oh, I didn't think my libido would be turned on again in my life. But since you've come back into it, my libido is alive and well. You've awakened that part of me.'" Their lives, said Yeates, were tied up with the newspaper cartoon strip, "Cathy," created by Cathy Guisewite. At the time, the cartoon depicted a single woman in her 40s with a frenetic, on again, off again love life. "Scotty asked me to marry him right before [cartoon strip] Cathy got proposed to. I said to friends of mine, 'I thought I was going to get married.' And they said, 'Of course you are, Cathy has been proposed to and your life always parallels hers.'" The cartoon strip Cathy was scheduled to wed that February.

Back in New Preston, Peck sat down Gail Puterbaugh and

Valerie Duffy for a talk about Kathy coming. Duffy said she thought, "Three women in this house? Oh boy! I mean we've always been very protective of Scotty." During Yeates' third visit, Duffy recalled, "Kathy and I were standing in the kitchen. I didn't really know her but I asked her age. She was four years older than I am. I said, 'Can I honestly say something to you, woman to woman?' And I thought, I don't know if this is going to work, but it was really, honestly, coming from my heart. I don't know her. I don't know if she's coming for the money—my initial thought was she's coming for the money. I don't know what happened [between Kathy and Peck] years ago, and I don't really care. I said, 'I really think you need to think about this. Really, really hard. You seem like a brilliant woman with a great job, coming from California to this tiny town of one [Peck's household]. You're giving up a lot, and if you married Scotty, you're not marrying Scotty, you're marrying Scotty and Gail.' And she just said, 'Thank you. Thank you very much.' And I think she took it the right way. After I'd said it I thought, how could any woman understand that? I've seen the old Scotty. I didn't see anything appealing about Scotty other than I loved him to death and would have done anything for him. So obviously, she must have a whole different [view of him]."

Housekeeper Duffy knew Peck was deteriorating and was concerned for his final care. She went to him, told him she didn't care who he brought into the house, how much money he had, or who he gave it to. "'But you always told me that if you got sick and died there'd be enough money so you could die in your own house, enough for nurses around the clock, and we wouldn't have to stuff you in some home somewhere. That's the only promise I want from you' He told me how much he had and he promised me, and I took his word. And [when he was dying] it worked. He did that, and Kathy went above and beyond. But she and Gail, Oh! Bad situation," she said.

During the third visit, said Yeates, Puterbaugh told her, "'When you come here you'll never be able to go to California again, you'll never be able to do anything.' She said, 'The drawbridge will be raised.' She said, 'Do you know what you're doing? You're crazy for coming here. You don't know what you're getting yourself into.' She was very negative," said Yeates, "and tried to talk me out of coming." Meanwhile, Peck told Yeates he intended to "call some old friends: 'Is that all right with you?'" She said, "Sure," but was wary enough to ask if they were "just friends, or girlfriends? He said, 'Just old friends.' And I said, 'Sure, of course, that's fine.' And so that was that."

In California she applied for a leave of absence, eventually granted effective the start of the September 2005 school year. Peck kept pressing her to come. "I was working until August 30. So it was very, very stressful because I said I wanted more time. And that's when the bad Scotty showed up. He called me—I was actually with my mother at the wedding of a family friend. I was kind of thinking all this was negative energy from Gail; he was very mad that I was with my mother. He said I should be there with him and not with my mother. And I said, 'Scotty, it's ridiculous to be jealous of my mother.' He was irate about it and said, 'Well, I'm calling this other friend.' And I said you tell me this is a friend not a girlfriend. And he said, 'Yes, she is, and you better like it.' I said, 'Well, wait a minute, Scotty. Wait just a minute.' I said, 'Listen, you know I won't come if you want this other woman. You have her come, you be with her.' I said, 'You know, play the field. You don't need me, if you want somebody else.' And he goes, 'No, I want you, she's a friend.' And I said, 'Well, I can't understand what you're talking about.' He said, 'You get here by'—you know he gave me like August 20th or some ultimatum—'or don't come.' I said I couldn't leave work until my leave of absence started. And he said, 'You better be here September 1 or don't bother coming.' And I said, 'Scotty? Scotty? What's wrong, sweetheart? What? What?' I said, 'You're mad about my mom?'"

Peck told her he'd had a friend visit for the weekend who said that if Yeates loved him she'd be in Connecticut. Yeates said she wondered, "Is he losing face with his friends that I'm not there? There's something that's wrong that I can't figure out. And then I thought, what is this woman that he's calling? And so I said, all right, I will be there on September 1. So for the next three weeks I pulled all-nighters to pack, and was wiped out by the time the moving truck came because I had been packing at night and working during the day." She arrived in Connecticut in September 2004.

While she was still in California, Peck was courting Yeates by clipping Cathy cartoons. He and Yeates would talk about the strip, "and I'd educate him about women," she said. Finally the departure date from California arrived. On September 1, she flew out to the East Coast. Peck was at the Hartford, Connecticut airport to meet her, "all dressed up and had roses. A man from I'll Drive You Car

Hire had brought him. It was very, very romantic." Within twenty-four hours that mood was shattered when Peck announced that in her absence he'd been regularly calling another woman, R, who lived in the Southwest.

"And that's when the alarm bells went off for me," said Yeates. "He was lonely while I still in California. I'd talk to him maybe fifteen minutes in the morning on the way to work and fifteen minutes on the way home, and that was all I would talk to him. So, he would talk to her for two and three hours at night. I didn't realize that he was so lonely and in some ways it was my fault, because I didn't realize it."

Once she'd moved permanently to Connecticut, she said, "He didn't need to call R, but then he would obsess about her and about me. He wanted her to come so that I could meet her, so that we could have a *ménage à trois*. I said, 'I don't sleep with women, and I don't sleep with people I don't love.' He said, 'Well then, maybe we can just get in our pajamas and watch television.' So he had this fantasy that was very upsetting to me. I thought, 'Oh my God, what have I done? What have I gotten myself into?'"

CHAPTER THIRTEEN
Peckian Fantasy vs Yeatesian Reality

Yeates dealt with the *ménage à trois* issue with humor. She set up her camera in a bedroom and persuaded Gail and Valerie to climb into bed with her, all dressed, but with their shoulders bare above the covers. That's what the photograph revealed. Yeates told Peck that was the only *ménage à trois* there'd be. It was a rare moment of all-round humor in a household becoming more tense with each passing day. As for R, the compromise Yeates and Peck made was that he'd just call R once every two months. "I could tolerate that," Yeates said, "and he kept to it."

In November 2004, asked why she would consider marrying a man already in the grip of Parkinson's Disease, and face an inevitable future geared to Peck's physical and emotional caretaking, Yeates replied she could handle it. She loved Peck, she said, and had since they first met. She said that prior to the Connecticut move, "I did a lot of research on Parkinson's. I did a lot of soul searching of myself. I'm not afraid of death or illness or my own death or illness. [I saw] my father die—it was a lovely time as well as a painful time. I had a fiancé who dropped dead of an aneurysm, alive one minute, dead the next. I didn't have a chance to say goodbye, or anything. I've had a lot of near and dear friends die, so I see death as something you can't avoid. Death is another adventure, another mystery. I have loved Scotty for 20 years, so it will be a privilege to be able to serve him and to love him."

Fifteen days later she was Mrs. M. Scott Peck.

It was still a period of adjustment, she said, "I came to give him all this love, and I realized it was too much." She said she was trying to gauge her next moves. "Even though I had more love to give him, an abundance, I realized I'd have to step back. It was not comfortable to give him so much love—because he can't handle it. If I gave him too much love he would turn it against me. It was too scary for him. It was tragic. Even though he'd been in psychotherapy, I don't think he learned how to cope with [his need for love]. He'd hide it, manipulate it, explain it. Even with Lily and his kids and people that loved him, if they loved him it made him angry. The rage. I don't know whether we were all getting charged for what he didn't get as a child. He was still sitting on that rage, that he didn't get that kind of love as a child. He was so angry. I mean I'm not enough of an analyst but it was very deep-seated," she said. "It's very hard to explain, but he didn't know how to give love, he didn't know how to get love."

Even months after Yeates' arrival, the boxes she'd shipped from California were still shoulder-high, unpacked, in downstairs rooms. When asked at the time if it was a presentiment about their relationship's difficulties, Kathy smiled away the implication and instead said, "There were several things. One is unpacking is not fun. And there was no real room to put stuff in the house. There was also no time, you know, when you're really busy. I was doing things with him that were far more interesting. There was no urgency. I would unpack quite a few boxes and be called away to do whatever. And then I would be like, where am I going to put this stuff. There was no place to put it. I was constantly trying to figure out what my role was. There were things that were set up before I arrived that Scotty didn't want changed. Lily didn't do grocery shopping. Gail did the grocery shopping. But I did the cooking, so I wanted to do the grocery shopping. Gail was totally threatened that I was taking away her job. She was afraid that Scotty was going to fire her or limit her salary. Gail in my opinion was about money. I was trying to be a wife."

Unlike her cartoon "Cathy" namesake, Yeates had the on-the-premises competitor Duffy had predicted. "Every time I tried to do something I was thwarted. I was either thwarted by Gail being insecure—and we'd 'have to wait until Gail was more secure' and all that—or I was thwarted by the fact that 'Oh, Lily spent too much money, so I'm going to give you an allowance.' Or, 'Lily did this so I'm going to punish this way.' So I thought, 'Okay, you know, he'll see in time. He'll see who I am, but for right now I'm going have to pay the price that Lily didn't pay, and deal with this neurotic secretary that has all these phobias.'"

Yeates said Peck wouldn't handle his affairs himself and had turned most of it over to Gail. "She was so familiar with everything he had to keep her. Gail had taken over," said Yeates, "and he let her. She thought she'd be with him at his death." Day in, day out, life in the household was electric with animosities, said Yeates. "Some of it was Gail's personality and some of it was my personality." Practically all of it was Peck's doing. "We were just at great odds. Gail is much more negative, would see the glass half empty. Even with people coming, she would have negative things to say. She was trying to keep people away. She was his bad guy, but I was much more open to people, I had many more friends, was much more interested, much more a community builder. I was much more spiritual and religious."

There was another issue—Peck's predilection for walking around the house naked. It was not a recent habit. Yeates tackled him about it, asked him not to do it. "I was trying to plead with him. Any kind of criticism he would not tolerate, and not tolerate it in a crazy way." She said she tried to explain his home was a workplace and that his behavior was inappropriate and illegal—as sexual harassment. Peck would repent, she said, go and dress, and the moment would pass. But if she went to the grocery store, Yeates said, when she returned he'd be naked again. "He'd say, 'I'm not ashamed of my body.'" Her decision was to step back and figure out how to deal with him. "His narcissism did not allow him to tolerate any criticism. There had to be another way."

It came one day when the yardmen were working in the garden, and Yeates needed to talk to them about the work. She told Peck, "'I'm going downstairs and talk to the men,' and I started taking off my clothes. He said, 'What are you doing?' I said, 'I'm going to go downstairs and talk to them.' I had my clothes off. And he said, 'Naked?' And I said, 'Yeah.' And he said, 'Why are you going down naked?' And I said, 'Well, you have no concern about your body, I have no concerns about mine. I'm going.' He stopped me and said, 'Okay, put your clothes back on and I won't take my clothes off.' The matter was resolved."

During an interview, asked if she had to be a strong woman to deal with Peck, she replied, "Well, I did, because when I was taking off my clothes I thought, 'My gosh, what am I doing?'"

All this was bubbling up and there was a wedding in the offing, though the dates and the details were far from resolved. Peck wanted to be married as soon as possible. He'd already booked the honeymoon, a 58-day luxury cruise around South America. He hoped and anticipated that his nephew, the Rev. David Peck, could marry them during an October visit. That proved impossible. Yeates' response to Peck at this news was that they could go to England. Peck demurred because he'd made a great fuss with relatives and friends for several years about his inability to travel any great distance. He felt the South America trip was test enough.

The first search was for a minister, then, they hoped, a locale might suggest itself. They both wanted either an Episcopal or Catholic priest. Yeates enjoyed going to church on a Sunday, Peck didn't. He didn't like getting up in a morning for a church service and preferred what he called his own "rogue" communion services: Peck as celebrant and preacher. The future Mrs. Peck decided it was too exhausting to keep fighting him "on the church thing." She attended Sunday services alone.

There were breaks in the wedding planning routine. Visitors came, including Yeates' mother, and California friends. There were Peck's friends. His back specialist Dr. Cameron Brown and his wife, Jodi, came for Halloween. The Pecks and the Browns decided to work on a book together, *Psychosomatic Spiritual Illness*. With that and the South American honeymoon in mind, the Browns decided they would join the Pecks on the Rio de Janeiro to Manaos segment of the South American cruise so they could work on the book. But there was still the wedding to get to, and through.

Peck's next suggestion on the marriage topic was they could be wed in the church where his daughter Belinda was wed, with his friend, the Rev. Stephen Bauman, officiating. Peck also wanted Melissa Bauman, a superb soprano, to sing Mozart's "Alleluia," as she had for the funeral of Peck's late executive secretary, Mary Ann Schmidt. Said Kathy, "The moment Steve [the Rev. Bauman] found out we were getting married, he came up immediately, sort of blew by me and just talked to Scotty and said, 'As your executor, as your trustee, you must get a pre-nup.'" When Peck told Yeates, she said, "Fine."

But she was not fine with replicating Belinda's wedding or including Mozart's "Alleluia" from a funeral service. She told Peck she wanted "our wedding to be ours and not have previous attachments to compare it to." When Peck asked Yeates where she wanted to get married, she suggested Peck's garden "as the most spiritual place I've been to here." He agreed and suggested a Thanksgiving weekend wedding, and "'we'll have to figure out a priest.'" In telephone conversations at this time, Peck was happily anticipating the wedding and honeymoon. In the home, there was talk of Peck's daughter Belinda and family coming up for the wedding. However, there were doubts the "pre-nup" could be prepared by Thanksgiving. Early December seemed the more likely. There was an issue as to how many people to invite. According to Yeates, Peck said, "If we have a big wedding I won't get to meet any of your friends, you won't meet any of mine. It will be a big bash and then we'll be exhausted, and I don't like to do that." She suggested, "Let's just make it a wedding full of love—a priest and you and me and two witnesses. And if you're worried about cost, we can bake the cake." It was set; all that was needed was a date, a minister and a bridal outfit.

Scott Peck had never in his life been into a shopping mall, she said, but she "dragged him to the mall anyway and made him sit outside the dressing room while I tried on wedding outfits. He was very sweet and did things like that. We were there for several hours until he was totally exhausted." She found a $300 white Liz Claiborne pants suit she liked and put it on hold, then bought a matching scarf at another store. The next day, with Jayne Amodio, a friend of her closest girlfriend, she went "to these fancy shops and I tried on beaded dresses and formal wedding dresses and just got the girly bride out of my system. Beautiful dresses. It was just fun to be with Jane to try on these dresses and get oos! and ahhs! and whatever."

They went to a second mall, said Yeates, because Jane wanted to purchase something from Filene's Basement. While there, Yeates saw the same pants suit she had on hold. "It was only $89, so I bought it, came home and said to Scotty, 'Honey, not only did I buy the suit that you like, I got it for $200 less.' So he was very pleased." For wedding slippers she wore white tennis shoes. Peck wore a navy blue suit with a pink tie with a wavy design on it. As for a minister, he and Kathy both thought the chauffeur from "I'll Drive You" cars had seemed particularly spiritual; an enquiry revealed he was not ordained. Yeates said that as Scott knew many ministers they should go through his list, but that didn't produce an answer, either. When approached, a Catholic priest friend of Yeates on the West Coast said he would officiate and asked her to contact her local Catholic church. When she was told there'd have to be annulments, and that the time frame was impossible, her Catholic priest friend said, "Never mind, I like weddings, they're a holy time, a happy time. I will come and marry you."

A date was set, December 3; only the matter of witnesses remained. When Peck suggested his executive assistant, Gail Puterbaugh, and housekeeper Valerie Duffy. Yeates retorted, "I only want people that have been supportive of us, and Gail has not. I mean Gail keeps questioning you and me and saying why do we have to get married. I said I don't want anybody that's questioning us. I want this wedding to be about God and about love, and that's all I want. When he suggested R as a witness I just looked at him. There was a part of me that wanted to fly off the handle; there was a part of me that was in disbelief. So again I kind of stepped outside myself. And I said, 'Sweetheart, I don't know R,' and I said, 'It's really important that the witnesses really be supportive.' He said, 'I don't know this priest but I'm trusting you with this priest.' And I said, 'I know, but if you rather that we do someone else, I can understand.' He said, 'Okay, we'll go with the priest.' He was calm about it and later denied that he even mentioned R. He had no recollection of it. None. I don't know whether it was the [Parkinson's] medications or whether it was just his getting out of a conversation."

The witnesses were Peck's friend and personal physician, Dr. Clark, and Sister Ellen Stephen. Yeates and Peck baked the wedding cake together and "had a wonderful time doing it." Because Peck wasn't having a bachelor's party, as a treat Kathy thought he might like to talk to R. She called R and said, "'Could you please call him as his bachelor party?' I said I'd like to give him that. And she said, '*You're* not giving it.' I said, 'I didn't mean it that way, R, I just wanted ...' so she snapped at me. I said, 'I'm just trying to make Scotty happy and I think this would make him happy, and I think you want to make him happy.' And she said, 'Well, while I've got you on the phone ....' and then we started talking."

Yeates said she told R, "You know it hurts me when he talks to you; it hurts me when you call. I don't understand what this relationship is.' I said. 'You know, I don't know what your integrity is. I know that he flirts with you and it hurts me.' I said, 'Woman-to-woman I don't know what you're getting out of this and it hurts.'"

Later, R did call Peck for his bachelor party as planned, and he was delighted to talk to her. She also complained that Kathy had questioned her integrity. Recalled Yeates, "He got off the phone and was mad at me—that I used that call to poison him right before the wedding." (Nonetheless, even after the wedding, Peck and R continued to call each other. For two months she'd be happy, Yeates said, then just before making the call Peck would start "tormenting" her with it. Once she said, "Go ahead and call," he no longer had any interest. She thought then, "'Gosh, I should have not gotten hooked,' but I did. I mean it hurt my feelings.")

When Yeates had tackled Peck about the calls to R, he'd replied, "I'm from another planet" and he hoped she was from that planet too. Yeates told him, "'I'm from planet Earth.' He wanted his way all the time, and once he got it his own way, he didn't want it. But if he wanted to make me unhappy he would bring up R. It was silly because we would be ecstatically happy." Peck had a pet name for Kathy, "Honey Bunny." Yeates said, "He'd even talk about having no libido—because that was a funny story. He was wedded to his funny stories. But he got erections. It was not that his libido was dead. It was far from it. Far from it. He'd gotten rid of porn films, so we got more and so he was very sexual."

They were wed, on schedule, on Dec. 3, 2004, and were set to depart for South America on Jan. 15, 2005, on the 58-day cruise.

(With the marriage, this narrative switches to first names for the women for ease of reading as there were now two Mrs. Pecks.)

As the new Dr. and Mrs. Peck set sail to circumnavigate South America, author Peck left behind his latest book, *Glimpses of the Devil: a Psychiatrist's Personal Account of Possession, Exorcism and Redemption,* to the untender mercies of reviewers. To those reviewers on the "Satanic possession" wing of Christianity, this was Peck telling about Satan the way it is. *Christianity Today* magazine's reviewer said Peck's account corroborated his own observations at two exorcisms, and he praised the book as courageous, and valuable for "theological reflection." To others, there was little evidence Satan was present just because Peck said Satan was present.

Prior to the Pecks' honeymoon cruise, the *Washington Post,* which had launched his writer's career with its review of *The Road,* gave *Glimpses* a one paragraph passing mention in a compilation of books under review. The *National Catholic Reporter* called on Dominican theologian Richard Woods, who closed his 800-word review stating: "Dr. Peck also seems to have transgressed the boundaries of professional ethics. But this is a matter for his peers to evaluate." Wrote Woods, "'Beware the man of one book,' said Thomas Aquinas (perhaps). Here, clearly, it would have been wiser by far for Dr. Peck to consult more widely than [Malachi Martin's] *Hostage to the Devil.* And if one is tempted to read something by M. Scott Peck, choose *The Road Less Traveled.*"

For the rest, reviewers who could ignore it did ignore it.

Peck gave a *Glimpses of the Devil* interview to the online magazine, *Salon.* There was no point in suggesting to Peck that he could no longer handle himself well in interviews. Consequently, he jumped on to his "group evil" hobbyhorse, and gave as an example the U.S. Supreme Court decision to award 1980 presidential election to George W. Bush over Al Gore. What he lacked in publicity reviews he suddenly made up for with responses from bloggers and columnists; none of it favorable. "Culture wars" radio commentator Michael Medved, a former Hollywood columnist, called Peck "an unhinged, bestselling" celebrity.

Aboard the ocean liner, happily away from it all, hoping for rave reviews he suspected would not be forthcoming, Peck and his new bride were on the high seas for two months of inescapable proximity to one another. "It was glorious," said the new Mrs. Peck, "because there were no distractions." Peck didn't want to meet a lot of people on the ship, or take many of the excursions. He was content relaxing on the balcony looking at the sights, smoking, sending Kathy out to reconnoiter, and occasionally joining in at meals or shipboard events, such as art auctions. He was not about to let his control of the situation slip, however. Kathy said it was all "very romantic, leading up to the cruise" although once it was underway he was difficult. He said they were to use the time to work on their marriage. He told Kathy, "I don't want you to be jealous of Lily, Gail or R."

"So we tackled each one," she said. "I wasn't jealous of Gail, although they had this strange relationship that I couldn't figure out. I wasn't jealous of Lily, although on the ship, in conversation with others, he kept saying, 'We did this' and 'We did that,' and people would look at me and I would shake my head, not me, his first wife. I told him, 'I'm not jealous of Lily; you just need to reference it. I talk about things I did with my first husband, but I say it was my ex-husband, or I don't even bring him up in it. It's fine. That doesn't bother me. As for R,' I said, 'it's not that I'm jealous of R, I don't even know the woman, but you use her to torment me. It's not about R; it's about the way you do it.' Criticism. He couldn't handle it. So we processed that."

Peck began his shipboard day on the stateroom balcony, in contemplation, or having a cigarette. Kathy brought breakfast back to the suite, "checked out the excursions and brought back information. He liked that." On the first leg of the voyage Peck contracted "cruise ship flu" and "was very ill with hints of pneumonia. That was because he'd keep going outside for a smoke on deck, despite the fact that he was stepping into the frigidity of a scenic beauty featuring fiords, glaciers and ice. For five days he was on antibiotics and used a nebulizer. It was the tangential stuff, pneumonia, that was very scary to me," Kathy said. "He would sleep and send me off on an excursion to scout out the town."

She didn't take the organized trips into the hinterlands, she said, but looked around, took some photographs, and returned to tell Scott what she'd seen. In all there were only two ports he did not visit himself, but he limited himself to two side excursions—one to visit volcanoes, the other to tour the Falkland Islands. On board, she said, "I'd meet people, some times he would meet people while we were sitting in the lounge waiting for an excursion or something. He'd say, 'Well, you're out here making friends.' I'd say, 'I'm not making friends. I was out doing stuff or listening to the lectures.' They had wonderful lectures. I went to art auctions, by myself. He'd be in the cabin and I'd come back and report to him. Then sometimes I'd drag him along on something, and he would gladly come and do it. Stuff like that. The only friends we made were the two lovely Romanian women maids who cleaned our room."

Peck and Kathy did periodically attend the on-board art auctions together. "There were some pieces that we liked in common. When we were on the Amazon I actually won a painting in the raffle. I was shocked and very happy about that. He was very happy when the picture came, he loved it and we hung it up. It looked like a lake scene, very colorful and happy," she said. Toward the end of the cruise, when the vessel arrived at Rio de Janeiro, Peck's friends Cameron and Jodi Brown, with their children, joined the ship. Kathy said, "We went out for lovely dinner and had a blast. Every day we'd spend some hours on the boat, then time exploring and whatever. When the Camerons left we had the last leg of the trip. Scotty was incredible amorous and loving and very adventuresome and just terrific. He had been terrific at various points, but he was also difficult. Then, whatever the chemistry was, it shifted to amorous."

In March 2005, the couple returned home to a house that was to function from then on through a combination of borderline civility and periodic confrontation, but not much fun. Valerie Duffy could recall only one day in the succeeding months when everything passed off pleasantly. Otherwise, it was dark clouds most days over the house across the road from Lake Waramaug. "Valerie's got a great wit. She's very funny and Scotty loved her for it," said Kathy. "She remained helpful. Gail wanted to control and was going to leave Scotty. I mean she couldn't handle me anymore. That was a big upset."

The crux issue was reasonably complicated. Just as Scott and Kathy were about to leave in January for their honeymoon, Kathy received notification from the State of California that as an employee in good standing she could "buy" five years of retirement, which she decided to do. She withdrew money for it from a retirement account. Because of their imminent departure to South America, however, Peck persuaded Kathy to let Gail handle the paperwork. Kathy said she protested, but Peck said, "'Now *you're* going to have trust me, and trust Gail. Gail will have to do this for you because you can't do it on the ship. She'll be fine. If she doesn't do it right, I'll cover the cost and make it right.' Okay. So I had no choice. I turned it over to Gail and explained what needed to be done. Gail said she would do it, and that was fine."

Spring arrived in New Preston. Later in 2005, with Kathy about to take Peck to the hospital in New Milford, Connecticut for exploratory gall bladder surgery, notification arrived from the State of California that Kathy's application had been denied because it had not been completed properly. Given Peck's condition, despite the fact she was upset, Kathy decided not to say anything. But Peck sensed something wrong and said, "I'm your husband and I want to know what it is." Kathy said, "So I explained to him what had happened." Peck said little that directly referred to the lost retirement, and instead suggested that Kathy invite a friend from California to help her unpack her boxes, which Kathy decided she would.

That pending visit, according to Kathy, annoyed Gail. Gail apparently told Peck, "I don't have anything to do. I'm here. Why doesn't she use me to unpack the boxes?" Peck reported to Kathy, "Gail is mad at you for having your girlfriend come." Kathy said, "When I went to Gail, she said, 'I can't talk to you, I can't talk to you.' I said, 'Why are you upset that Bobbie is coming here?'" But that wasn't the issue; it was the denied retirement benefits. Kathy said Gail insisted, "'Scotty told me that I did everything right on that paper, Scotty told me that.' I said, 'Well, if he told you that, he didn't tell me that he told you that. It got denied, Gail, so obviously you didn't do everything right. It got denied because of it not being done correctly.' Gail got all defensive about that. Bobbie didn't come."

The situation at the house on Bliss Road was deteriorating

rapidly. Kathy needed to fly out to California to be temporarily reinstated in order to properly retire later in the year. Gail told her, "'When you come back, I'm going to take another job.' She was telling Scotty she couldn't stand to work in the house with me anymore," said Kathy. "And Scotty was livid at me. I said to him, 'Why should you be mad at me? She messed up my retirement and you said you'd make good on it'—which he never did. 'If she wants to leave, fine. But she made a mistake, so she can't admit to making a mistake and it affects the rest of my life. So why yell at me?' He was yelling and screaming. He was afraid he was going to lose Gail because Gail had so much information. Gail felt my frustration and knew that I was judging her as incompetent. Just like Scotty couldn't be wrong, Gail cannot be wrong. So they're very similar in personalities."

Kathy said Peck would complain about Gail but she didn't dare to because Peck would "get mad at me. He'd set up a triangle with Gail and myself [and] would play us against each other and then say, 'I hate it when you two fight.'" Before and after the honeymoon Peck constantly added kindling to this incendiary situation.

His mischief had started lower on the annoyance scale just before their marriage when Peck told Kathy that Gail would give her a check for her allowance once a month. Kathy protested. Peck would hear none of it. Kathy said Gail would gloat when handing over the allowance, which was also the housekeeping money. Kathy mentioned again that Peck put her on an allowance because of Lily's spending. "He projected a lot of stuff he got mad at Lily about on to me—'You know, Lily had shoes she never wore.' I'd just say, 'Okay, some day you'll realize I'm Kathy, not Lily. I'm sure I've got flaws but I don't have the same faults that she had. And I'm not secretive.' He was very tight. He was frugal. He loved counting his money on the stock market every day and didn't see any reason to spend money. He would spend a ton of money on a trip and then wouldn't spend any on stuff on a house that needed to be repaired."

His tightfistedness extended to his garden. In California, Kathy had been a keen gardener. Peck said she couldn't have a little plot in *his* garden, though he later relented on the point and told her to talk to the gardener.

Kathy said she put up with so much because "there was something—I don't mean this in an arrogant way—but there was a reason why he chose me. I don't know if in the bigger scheme of things God knew he was dying and wanted me to be with him—because he knew I would be steadfast and could handle it; that I would be there for his care and his wishes about dying at home." During several conversations at this time and later, Kathy would reflect on the relationship. "There was a constant struggle between the light side and the dark side of Scotty. I could see into the light side but wouldn't tolerate the dark side. I mean I challenged him on so much," she said. "Sometimes I'd feel guilty because I was really challenging the dark side he'd used as a coping mechanism for so long in his life. He realized I wouldn't roll over the way Lily rolled over all those years. I wasn't going to roll over, I mean we were either going to work it out or not."

She saw the complicated man and the simple good he had done, she said. "Scotty's writing was done in a beautiful, simple way. So many people that read his work felt they could have written the book themselves. He resonated with something in their own lives; they felt he was reading their minds. It rang so true that they felt a closeness to him, that he was speaking for them, inspiring them, challenging them." Asked if she felt the same way, Kathy said no. "Our very first time together, our first meal together, I was calling him stuffy and pompous. He was used to people kissing up to him and I didn't. I mean I wasn't rude, but I certainly disagreed. I spoke my opinion and challenged him on some things. I'd met famous people. I'd had my arm twisted to donate a room to him at my bed and breakfast."

Christopher detachedly watched the household turmoil. He said, "Scotty was always able to surprise us. I think a thing that surprised me about Scotty is that women found him attractive. I just couldn't understand it. Also, that he'd gotten out of forty years of marriage [then] married so quickly. He explained to me he wanted a nursemaid. He wanted to be babied. And by golly, he got it in Kathy. Kathy was very strong, she had a year where she always stood up to him on whatever. I would say that she was thinking of leaving him from the moment she got to Connecticut. But by the end, even before Scotty had been diagnosed with whatever, I think she was starting to crumble. He was able to give people the impression that they didn't really have a choice, they had to be there to love him."

Asked whether, during this period, he'd witnessed his father's ability to be cruel, the son said, "I've seen lots of it. I've heard it said that people interviewing Nixon couldn't believe they were speaking with Nixon because it seemed like somebody doing an outrageous caricature of him. Scotty was the same way. It just became more and more unfortunate. I saw the same qualities and cruelties very early in life. The difference was in degree—he lost his capacity to control. I don't think he was feeling differently about things; he wasn't filtering, editing what he was saying. And he was never terribly good at it anyway. On principle he believed that in being open and honest about certain things, he was just sticking by his guns."

During 2005, housekeeper Valerie said, "I saw the cruelty recently, but I have to be honest, I think it was Scotty losing control [of himself and everyday affairs due to the Parkinson's] and knowing he was losing control." Gail expanded on the situation. She said, "I mean I loved Scotty, but I didn't deal with him. Scotty for a long time had been me, me, me. Scotty would give everyone their fifteen minutes and then they'd shut up. It was definitely his ideas, his thoughts, and once you'd learned you stopped being hurt by it. He was definitely so focused he didn't even see what was going on in his own home."

Asked about her relationship with Kathy, Gail said, "It was hard for her to understand that Scotty did confide in me the way he did. I don't know if it was right or not, but that was the way we'd worked for years and years. I think one of the main problems between us [Gail and Kathy] is that I knew what their marriage was and she knew it. So I knew their fights, I knew every day of it. I know this—Scotty played us. I don't know if Kathy mentioned that. He loved using us against each other. He liked having two women arguing over him." Asked if she thought Peck was a spoiled brat, Gail replied, "Yeah, in a lot of ways he was. Yes." As Gail perceived things, Peck hired people "he wanted what he wanted in his way. As boss he was entitled to it. He wanted Kathy to come from California under certain conditions. He bought someone to take care of him. I don't believe he was in love with Kathy." Gail said that when she told Peck, "'I will stay with you until that woman comes back from California, and then I'll leave you,' he started crying and he kept saying, 'You can't do this to me.' I said, 'I cannot not do it.'"

"Kathy and I talked, later," said Gail, "and Kathy said they'd had a major fight about that, part of it instigated by him from the start. Kathy and I never stood a chance of getting along. Two women in the house with different parts of this man. She does not like me now. I don't like her." Then Gail added, "On some level, if we could sit together in a room, we'd start laughing at how we feel. But I don't see it happening."

Valerie viewed the deteriorating situation this way. "I don't like to hurt feelings," she said, "but [Gail] was jealous in her own way. Gail liked to plan things, so her life was planned that she was going to take care of Scotty, and when he died we'd be at his deathbed and everything was going to be organized. When Kathy stepped in Gail was stripped of all those things. But Kathy was trying to be a wife. You know, do what we [Valerie and Gail] do, but as a wife. And was Gail quitting? Gail was going to quit. But then Scotty got sick." To Valerie, Peck "loved control and in the end, after Lily left, Scotty gave up control. He had no idea he'd done it. Gail controlled him and he allowed it. I never saw Scotty out of control when he was married to Lily. He was controlling, but he wasn't out-of-control mean. Scotty was a brilliant man but he had no commonsense. He liked control, but he had this fear we used to talk about: 'When I die. When I die.' I'd always say, 'Well, are you dying soon, because I have a schedule.' Then I'd say, 'Well, what's your worst fear?' He said, 'That I won't have control of my life.'"

One way or another, everyone in the household who was close to Peck was lectured, or worse, bullied. Peck used "truth" as a weapon, said Gail. "He would lay people's faults bare, tell them what they were really like, then back off and excuse himself by saying he was only telling the truth. He had no idea of how to be socially adept, not even little whites lies—I mean we all do them: 'Oh, you look nice.'" Instead, said Gail, "Scotty would say, 'Jesus Christ,' and take people apart. I said to Kathy, 'I don't know why you don't go running and screaming into the night 'cos he's not going to change. That's not his goal. Everybody else grows and changes for the best, but Scotty doesn't have to.' He was actually creating a worse situation with Kathy than he did with Lily."

Within the household, said Kathy, "Gail loved Scotty and so they had a constant, flirtatious relationship. I came to realize that Gail was Scotty's best friend." And that there were two Scott Pecks. Kathy described Peck at that time as "just a residual-like dry drunk. The personality was already created from the alcohol and the drugs, then the combination of them. He prided himself that he went through therapy and talked about how he'd been cured. I think he just learned how to drive his neuroses deeper underground and how to control them. He could—because he was so intelligent he looked sane. And so these insane things. The good Scotty was really, really good. The good Scotty was so much more intelligent, insightful, brilliant—more so than anybody. Most of his friends got the good Scotty. He kept the bad Scotty for the people closest to him, whether it was to test them, or because he couldn't keep that Scotty in the box all the time. I mean he'd be screaming at me and then the phone would ring and he'd be all sweetness and light. He could definitely bracket in—most of his friends had no idea of the dark Scotty. They got someone who was charming, intelligent—all those things; you couldn't find anybody better. He would challenge you with thoughts and conversation and delight you with stories and make you laugh, challenge your thinking, and it was wonderful. They got a wonderful friend."

As Gail went over the root issues, she explained that she'd worked with Peck for so many years when he had a wife who wasn't interested and didn't care and then, suddenly, there was Kathy, "someone in the picture who does care, and does resent my being there and being such a part of it. He certainly pushed buttons in Kathy and I." Gail said that as she reached the point when she'd had enough and told Peck she was leaving, it was because "I had no more endurance. No more. I just couldn't do it. I said to him, 'I come to work crying every day. I hate being here.' And I'm sure Kathy felt the same way when she went downstairs. So we were locked in a terrible battle."

Then everything changed. Peck became ill.

It started simply enough. His skin was yellowing with jaundice, his stools were light, and he was diagnosing himself, convinced it was the gall bladder. He was not in pain. His blood sugar was extremely high, but he ate a lot of sweets, really craved them. Finally he called Dr. Clark, who admitted Peck to the nearby hospital for tests. Peck was buoyant, said Kathy, so she went to airport to collect her mother who was arriving for a visit. At the hospital there was an MRI that showed nothing. There were more tests, and Peck accused the staff of withholding information. There appeared to be a blockage in the liver. A stent was inserted, and within a couple of days Peck was back home. There was much discussion with his physician friends regarding where Peck should go for more comprehensive testing. Finally, on the advice of his endocrinologist friend, Dr. Robert Hatcher, Peck decided on the Mayo Clinic, in Rochester, Minn.

On the Friday he was released from the local hospital, he and

Kathy and her mother went to see the play *Equus* at an outdoor theater where they picnicked on the grass. By the Sunday he was complaining of feeling unwell, but refused to return to the hospital. On Monday he was in such pain he had to be admitted, and his condition was rapidly worsening. "Lily showed up at the hospital," Kathy said, "and he didn't recognize her and said, 'Who are you?' She said, 'I'm Lily.'" Kathy left them alone and went for a 45-minute walk. When she returned, she said, they were just "talking about this and that."

The hospital was waiting for the ambulance that would take Peck to the Mayo Clinic jet that was standing by at a nearby airport. It had been late arriving. With more delays, Peck was going into shock, said Kathy. Finally the plane took off on a flight that was hampered by thunderstorms and rerouted. "His blood pressure was 40 over 30," she said. On arrival at Rochester airport Peck was transferred from aircraft to ambulance and from ambulance straight into the Mayo intensive care unit at St. Mary's Hospital. He was there for the next week, his condition up one moment down the next until the Sunday, at which point Peck was not expected to live. His son Christopher arrived.

Kathy said Christopher was nonchalant and told her, "He's been at death's door many times." Peck asked that his daughter, Belinda, come from Texas. Belinda asked Kathy if she was certain, because, when Peck had been transferred out of the intensive care unit, Christopher said, "See, I told you he wouldn't die." Belinda was reluctant to make the journey unnecessarily as the next day was her children's first day back at school. Belinda made the journey to Rochester. By the time she and her husband arrived, Peck had rallied, his temperature had broken, and the excruciating pain in one leg had passed. As Kathy described it, the meeting "was an opportunity to reconcile, and Belinda sincerely tried. Scotty, because of his narcissism, just could not admit he was wrong."

Peck, sick and confused and still being willful, told Kathy it was good that he and Christopher had reconciled, and that that Christopher would now come to visit them. When Kathy told him not to count on it, Peck became angry and accused her of trying to drive a wedge between father and his son, whereas, Kathy said later, she'd worked for two weeks to persuade Christopher to visit.

Six months earlier, Dr. Gerald May, the psychiatrist who gave Peck's *The Road Less Traveled* its second review, had died. At the time, Peck was writing an introduction to May's book, *Dark Night of the Soul: A Psychiatrist Explores the Connection Between Darkness and Spiritual Growth.* Kathy said Betty May wrote to Peck, and "I could see in the way she was talking about their children, and the relationship they had as a family, that it moved Scotty and it hurt him. He said, 'I wish I had that kind of relationship with my children.' It hit him very deeply. He really did tear up because he really envied people when families had a good relationship, but he was his own worst enemy with his family. I mean it was with the people that loved him most he showed his darkest side, and that was very hard on him."

"Scotty never knew how to be a father," Valerie said. "I judge that because I had a wonderful father. I think kids need to be patted on the back. Kids do things we don't like. Kids do things that we don't want for them. He just didn't know how to be a father. I felt very sorry for Christopher. In a way I think Christopher always tried. I think Scotty liked to play games and analyze. You may be a psychiatrist but you can't get inside your kids' heads because a part of it is your own head and you don't even realize it. I really don't know much about Belinda and Julia. Belinda has been back and forth and Belinda to me is the good daughter. How she handled it really, I don't know. Christopher had cut off communications [with his father] for a while. I said to Scotty—this was after Lily left—and he was writing to Christopher, 'Scotty, if [for] Christopher to survive it means cutting off communications with you, you have to accept it. I mean kids do things we don't like all the time. But Scotty, you have to learn how to be a father and it's kind of late.' I got the silent treatment, which means I hit a sore spot."

The Mayo Clinic diagnosis was in. Peck had pancreatic and liver cancer.

CHAPTER FOURTEEN
His Bed by His Window

Peck returned home to New Preston, to a hospital bed in an upstairs bedroom with plenty of windows. A good friend to his friends, Peck was soon seeing them all as two-day visitors. The calendar on the kitchen wall filled with entries, two days marked, "Guy, Guy" (psychologist Jim Guy from California), "Kaz, Kaz" (Kazimier Gozdz from California), "ES." (Sister Ellen Stephen from the convent). There was a constant, organized flow of well-wishers and those coming to say what they knew were final goodbyes. As far as unconditional love from friends was concerned, Peck was having a reassuring several of weeks, though his condition was deteriorating. It was the double bind, the pain of cancer plus the befuddlement and rapidly decreasing mobility caused by the Parkinson's.

Said Kathy, "He didn't have pain, he had nausea so would throw up a lot, bile, all of his stomach. And as he was in bed, his lungs of course were filling with fluid because he wasn't able to exercise. I was afraid he was either going to aspirate vomit or get into a coughing spell and drown, the way a friend of mine did from pneumonia. He was gasping for air, and desperate." The inevitable deterioration continued, later visitors were finding a Scotty who could no longer hold a conversation, though he'd occasionally say things. Kathy was with him most of the time, often saying prayers aloud. If she squeezed his hand, he'd squeeze hers in return. There'd bursts of talking, isolated, talk of letting go, no talk of God unless Kathy mentioned God. He'd groan. If Kathy asked him was he in pain, Peck would reply, "No, I'm just letting go."

Peck could still get furious. A few days after his return from the Mayo clinic, Kathy and a visitor from California were in Peck's room. The visitor said to Kathy he would give Peck some marijuana to help combat his nausea. Kathy said to wait until she telephoned Dr. Clark to see if the pot might adversely potentiate some of the drugs Peck was on. Peck became furious, yelling at Kathy for daring to interfere with his medical care. She, equally tartly and emotionally, retorted she'd been taking responsibility for his medical care day and night for the past two months, and it was because she was there she'd break the Peck family spell of the Peck men never having their wives by their bedside when they died. They were yelling and screaming at each other, she said. She was crying even as she recalled the evening.

There were other major household tremors and tremblors. Peck had written a codicil to his will giving Kathy an additional bequest, a codicil he later revoked; he was ratcheting higher his bid to control, and didn't care who was hurt. At the Mayo Clinic, said Gail, he told her he intended to divorce Kathy when he returned home. Once home, it appears he was telling Kathy he really did want her better provided for while insisting to Gail he was going ahead with the divorce. The final bitter details around this, and the mutual recriminations and antagonisms Peck viciously fanned to a great heat between the two women, can be charitably be blamed on the dying Peck struggling in a fog of pain and fear and morphine derivatives. Less charitably it might be surmised he knew precisely what he was doing as he tried to exert his power one last time.

"On the [final] day he was really lucid," Kathy said. "Gail and I were in there—and I think he realized he was losing it as far as mental cognition. He said, 'Gail, I have put Kathy through more in one year than I have put you through in nineteen.' He said, 'I had to test her love and she loves me and I love her.'"

The competing issues of divorce versus adequate coverage would become moot as Peck slipped further, leaving a bitter interpersonal bequest of his own making, whether deliberate or delusional.

He would have bursts of good humor, and, if provoked, recall. Kathy commented that one point Peck "was trying to tell one of the nurses a joke. It was close to his death. He could still understand what was being said to him, but his mind had a loose wire and wasn't connecting—so he had trouble maintaining the length of the joke, and I would prompt him by saying a line." But Kathy's line was not verbatim, "and then he would correct me with the verbatim version," she said.

It is impossible to know in those final few weeks what he really wrestled with internally, psychologically, spiritually. All the time he was sick at home, at the Mayo Clinic, and back home again, he never raised the topic of God or God's grace in terms of his own dying. At a point when Peck was still communicating fully, his endocrinologist friend, Dr. Hatcher, "told Scotty he needed to cut

down on the number of visitors: 'You need to have a quiet time,'"
Kathy said. "Out of the blue Scotty said, 'I want to be Catholic.'
Bob and I both said, 'It's fine.'" There were no visitors on the
calendar for the following day, so Kathy suggested they pray over
it. Peck said, "'Unh-uh.' So he didn't really mean it," said Kathy. "I
mean I was shocked because I was turning to God the whole time.
There were so many times he was sleeping I was in prayer. I mean
because I had no choice. It was the only place I could go for
comfort."

Kathy continued, "I don't know if he was angry at God, he
never expressed that. But there was no real connection to God.
Sometimes I felt it was a real conflict between us because there
were times—even on the [honeymoon] ship I wanted to go to
church, and he wanted to have communion, two of us. I went to
the two churches on the ship, the Catholic and the
nondenominational one. I told him later and he was upset. I said,
'Well, we had our communion, but Scotty, it was not authentic.
There was no connection to God. It was your way of using God to
give me a lecture about 'God, I'm going to talk to Kathy when we
get to the Falkland Islands about this or that.' That's not a prayer.
That's not communion, community.' I said I needed something.

"There were times when his connection with God was a sham. I
don't know what he thought he was doing. I don't know if he really
thought he was communicating with God. I mean he could
certainly talk the talk and convince many people. And I know how
much he loved God, and how much he cared. [But he had this] fear
of even the love, I mean to let God's love in. I mean if he could let
any love in he could let God's love in. Not to experience God's
love is sad. I don't know whether it was his adult arrogance that he
couldn't let God love him. But I think it had to do more with his
childhood. I think it was all back to that."

Nonetheless, "the last two and a half weeks of his life he was
wonderful to me," said Kathy. "Finally we were loving each other,
he was the man I came here to love. He was being very sweet. But
up to that point he was a little monster." The end was very close,
the coma was not continual but during the periods he emerged
from it his thought patterns were generally disconnected and
erratic. At one point he was telling Kathy about the wings, all sorts
of fluttering wings he could see and hear.

The days had dwindled down to the final three. On Thursday
Sept. 22, 2005, Kathy said, he was vomiting, desperate and gasping

for air. "He grabbed me and said, 'Honey Bunny, don't let me die. I'm afraid, help me! Help me!' So you know, we got him calmed down." On Friday morning, as the nurses were busying around, said Kathy, one of them mentioned something about it being "over there," and Peck burst into the World War I song, "Over there, over there ...."

On Saturday morning he was being cleaned up, the nurses were with him, and he said, "Good morning." One person present was George Moscoff from California. Moscoff, on his own initiative, had much earlier created a Scott Peck website where many friends and acquaintances posted their thoughts about Peck, along with reminiscences. Moscoff, plus Peck's friend Phil Mirvin, and Kathy, were all in his room. Gail and Valerie had visited him that morning. Phil suggested to Kathy they go for a walk. They did and George remained with Peck. Later, when it was time for the nursing shift change, Kathy went back upstairs and George went down.

Peck's eyes were closed. Kathy said, "He was breathing quietly, sleeping inside a semi-drug-induced comatose thing. The nurses were counting pills between shifts, and I was with Scotty alone. I was telling him about the light on the trees. I was telling him what a light he had been to me and to so many people. I was telling him it wasn't always the best of times but I forgave him for all his shit. And I apologized for any shit I gave him. I was talking about South America and the fun times we had over 21 years, and thanking him for all that. And I told him I loved him very much. I just wanted to say a prayer. I'd been saying things like, you know, made up prayers, 'Dear God, please save Scotty,' kind of thing. And then I said the Lord's Prayer. And as I said Amen, he died and left. He absolutely died when I said Amen. He sighed, and then I looked at him, and I looked around the room, and looked at him again, and I said, 'Oh my gosh, my darling, be with God, and thank you.' And at that point it was a perfect death. It was his final gift to me and my final gift to him. It couldn't have been better."

Later, at Peck's memorial service, his friend Dr. Clark said, "Doctors do sometimes make the worst patients and Scotty refused a medication I knew would have eased his suffering. Consequently he suffered more than he needed to, and consequently that was painful to watch. He resisted Kathy's efforts to care for him even though she'd become expert in his care, at this point truly his 24/7 guardian angel. With only ten days remaining in his life a remarkable transformation occurred, for reasons I do not

171

understand. Literally overnight from one day to next that lifelong deep-seated need for control vanished completely. I'd never seen anything quite like it. He literally surrendered his care, and I believe his whole being, to Kathy. Just a few days later, on a bright, sunlit Indian summer day, he died peacefully in her arms. At peace. At long last."

There was a family burial service at the little church in Quaker Hill, the church closest to where Judge Peck and Elizabeth Peck had their final country home, and where they are buried. Scott had bought a plot there, though the cemetery is now "closed," there is no room for further grave sites. Peck was cremated. The Rev. Peck, already en route to see his uncle, instead arrived in time to participate in service. The Rev. Stephen Bauman gave the eulogy.

Present in the little Quaker Hill church was a handful of family members: Kathy; Lily, two of Lily and Scott's children, Belinda—with her husband and children—and Christopher. The Rev. Peck's sisters, Heather and Lisa attended, with their mother. There was an additional group of close friends. The press announcement of M. Scott Peck's death stated Lily and Scott had only two children. No names were mentioned. The Pecks' second daughter, Julia, was simply not acknowledged. Peck was gone; it was too late now to undo the emotional knots of tightly tied family pains.

What remains remarkable about Peck's closing months is less Peck's often outrageous behavior than the candor with which Kathy, Gail and Valerie (and, on the sidelines, Christopher) could still address their relationship with Peck in a detached manner. The three women were able to display love for Peck, each in her own way, despite a disunited front. They were able to talk of his failings while keeping his strengths in perspective, even after his death.

Valerie said, "The last week I was going to see Scotty every day because that's all I needed. I have no hard feelings, no regrets in any way, shape or form with Scotty. The day he died, I was sitting on his bed, a few people here and there, I knew it was coming—Gail walked in and goes, 'Don't you ever go home?'" Valerie said she and Gail had "always been very protective of Scotty and Lily. Very protective. I would not trash him, but I will be truthful. There's a whole big difference. I miss him everyday."

Gail said she'd "given it some thought, and what comes back to

172

me is that Scotty was the focal point of our problems, our disagreements and everything else, and was also the focal point for us at the end. I think we did try hard to do what was best for him at the end. Kathy and I knew Scotty was a major part of the problem and we both were terribly sucked into it. But towards the end we rose above it to give him what he wanted, and honor what he wanted."

Kathy said, "I'm much more honest than Scotty was. I'm not going to lie. I don't want anything I say to be used critically against him, but I don't mind it being used honestly. Scotty was such a paradox. On the one hand I feel terribly sad and upset that we didn't have more time. On the other, incredible gratitude we had the time that we had. It's such a mixed feeling."

Three days after Peck's death, Gail wrote, "Coming to work today was terrible. To know he is no longer in the house is terribly sad. There has been no man in the past, present, and God, I hope not the future, that could infuriate me more, make me cry more, make me want to strangle him more, or create such devotion and loyalty. I will miss him terribly. Sooo, here's to your book about him. May it make people think and know about him better (all parts of him)."

In a closing email Gail said she did not want the final months of Peck's life depicted as merely a conflict between her and Kathy.

The final months, in fact, are the portrayal of a man crying out as he sank deeper and deeper into Parkinson's. It is a portrait many Parkinson's caregivers will recognize instantly. As the disease tightens and further tightens its grip it can squeeze out more and more anger. The sufferer lashes out, ever more fiercely, at those nearby, until that consciousness begins to finally slip away. In Peck's case, the Parkinson's exacerbated the simmering fury of a man who'd been lashing out all his life because he felt unloved. The disease magnified all the underlying hurts, and amplified the anguish. Amplified, it emerged as cruelty in a man who, finally, totally lost control.

Kathy took refuge in the best of it and acknowledged the worst of it: "A wedding day, filled with love and joy. And times when he would steam with anger and give me such a steely stare. I remember the sound of his breath as he slept, and it's hard for me to go to bed and realize he's gone; the way he felt in my arms, and yet what solace he brought as well as the pain. For every dark moment a moment of such brilliance it was overwhelming. I try to remember the man that he was—not the one I would like to build out of fantasies and 'if onlys,' and things to comfort me."

There was no general announcement or widespread invitation to the Nov. 12, 2005 memorial service in Christ Church on New York's Park Avenue. Again, the Rev. Stephen Bauman officiated. He had buried Scott's father, Judge Peck from this same church. Attendance at the memorial service was just by word of mouth and about a hundred people were present. Kathy, and Lily and her family, were up front, in different pews. The Rev. Peck included Julia in the public prayers for the family. Kathy's printed tribute alternated between the hilarious and the moving. Appropriately, near the conclusion, it stated: "To those of you he may have hurt, I truly believe that the Scotty that left us on September 24 would offer an apology and ask your forgiveness."

Kathy said the bulk of Peck's approximately $4.5 million estate (not including the house), was divided between Belinda and Christopher. Kathy inherited the house and "a small sum of money." (A local realtor said he valued the house at "around $1.5 million, somewhere in there.") Gail, a co-executor, was left $300,000. Asked if she had been fairly dealt with by Peck in his will, Gail replied, "Less so than her, I'll tell you. You know, for less than a year's work that's not bad, regardless of how she wanted to cry and wear his robes. But I don't want this to be about Kathy and I. It was a doomed situation, it really was, looking back at it. He tweaked it all along. And in the end she has succeeded in erasing me from him."

Apparently there were legal confusions left behind too as Gail said, Peck "had X amount of attorneys, and one didn't know what the other one did and it was confusing. It was Scotty. We all miss him and kind of shake our heads and go, 'Oh, how typical.'"

Kathy joined a grieving group, "a lot of women in the same place." She said, "It's been very helpful. It brings up so many questions: it is better to have loved? But it's interesting how grief just waits in ambush, like Cato [Burt Kwouk] in *The Pink Panther*."

"Meanwhile," she said, she'd read a book that "describes Scotty's condition perfectly, *Controlling People* by Patricia Evans. It has helped me understand Scotty and has been a major relief. I understand him, and my reaction to him, and Gail. Their pathologies were a perfect match."

Alone in the house on Bliss Road, Kathy said, "What a paradox. It is so apparent—I get letters every day from people who don't know that he is dead—thanking him for the incredible contribution he made to their lives. And I must say that every day there is some insight into myself that he has also made possible. I think the thing that has moved me so much is that Scotty lives on through the things he's written and done that has affected our lives, and I think that sometimes there's something—a quality or action in my own life—that makes me smile and think, that's a part of him living in me. He lives on in the people who have read or known him."

She went to stay for a while in Florida with friends before returning to New Preston. When she attended the "King Tut" exhibit she noted a quote from Howard Carter, who discovered Tutankhamun's tomb. She felt it was apt for Peck: *The mystery of his life still eludes us. The shadows move but the dark is never quite dispersed.*

The Rev. David Peck, viewing his uncle's death in the light of the deaths of his grandfather and own father, said, "There are interesting spiritual and theological and psychological issues here: he who dies last with the most toys wins. Scotty has certainly won among the men of his family. It is human nature and tragedy that even when one reaches this, there is an emptiness; because, of course, it is reconciliation, forgiveness, love, that is missing, and by definition unforthcoming. We are simply left with our appetite for approval and no one left in the restaurant."

Peck was that solitary diner. Distrusting people, distrusting love, finally distrusting himself, he placed—to the extent he was capable—what little fragment of trust remained, in God. And hoped God understood. He'd written:

"The prevailing Judeo-Christian view of the world is that this is a naturally good world that has somehow been contaminated by evil. My own view— speculation—is that maybe it is the other way around: we live in a naturally evil world that has somehow been mysteriously contaminated by goodness. There is no question that evil is a mystery, but I think the mystery of goodness is an even greater mystery."

No, the greater mystery is always the flawed healer, the paradox, in this case a narcissist who could not break through the brambles and briar patches of his life. Yet, the same man who, through one book, could elevate the lives of tens of thousands, possibly hundreds of thousands of people.

BIOGRAPHER'S NOTES

M. Scott Peck wanted a "warts and all" biography. He did not object to, or hide, much of the darker side of his personality and behavior. Equally, he was determined that people around him not be further hurt. He agreed in advance, in writing, that he would not see this manuscript or any draft of it prior to publication, and yet would cooperate. In turn, I was not to contact his wife, Lily, or his children, whereas if they contacted me that was up to them.

After Scott Peck's death, Kathy Peck, Scott's second wife, in a move not prompted by me, arranged matters so that indeed I did interview Christopher Peck, Scott and Lily's third child and only son.

It must be said that during our sixty or seventy hours of interviews and tape-recorded telephone chats, Peck's decision to stay with the truth on difficult topics was generally steadfast. I also had full access to twenty hours of interviews with Peck conducted in the late 1990s by the psychologist Dr. James Guy of Pasadena. The tapes were transcribed and remained in Peck's keeping. Peck made them available to me. I am grateful to the generosity of both men. Because Peck gave many of the same answers to Guy's and my similar questions—occasionally word-for-word identical answers—Guy's interviews are woven in with my own (begun half-a-decade later), except where otherwise indicated.

Peck was a performer many of his answers were a verbatim repetition of paragraphs in his books, or anecdotes or jokes he'd regularly told, or during questions-and-answer sessions following his talks. His recall of what he'd written or said was uncanny. He was also constant in attempting to superintend the content of the book.

"I've sent you a long, nasty letter," said Peck, on the telephone. He was in a New Milford, Connecticut hospital bed awaiting gall-bladder surgery.

"I'm still trying to push something on you," he said.

"That's fine," I said. "I'll read it and ignore it, like the others."

"The anaesthetist just walked in."

"That's fine, I'll call you back. What? Half an hour?"

"I'd prefer you'd call me back next week, because I'm tired."

And so it was, but not quite as planned. For by the next week Peck was in the famed research center, the Mayo Clinic in Rochester, Minnesota. It was not merely gallbladder, it was pancreatic cancer. His kidneys shut down, he was on dialysis. On Sunday, 14 August, when I returned home extremely late from a vacation noted for thunderstorms and delayed flights, there was a voicemail from Kathy Peck at the Mayo Clinic. Scott was not likely to last, and if I wanted to talk to him I should call.

I tried several times the following morning. Finally, just before noon, Kathy answered the telephone. Scott had bounced back. He and I chatted for a brief time. His voice was weak, his spirit wasn't. We joshed and exchanged pleasantries for a few minutes until his voice faded. I reminded him that we'd an agreement that he'd never see the manuscript. What he didn't know, I told him, was that because of his condition—no longer able to read—it had always been my intention to take the book, on publication, to his home and read it to him. "How parental," he commented, not critically. I continued, bluntly but essential to the topic, that as he know he would not live long enough now to know what the book said, once he was back in New Preston from Mayo, I would come to New Preston and read him the draft Introduction and two chapters. I knew which two chapters I intended, one about his books and one about FCE and his friends commenting on Peck's personality. He was deeply touched that I would do so.

A couple of weeks later I made my way across the flagstone patio, past his SUV with its "THLOST" license plate, past the large rounded stone engraved in Roman lettering, "In Search of," to the side door. Gail was there; Kathy was upstairs with Scotty. Later I saw Valerie. Two nurses were on the upstairs level when I went into Peck. He was on his back in a railed bed. I stood to his left side, took his hand and held it as I said a short Celtic prayer aloud. He winced at several of the words, or phrases, or cadences. I'd sent him a copy of the book it came from when we first began our conversations.

It was the first of his thrusts and my parries. The paradoxical M. Scott Peck both did and did not want a biography written about him, and both did and did not want me to write it. He tried hard, unsuccessfully, to make it a collaborative effort. We had several serious areas of disagreement, and he never actually ceased trying to influence how I'd say what I might say.

During our hours of interviews we were generally cordial

conversationalists; he was sometimes delighted with the questions, even if they were tough, yet on occasion would chide, goad, and say the question indicated I failed to understand him. I would always reply that such was the risk of cooperating with a biographer. As he did with most people he met, Peck felt he had something to teach me. I made it clear I had no wish to become the student. I remained a detached observer and listener, and resisted his blandishments—and occasional barrage of lengthy letters—to be more than that. He only rarely bristled or brooded during out hours of conversations.

It was when I'd suggest that in his admission of infidelities or admission of failure as a father he showed little evidence of remorse that he truly went on the defensive. Later, on the telephone and in person, he would periodically return to that observation and attempt to develop his comments further, usually more in self-exculpation than explanation. Knowing his life was not unblemished, he'd remark one doesn't have to be a saint to be a prophet.

Finally, he felt I had thoroughly misunderstood his relationship with God and his role as a Christian prophet and pilgrim. And in that long, nasty letter he let it all pour out. It hadn't been the first time.

But let him speak for himself in excerpts from a small selection of his letters and emails to me. About the book (29 September 2003): "I am excited and intrigued about your suggestions of writing my biography. I recognize that you are talking about something other than a fully authorized biography but do not consider this to be a barrier to our continuing to work together, although before becoming totally committed I would like to have more discussions with you as to precisely what an unauthorized biography might mean." (I told him it meant he would not see any drafts or the final manuscript prior to publication.)

"Hot dog! It looks as if it's going to be a go, and I'm as excited as a child [2 October 2003]. You are inked in my calendar for 18-19 December. I had fantasized the possibility that one of my children would approach you in desire to be heard. Should that happen with any of my children, it is their responsibility and not yours. Not seeing your early or final drafts doesn't bother me because I think I will have an idea of the tone of book for the reasons you state.

"Reflecting on our talk yesterday [3 February 2004] about me not taking time off to be a good father, etc. I was being a bit one-sided. I am a responsibility-holic. Throw some responsibility out in the middle of a group and I'm likely to dive for it while others sit there. This also means that I tend to take on lots of guilt that I probably shouldn't.

"I am an evangelist for many things [3 March 2004] including Jesus and Christianity. But above all else, although distinctly related to the two, I believe I am an evangelist for (or is it of?) 1. The Truth and 2. The concept of life as a pilgrimage. In that order. Can you believe such brevity and conciseness.

"Sorry to have dumped on you the way I did last evening [15 August 2004]. Most of it you didn't deserve (I hope). That was twenty-five-plus pent-up years of resentment. The question for my therapy and perhaps for the book is why I haven't done it before. But I'm grateful to you because I had to start with someone somewhere. It is a compliment to you that you apparently felt safe to me. What popped me off was my awareness of how defensive I felt after our Friday afternoon session, how old that defensiveness was and how inappropriate it was. Ergo, high time I went on the offense. It was not a polished offensive and I apologize to you for that. I guess that my biography strikes me as a matter of such consequence because it seems to a potential opportunity to offer the public a glimpse of the hand of God at work."

Finally the "long, nasty letter," a missive of almost 4,000 words that arrived in three batches. Main points included his dismay about my Tom Lehrer remark, and my question regarding some of his liaisons. It was also his strongest plea for a collaborative biography. He indirectly accused me of having an adversarial attitude towards him, of asking others about his marriage, and intending a book that tended towards sensationalism. He repeated an earlier charge that three people I'd interviewed "opined that you 'were certainly doing me no favor,'" that the book "would not be a complimentary one," or that you "did not comprehend what I was about. They advised I should stay clear of you.

. "I have not taken their advice because I like you and sort of trust you. Yet there are reasons I cannot discount their advice. In particular there have been a number of occasions when we have been totally out of synch. I'm not sure whether it's been a mad hundred-yard dash or a marathon. I thought what you read to me about my being non-denominational was understanding and an elegant apologia and clear explanation of the dimensions of my ever enlarging faith. I wonder if it would be interesting for us to talk about why I talk so much?"

I did not pry into his married life. Any comments on it essentially arise voluntarily from others in the three closing chapters. I did early on ask many interviewees about their impression of Lily, for they would be my only guide to her character. Even at the memorial service, when I introduced myself to Lily and two of their children for the first time, I assured them I was simply letting them know who I was and was not asking for an interview. Whenever I was in Peck's home, he and whoever was present knew, because I made it clear each time I entered, that anything I heard in casual conversation was not part of the book, that if I wanted information I'd formally ask with a tape recorder running.

One of his Peck's written communications of length was a list of his "significant contributions." It is a list significant because once more it illustrates, even just weeks before his death, how acute his mental facilities remained when he was focused. It is a valuable summary, severely edited to present it here:

> ➢ *The Road Less Travelled* did, I believe, break dramatically with traditional, Freudian-oriented psychiatric thought in that I proposed that most psychological disorders are disorders of consciousness of the conscious mind, not the unconscious.

> ➢ I have repeatedly taught that most psychological disorders are "thinking disorders." For example, narcissists are people who cannot think about others; obsessive/compulsives have great difficulty in thinking about the big picture; passive dependent people cannot think for themselves, etc.

> ➢ Until I wrote "The Healthiness of Depression" (in *The Road*), depression was thought of solely as a bad thing and was not seen as a somewhat graceful signal of there being something wrong which we needed to work on. Indeed, I believe there is evidence for a depression centre in the brain, depression serves a life-saving function just as anger does.

> ➢ I am the first to have been explicit about ways in which I actually used religious concepts in the course of psycho-therapy (*The Road* and other books).

> I believe I was the first to suggest that Evil should be considered a disease and should have a specific place in the diagnostic manual of psychiatrists.

> I do not know if there has been any other sociological analysis of group evil other than *Little Brown Brother*, written a century ago about Philippine-American War, but I think my sociological analysis of My Lai, if not totally original, is generally considered to be the best such analysis around.

> For generations we have been locked into "nature vs nurture." No one else has suggested it is more complicated, that it is obviously "nurture and nature and God."

> Although fiction writers offer innumerable examples of the death of romantic love in human relationships, to my knowledge I was the first psychiatrist ever to specify it was a norm.

> I am struck by what a seminal work *The Road Less Travelled* was.

Then came my final visit, to read the Introduction and two chapters to him. He was physically brave. He's said he would hold off the morphine derivatives in order to be at his most clear-headed when I read to him and asked him questions. He insisted, for part of the first day, and with extreme physical difficulty, on leaving his bed, being wheel-chaired to the electric stairs, and once downstairs, being interviewed in the sunroom as before. He could not sustain that for long and instead was assisted to a day bed.

I read to him the Introduction. He listened, commented, asked questions for clarification, or would have me repeat a sentence. He occasionally made a demurring sound, at times expressed approval. That done, and to get the worst over first—most of my first questions were factual checks from earlier conversations—I asked him about his children coming to see him at the clinic. His defensive answers were indicative of the pain he felt at having alienated them all. Later, upstairs, after reading him a chapter, he again had comments and questions. We had a brisk discussion. It changed nothing.

Peck lay there, propped up on his bank of pillows in the sunlit room, tubes keeping him in bodily balance, nurses occasionally coming in and out, Kathy and others occasionally stopping by to listen to parts of the reading. I asked him, given all that he had written about death, given his advice to Christians to accept they still would be afraid, and given his own reliance on God, what was it like, now, facing death?

He replied, "It's like waiting for the postman." (He didn't say "mailman.")

I said, "That's it? That's all you feel?"

And he said, "Yes, waiting for the postman to come."

The following morning I read him a chapter replete with many comments about him from FCE colleagues and friends. At times others were in the room, listening, other times not. He was alert, would stop me, make a comment, ask a question. Once the reading was done, I had a couple of questions. We were alone when I went around to his left side and took his hand. As on my arrival, I prayed aloud, softly. He closed his eyes.

I squeezed his hand, said, "Goodbye, Scotty, God bless." He kept his eyes squeezed tightly closed; applied pressure to my hand, said nothing. I left.

ACKNOWLEDGMENTS

Scott Peck's public saga began with reviewer Phyllis Theroux's landmark assessment of *The Road Less Travelled* in *Book World,* the *Washington Post,* 27 September 1978. For permission to use it in its entirety over chapters seven and eight I am particularly grateful. Thank you, Phyllis.

This book opens with the phrase, "Life is difficult" (epigraph to Chapter One), from *The Road Less Travelled,* by M. Scott Peck, MD. Copyright © 1978 by M. Scott Peck, MD. Reprinted with the permission of Simon and Schuster Adult Publishing Group.

Jonathan Dolger of Jonathan Dolger Literary Agency, New York, as Peck's literary executor, kindly gave permission to excerpt the material regarding the Rev. Malachi Martin from the closing chapters of *Glimpses of the Devil: a Psychiatrist's Personal Accounts of Possession, Exorcism and Redemption* (2005).

The material reprinted from *The Hartford Courant* (23 February, 1986), specifically from its *Northeast* magazine article, "On the Road with M. Scott Peck" by Gary Dorsey is "Copyright, 1986, Hartford Courant. Reprinted with permission."

My thanks to Ben Yagoda for permission to quote at will from his on the road with Dr. Peck article in *Connecticut Magazine.*

Quotations from *Aurora* magazine's interview with Dr. Peck are used "With Permission of Athabasca University's *Aurora.*"

I talked about Dr. Peck with Dr. Gerald May, and acknowledge the now late Dr. May's permission to quote from his review of Peck's book in the *National Catholic Reporter.* My thanks to the *Reporter's* editors, Tom Roberts/Dennis Coday, for permission to quote extensively from May's review, from my Peck essay, and other kindnesses. Similarly, I am grateful to the Rev. Richard Woods, OP, for permission to quote from his review of *Glimpses of the Devil* in the same publication.

The Rev. John W. Donohue, SJ, kindly gave permission to quote from his article on Dr. Peck in *America* magazine.

I acknowledge the quotation in chapter two regarding Sullivan & Cromwell is from *Dulles and their Family Network,* by Leonard Mosley (Dial Press/James Wade), and I am grateful to Sullivan &

Cromwell partner John L. Warden for providing a copy of Judge David W. Peck Senior's contribution to the firm's *Centennial Book*, for details regarding the firm's early Jewish partners, and other information.

I acknowledge two one-line quotations, by Eleanor Roosevelt and U.S. Senator Joseph McCarthy, from William Manchester's *The Arms of Krupp* (Little, Brown & Co.), also in chapter two.

The antepenultimate and penultimate paragraphs of chapter fifteen are from *The Door* magazine. To Harry Guetzlaff and all those in times past associated with *The Wittenburg Door* and *the Door*, I am grateful for permission to quote those and other items. (I'm particularly grateful to them for the opportunity to finally use the word "antepenultimate" in print.) Dr. Peck's quotation regarding Thomas Merton is taken from Peck's Introduction to *A Thomas Merton Reader*, by Thomas P. McDonnell (Random House).

I acknowledge quotations regarding Peck from the *Watchman Expositor* (Rick Branch) and H. Wayne House's article M. Scott Peck, "Travelling Down the Wrong Road" (Christian Research Institute), and the line quoted from Roy H. Smith's article in *Pastoral Psychology* (Volume 49 (3), January 1992, 179-187). My thanks also to Dr. Hendrika Vande Kempe for permission to quote from her chapter, "Historical Perspectives: Religion and Clinical Psychology in America", in *Religion and the Clinical Practice of Psychology* (1995). To Cindy Lollar for an interview and permission to quote her article in *Campus Voice*, my thanks.

My thanks to Dr. Melissa Jones for permission to quote from her research into the religious revival of the 1960s and 1970s. My thanks to Jonathan Yardley of the *Washington Post* for permission to quote from one of his columns (*Book World*, 10 January 1988) a remark concerning the writings of John P, Marquand. Similarly, Michael Dirda kindly allowed me to quote from his 13 February 2003 essay in the *Washington Post*'s *Book World*. And while I did not quote from *Marquand: An American Life,* by Millicent Bell (Atlantic Monthly/Little, Brown & Co.), I did read it for the period Peck was close to Marquand.

Andrew Billen of *The Times* of London gave permission to quote from his interview with Peck, Peck's final interview of any length in a newspaper.

I suppose I could write a book without the assistance of Jean Blake, my aide-de-camp for three decades, but it would be a sorry thing and I wouldn't want to attempt it. Once again, thank you, Jean.

Genuinely appreciated is the generosity of Dr. James D. Guy, executive director of the Headington Institute in Pasadena, California, a psychologist and friend of M. Scott Peck, in making his interviews with Peck available. And while in Pasadena, my thanks to Michael Murray of Fuller Theological Library and the archive staff's assistance—and that of my wife Margie—in perusing the Peck files.

For assistance with this North American edition I am particularly grateful to the "Henley-on-Thames" crew; to my good friend Jeff Bubier for legal advice—and lunch; to Mark Harvey for the book's design, and his friendship; to Alix Tobey Southwick for proofreading—and crabcakes; to Pat Frascati for transcribing—and laughter; to Toni-Ann Ortiz for tracking down the cover photographs—and more laughter; to Jonathan Olson for permission to use the photographs, and to Jeremy Hess at Gasch Printing.

ABOUT THE AUTHOR

A former European bureau chief of *Forbes* magazine, retired journalist Arthur Jones had a long association with the U.S. weekly newspaper *National Catholic Reporter*. Jones has published a novel, *The Jesus Spy*, and 12 non-fiction books, including a well-received biography of Pierre Toussaint, a 19th-century freed slave regarded as a saint in his own lifetime.

Visit **arthurjonesbooks.net** to find out more.

Made in the USA
Monee, IL
16 January 2023

25399444R00114